THE STRUCTURE

OF ENGLISH

AN INTRODUCTION TO THE

CONSTRUCTION OF ENGLISH SENTENCES

Charles Carpenter Fries

PROFESSOR OF ENGLISH AND DIRECTOR
OF THE ENGLISH LANGUAGE INSTITUTE
OF THE UNIVERSITY OF MICHIGAN

HARCOURT, BRACE AND COMPANY · *NEW YORK*

To P. H. F.

C O N T E N T S

PREFACE   vii

I   Introduction   1

II   What Is a Sentence?   9

III   Kinds of Sentences   29

IV   Sentence Analysis: Meaning or Form   54

V   Parts of Speech   65

VI   Function Words   87

VII   Parts of Speech: Formal Characteristics   110

VIII Structural Patterns of Sentences   142

IX   Structural Meanings: "Subjects" and "Objects"   173

X   Structural Meanings: "Modifiers"   202

XI   "Sequence" Sentences and "Included" Sentences   240

XII   Immediate Constituents: "Layers" of Structure   256

XIII Practical Applications   274

INDEX   297

Preface

The early plans for my *American English Grammar* [1] provided one chapter (later two chapters) for a treatment of the sentence. As the work progressed, however, two circumstances forced me to exclude the material on the sentence from that publication. The study of the sentence became too large to be treated satisfactorily in two chapters and was so steadily growing in bulk that only a separate book could handle what seemed absolutely essential. In addition, in spite of considerable progress, the study was not ready. The pressure of matters connected with defense and war, the problems of the teaching of English as a foreign language, made it undesirable to delay longer the publishing of the materials then practically finished. And thus the work on the sentence, although almost completely pushed aside, continued to grow. Only during the spring of 1948, thanks to a sabbatical leave, could the study be given the kind of consecutive concentration required for satisfactory writing.

In the meantime, however, beginning in 1946, it became possible to obtain an entirely different kind of evidence. Instead of the letters collected and studied for the *American English Grammar* I procured the means and the opportunity to record mechanically many conversations of speakers of Standard English in this North Central community of the United States. Altogether these me-

[1] Published as English Monograph No. 10 of the National Council of Teachers of English, 1940.

chanically recorded conversations amounted to something over 250,000 running words.

The materials here presented do not, as in the earlier book, center attention upon the "grammar of usage"—the problems of social class differences. Here the discussion deals primarily with the "grammar of structure"—the construction of our utterances— and offers an approach to the problems of "sentence analysis" that differs in point of view and in emphasis from the usual treatment of syntax.

Many matters have been excluded from this introduction. I have assumed that the morphemes have been identified, and have not touched the problems of the process of identification nor those of the establishing of lexical meanings. I have tried to center attention upon the results of my analysis of the evidence rather than upon the procedures of that analysis, and have sketched only briefly certain of the procedures. Throughout the presentation I have tried to stress the patterns of English structure and have sought in the evidence the frequently recurring "sames." Deviations from the frequently occurring patterns have been noted when they appeared in the material but I have not gone outside the limited body of my particular evidence to seek for possible exceptions. I have assumed that fifty hours of very diverse conversations by some three hundred different speakers would cover the basic matters of English structure. I hope that the generalizations made here will be regarded as summaries of the facts as they appear in my evidence and as tentative formulations for English practice in general.

One section of my study I have excluded from this book and plan to publish in a separate monograph, because it seemed to need more extended treatment than would fit the scope of this introduction. It is the material concerning the function words used with Class 2 words—the matters of "aspect," "tense" and "time" in English expressions.

One cannot produce a book dealing with language without being indebted to many who have earlier struggled with the problems and made great advances. To record all the sources of help and suggestions is always impossible. Like many others, I am very conscious of immeasurable stimulation and insight received from Leonard Bloomfield. Some particular contributions need more specific acknowledgment. Kenneth L. Pike's comments upon the first four chapters led me to include more fully the exact procedure of arriving at the units to be analyzed. He and Robert Lado and Yao Shen read the completed manuscript and offered many very helpful criticisms. Throughout all the long process of collecting the material, transcribing the discs, recording the instances, analyzing the evidence, and writing the manuscript, I have had the co-operation of the various members of my family and the patient help of my wife, Agnes Carswell Fries, whose devoted assistance made the work possible.

CHARLES C. FRIES

Ann Arbor, Michigan
April, 1951

I. Introduction

The reader should know, first of all, that he will *not* find in this book the usual analysis of sentences that pupils have struggled with and the schools have taught for more than a hundred and fifty years. Modern scientific study has forced us to abandon many of the older commonly held views of language and has provided us with new principles and new assumptions which underlie new methods of analysis and verification. But the cultural lag in assimilating the results of this modern scientific study of language has been so great that the views and practices of a prescientific era still dominate the schools. That this is so in matters of language is not surprising, for, in many fields of human endeavor, belief and practice have clung to traditional and conventional procedures long after the scientific evidence was available upon which they should have been repudiated. In medicine, the practice of bleeding patients for many simple ailments rested upon a view of the nature of human blood and its function in the human body which stemmed from Galen and ancient Greece. In 1628, William Harvey published his great book proving the circulation of the blood, with all the evidence really necessary upon which to discard the general practice of bleeding. But bleeding as a medical procedure continued for more than two hundred years after Harvey's book. In fact, it was just about 170 years later that George Washington was bled heavily four times in one night as a treatment for his quinsy. With our increased understanding of the nature of human blood, great blood banks have been created from which new life has been put *into* the veins of many patients. The lag in the social acceptance of linguistic advances has been nearly as great.

The linguistic approach adopted here will differ, therefore, from that made familiar by the common school grammars, for it is an attempt to apply more fully, in this study of sentence structure, some of the principles underlying the modern scientific study of language. This different approach is not difficult in itself but it may at first be somewhat confusing to those whose thinking in linguistic matters has been channeled by the traditional methods and materials of grammatical study. Even the well-known definitions of the sentence and its parts must be forgotten if the terms themselves are to be retained. The reader will certainly be confused if he constantly seeks to translate the statements he finds here into the old grammatical terms as he has customarily defined them and as he has employed them in practice. He must *not* conclude that the approach here is simply or primarily a new set of terms for the same old grammatical materials. As a matter of fact, in order to avoid some possible confusion, technical terms of all kinds are avoided wherever possible, and longer, more cumbersome descriptive statements often used in their stead. The difference between the approach used here and the older approach lies much deeper than a mere matter of terminology; it rests primarily upon a fundamentally different view of the nature of "grammar"—a view that has given tremendous enthusiasm to students of the "new" grammar and fresh hope that the results of their study will become increasingly useful for insight into the nature and functioning of language.

The many different values claimed for the traditional study and analysis of sentences in the schools have each been challenged during the past fifty years, and the amount of time devoted to "grammar" in this sense has fluctuated greatly as the advocates or adversaries of "grammar" have held power. Too often those who have opposed the conventional grammar analysis have had nothing to offer as a substitute, and no practical suggestions as to how an understanding of the mechanism of our language must be gained.[1] This book tries to provide the fundamental descriptive analysis upon which such practical textbooks can be built. The study presented here attempted an analysis of a large body of actual English speech observed and recorded in a university community in the North-Central part of the United States. It is, frankly, as its title indicates, an *introduction* to the structure of English utterances—not a complete descriptive treatment of all the features of that structure. The range of the precise topics discussed appears in the table of contents. This introduction is offered in the hope that it will provide the stimulation and perhaps the basis for the many additional studies of present-day English that we need.

The point of view in this discussion is descriptive, not normative or legislative. The reader will find here, *not* how certain teachers or textbook writers or "authorities" think native speakers of English ought to use the language, but how certain native speakers actually do use it in natural, practical conversations carrying on the various activities of a community. The materials which furnished the linguistic evidence for the analysis and discussions of the book were primarily some fifty hours of mechanically recorded conversations on a great range of topics—conversations in which the participants were entirely unaware that their speech was being recorded. These mechanical records were transcribed for convenient study, and roughly indexed so as to facilitate reference to the original discs recording the actual speech.[2] The treatment here

---

[1] There have of course been some, as for example, Otto Jespersen's *Analytic Syntax* (Copenhagen, 1937).

[2] With the recent development of mechanical devices for the easy recording of the speech of persons in all types of situations there seems to be little excuse for the use of linguistic material not taken from actual communicative practice when one attempts to deal with a living language. Even though the investigator is himself a native

is thus also limited by the fact that it is based upon this circumscribed body of material.

Often linguistic students are censured for devoting themselves to the "language of the people" rather than to the language of "great literature." Perhaps a misunderstanding of the precise task of the linguist underlies these criticisms. A linguist usually is concerned with finding out how a language works in fulfilling all the functions of communication in the particular social group that uses it. "Great literature" is only one of those functions and on the whole a very limited one comparatively. It is comparable in a way to the hothouse plants and flowers developed by the florist. The practices of the florist in creating especially beautiful specimens, as well as the work of a Burbank in producing seedless oranges or seedless raisins, rest upon an understanding of the nature of these plants as the scientific botanist reveals it. For the botanist's work, the plants as they occur in nature furnish a more satisfactory basis for study and investigation than do the specially developed, more beautiful specimens of the florist's hothouse or the cultivated garden. The scientific linguist doesn't attempt to investigate the creation of great literature; he has devoted himself to the difficult task of discovering and describing the intricate and complicated mechanisms which the language actually uses in fulfilling its communicative function and which the literary artist also must take as basic in his expression. As a scientist the linguist is searching for pure knowledge. To know the facts and to understand the language processes are to him ends in themselves. He usually leaves to others the business of applying practically the knowledge he has won. The fact that his particular task first

speaker of the language and a sophisticated and trained observer he cannot depend completely on himself as an informant and use introspection as his sole source of material. He has a much more satisfactory base from which to proceed with linguistic analysis if he has a large body of mechanically recorded language which he can hear repeated over and over, and which he can approach with more objectivity than he can that which he furnishes from himself as informant.

takes him to the language of the people as used in the practical affairs of life rather than to the creations of literature does not mean that he is hostile to literature nor that he ignores literature.[3]

For the linguist, the continuation of older forms in the language of the uneducated is an important fact of language history—just as important as the changes made in the language of the socially accepted. The particular areas of use of differences of language practice, geographical as well as social class differences, are important matters of his study, for language forms communicate not only their denotative meanings but also the connotative suggestions of the usual circumstances of their use. A linguist records and studies all the actual forms and uses of the language that occur, but that recording and that study, of Vulgar English as well as of Standard English, *should certainly not be taken as evidence that he therefore recommends or believes that the forms of Vulgar English can or should be substituted for the forms of Standard English.* If he is a good linguist he is very careful to note the precise areas of use in which the language forms are recorded, and he understands the problems of trying to learn to substitute the forms of one "dialect" for another. He understands, perhaps more completely than others, the nature of the task that the schools have undertaken when they assume the burden of teaching every child to use Standard English and, accordingly, he sometimes urges the limitation of that teaching to the actual forms of Standard English, as a scientific description reveals them, and the abandoning of attempts to teach forms that do not occur in the actual speech of native speakers of Standard English, forms that have become shibboleths of the classroom.

Unfortunately this insistence upon examining the actual facts of

---

[3] This does not mean that the language materials used in great literature do not interest the scientific linguist nor that his techniques and principles should not be exploited in the study of certain literary problems, especially such problems as those of style and literary form.

usage, as a starting point from which to proceed to clear a crowded teaching program of matters that can safely be ignored, has aroused considerable opposition from those who do not understand the point of view of the linguist. They interpret the issue as a struggle of radicals against conservatives. The conservatives, they believe, stand for "correctness," and they urge that "it is the part of the schools to teach the language strictly according to the rules . . . rather than to encourage questionable liberties of usage."[4] The radicals, on the other hand, are thought of as those who would follow an easier path and accept all sorts of "errors" whenever these "errors" are widespread—a policy which the "conservatives" believe would undermine the defenses against the "wretched English heard everywhere" and allow the floods of crudity to wipe out all accuracy of expression and sensitivity to elegance. Thus these two names, "conservative" and "radical," have for some become the two extremes of a scale by which to classify those who discuss language questions. The linguistic scientist is usually placed well to the left and called a radical or a liberal. If, however, a conservative in language matters is one who insists upon noting with precision all the varied circumstances surrounding the use of language forms and insists upon employing these forms with all the accuracy which they allow, and if a liberal or radical in language matters is one for whom in practical use "one form is as good as another" just as long as the gross meaning is understood, or if a liberal is one who believes that "if a language form is used *anywhere*, it is all right to use it *everywhere*"—then the scientific linguist is *not* a liberal but must be classed as an ultra-conservative. If, on the other hand, a conservative is one who believes that accuracy and precision of language are to be measured by the rules of the common school grammars and the handbooks, and if a liberal or radical is one who turns away from authoritarian rules to the modern techniques of historical linguistics, of lin-

4 *Christian Science Monitor* (Boston), February 23, 1921.

guistic geography, and of descriptive analysis, as a means of under-standing the significance of language phenomena, then the linguist *is* a complete liberal or radical.

Too often, it is true, the linguistic materials upon which teachers should build are presented in a form and in a language quite specialized and remote from that of educated laymen. Perhaps the solution is for more teachers to try to understand the scientific work in linguistics and for more linguists to try to write so that they may be more widely understood.

This book is addressed, in its form of expression, not primarily to the specialist in linguistic analysis, but to the educated lay reader who is interested in learning something about how the English language accomplishes its communicative function—about the mechanism of its utterances. Educated lay readers include the teachers in our schools and colleges—teachers in general, as well as those who must deal with the English language in particular, and those who attempt to teach foreign languages to students whose native language is English. In writing, therefore, I have tried to use explanations and illustrations, and terms, that will attach to the common experience of these educated laymen. Most of the examples appear in the conventional spelling, in spite of the difficulties this may incur, because the use of even simplified phonemic notation would probably put the book beyond the patience of many lay readers.

It is my hope, however, that the linguistic specialist will not, because of this attempt to address the educated layman, impa-tiently discard the book with a hasty skimming, assuming that it is merely a popularization of well-known materials, and miss my effort not only to challenge anew the conventional use of "mean-ing" as the basic tool of analysis in the area of linguistic study in which it has had its strongest hold—sentence structure and syntax [5]

---

[5] Otto Jespersen insists, for example, "But in syntax meaning is everything." *A Modern English Grammar* (Heidelberg, 1931), IV, 291.

—but also to illustrate the use of procedures that assume that all the signals of structure are formal matters that can be described in physical terms.[6]

Throughout the whole study I have tried to free myself from the channeling of traditional thinking about the sentence and to view the facts of the language as freshly as possible, in terms of the assumptions under which the work is done. It is not to be expected that I have succeeded at all points. I have, however, tried to state the special assumptions underlying the approach and enough of my step-by-step procedure to make possible the checking of the results obtained here, as well as to reveal the weaknesses that must exist.

[6] This challenge of the conventional use of *meaning as the basic tool of analysis* must not lead to the conclusion that I have ignored meaning as such, nor that I deny that the chief business of language is to communicate meanings of various kinds, and that the linguistic student must constantly deal with meanings. "To put it briefly, in human speech, different sounds have different meanings. To study this co-ordination of certain sounds with certain meanings is to study language" (Leonard Bloomfield, *Language* [New York: Henry Holt and Co., 1933], p. 27).

It does mean, however, that in the study of sentence structure I believe certain uses of meaning constitute an unscientific procedure and have not led to satisfactory, fruitful results. As a general principle I would insist that, in linguistic study and analysis, any use of meaning is unscientific whenever the fact of our knowing the meaning leads us to stop short of finding the precise formal signals that operate to convey that meaning.

On the other hand, this study assumes that we must control enough of the meaning of the utterances examined, that we can get from an informant (ourselves as native speakers of the language, or others) such a response as to determine whether any two items are the "same" in a particular aspect of meaning or "different." See the discussion in Chapter IV, and footnote 7 in Chapter V (p. 75).

II. What Is a Sentence?

More than two hundred different definitions of the sentence confront the worker who undertakes to deal with the structure of English utterances. The common school grammars continue to repeat the familiar definition, "A sentence is a group of words expressing a complete thought," although this ancient definition (which antedates Priscian c. 500 A.D.) quite evidently does not furnish a workable set of criteria by which to recognize sentences. In actual practice we often ignore the definition with its "complete thought" as a criterion. If, for example, a reader attempts to count the number of sentences that occur on this or any other page of print, he usually does not stop to decide whether each group counted expresses a "complete thought." In fact he may not read a single word of the material nor even attempt to discover what the discourse is about. He simply gives attention to the marks of end punctuation and to the capital letters with which, in our conventions of writing, we begin sentences. The practical definition used to count the number of sentences in any written material would thus be phrased as follows: A sentence is a word or group of words standing between an initial capital letter and a mark of end punctuation or between two marks of end punctuation.

The student, however, very often finds his writing condemned because of his "sentence fragments" and "comma splices." His teachers insist that the groups of words he has marked with capital letters at the beginning and periods at the end are not "sentences" in that they do not contain a "thought." Sometimes they insist that these marks for the boundaries of some sentences include too much material for one sentence and should therefore be changed to indicate the several "sentence" thoughts "spliced" together in the larger group. Sometimes they insist that the word groups marked off with the signs of "end" punctuation, although they are not "sentence fragments" as such, in that they do contain a "thought," still are "insignificant" sentences, and need to be joined in order to make a "complete" thought.

To remedy such pupil practices teachers give their students vague admonitions to develop "a sentence sense" and "to feel out" the sentences they have written in order to determine "whether the thought is complete or not."

> The best way to tell whether our sentences are complete or not is to "feel them out." Incomplete sentences do not make sense. . . . It is really not difficult to tell a fragment from a complete sentence. We seem to "feel" instinctively when a thought is stated completely. . . . Another very common error in pupils' themes is the "comma splice" . . . they sometimes join two of their sentences together with a comma. If you have learned to "feel out" the complete sentence unit, you will not be likely to make this error. . . . The best way to find such errors is to read one's own sentences aloud "feeling" carefully whether the thought is complete or not.[1]

If the following paragraph is read aloud with normal intonation to a group of teachers, and these teachers are asked to record simply the number of sentence units to be marked by the punctuation, there will be considerable disagreement. Usually with a dozen or more teachers the count will vary surprisingly; every number from three to nine will be indicated.

[1] F. G. Walcott, C. D. Thorpe, and S. P. Savage, *Growth in Thought and Expression* (Chicago: Benjamin H. Sanborn and Co., 1940), II, 31, 32, 35, 37.

Behind all of them lay two fundamental causes, which most Germans have persistently refused to admit. One was the failure of the will to do; the other was the almost organized abandonment of the currency to its fate. This is why I have all along maintained in these columns that there has never been anything vitally wrong with the country itself. Her soil is as productive as ever. The bosom of her earth is still a treasure house of coal and iron. The people have not lost their craft or cunning. The country escaped war ravage. The only concrete thing that went to pot was the currency.

Teachers have never succeeded in agreeing upon a set of criteria to determine just what and how much can be put into a word-group punctuated as a single sentence.

On the other hand, the student in his reading finds single words punctuated as sentences and word groups that consist of hundreds of words. The 1943 report of the President of Columbia University contains one word-group, punctuated as a single sentence, which fills eleven pages and consists of 4,284 words.[2] Within this one sentence ten paragraph divisions are marked. As a matter of actual practice most of the consideration given to the sentence in the schools centers upon the punctuation of written material.

Of course, our only difficulty with complete sentences comes when we write. We usually speak in complete sentence units without much difficulty, but when we write, we have so many other things to think about that we get lost.[3]

Theoretically many teachers would disagree with this statement and insist not only that conversation abounds in sentence "fragments" but that one of the most important objectives of school English is to develop in students "the ability to speak, in con-

[2] Report of the President of Columbia University for the Year Ending June 30, 1943. 44th Series #3, December 2, 1943, pp. 5–16.
[3] Walcott, Thorpe, and Savage, *op. cit.*, p. 34.

versation, in complete sentences, not in broken phrasing." [4] Practically, however, they devote their time to the sentences as marked off by punctuation in their students' writing. Discussions of the sentence, for students and for teachers, deal with "the types of sentences that appear in good prose." Sometimes these discussions take note of fragmentary sentences, but these are always the "fragmentary sentences" that appear in writing.

> Modern writers are making increasingly greater use of snatches of phrases and subordinate clauses set off as sentences even when the missing elements are not always immediately apparent. They do this particularly in situations in which they are concerned with communicating the psychological processes governing the minds of their characters. [5]

It is writing and the writer's practice of using graphic devices to mark off units of his writing which are the objects of the teacher's consideration. The rhetorical sentences of written composition rather than the grammatical sentences of living speech have occupied the attention of most teachers in their search for some rule, some specific directions, that would furnish students a clear and definite guide for the use of "starters and stoppers"—the punctuation to mark the beginnings and ends of sentences.

For these guides they have turned to the theoretical discussions of the sentence as these have appeared in the grammars and in the books that have dealt with the definitions of the sentence unit. Some of the two hundred–odd definitions have attempted to indicate quantitative limits for the material that a sentence should

---

[4] C. S. Pendleton, *The Social Objectives of School English* (Nashville, 1924), p. 36. Of the 1,581 objectives listed and ranked in order of importance according to the judgments of a large body of experienced teachers of English this objective was in second place of all those that were put into the group of "the greatest importance," "outcomes to be attained at all costs."

[5] Russell H. Barker, *The Sentence* (New York: Rinehart and Company, 1939), p. 8.

or could include. Examples of these statements are the following:

> 1. Speech is made up of separate sayings, each complete in itself . . . these sayings are sentences. Any complete meaning is a sentence.[6]

But how much must one know in order to have a "complete" meaning? Is it enough to know that a particular identified book is red in color? Or must I know that this red book contains accounts, and that these accounts are those of a particular family, and that they are accounts of income, and that the income is that of three years ago, and that the head of this family is charged with income-tax evasion, and that this particular book has been lost and that there is a reward for its recovery, and that the red color is the only mark of identification for the account book of this particular year? How much of all this is necessary for a "complete" meaning and how many complete meanings or sentence meanings are there in all?

> 2. A "complete" thought, or what we may call a *sentence-thought* is therefore any idea or group of ideas that is felt as answering to one impulse of attention. Not the amount of meaning but its being felt as *directed* is what makes it complete. . . . The only limit to the possible length of the sentence is the number of ideas that can be grasped in their relations in one act of attention.[7]

> 3. The completeness or incompleteness of a communication is wholly a matter of the intent or idea in the mind of the speaker.[8]

---

[6] Alexander Bain, *A Higher English Grammar* (London, 1879), p. 8.

[7] Alfred D. Sheffield, *Command of Sentence Patterns* (Chicago: Scott, Foresman and Co., 1924), pp. 34, 37.

[8] Janet Rankin Aikin, *A New Plan of English Grammar* (New York: Henry Holt and Co., 1933), p. 14.

4. A sentence is an utterance which makes just as long a communication as the speaker has intended to make before giving himself a rest.[9]

This search for definite quantitative limitations of content for the sentence unit has not produced acceptable and workable criteria.

More frequently the effort to define the sentence has turned to attempts to indicate the *constituents* of a sentence thought, and teachers have sought in the identification of these constituents the criteria for completeness. For centuries [10] it has been insisted that, for completeness, every sentence must have a word representing a person, place, or thing, and also a word "asserting" or "saying something" about that person, place, or thing. There must be a "subject" and a "predicate." This statement of the parts which a sentence must contain occurs in most school texts that deal with grammar in any way.

Here then is the secret of every sentence: first we always name some object or place or person or thing; and then, second, we say something about that object or place or person or thing. Unless we do these two things, we are not making complete sentences. . . . The subject will always be the object, place, person, or thing that is being talked about. The predicate will always be what is said about that object, place, person, or thing.[11]

---

[9] Allan H. Gardiner, *Theory of Speech and Language* (Oxford: Clarendon Press, 1932), p. 208.

[10] Cf. the following from the thirteenth century: "*Ad perfectionem locutionis duo sunt necessaria scilicet suppositum et appositum. (Suppostitum est illud, de quo fit sermo, appositum est illud, quod dicitur de supposito.*)" Quoted from Delbrück: see Eugen Seidel, *Geschichte und Kritik der wichtigsten Satzdefinitionen* (Jena: Jenaer Germanistische Forschungen [Bd. 27], 1935).

[11] Walcott, Thorpe, and Savage, *op. cit.*, I, 61, 62.

Two elements are necessary to the expression of a complete thought: (1) a subject which names a person or thing or idea about which a statement is made; and (2) a predicate which makes a statement about the subject.[12]

It is certainly true that many of the English expressions that we call sentences have the parts indicated in these quotations. But difficulties arise when we state this descriptive fact as a definition and then assume that its terms furnish adequate criteria for identifying and separating sentences from nonsentence word-groups. Use of only these criteria would make us accept as sentences many expressions we now usually call nonsentences. A situation such as that in which a dog is making the noise called *barking* can be expressed by the utterance *the dog is barking*. This expression we accept as a sentence. It fulfills the criteria indicated above—the word *dog* represents an animal, the word *barking* an action, and the action is attributed to the dog as performer. But the word-group *the barking dog*, expressing the same situation, also contains all the indicated criteria. An animal is named, the *dog;* an action, *barking*, is ascribed to this animal, the *dog*, as performer. Nothing in the criteria contained in the definition above will serve to guide us to accept *the dog is barking* as a sentence, and to exclude *the barking dog* as a nonsentence. The same is true of such word groups as *the red book, a beautiful white dress with a wide lace hem, who the man is, why he will come*. The statements in these textbook definitions quite obviously do not furnish the actual criteria we use practically in such a situation.

These statements fail us, not only when we assume that every utterance having the two constituents can be accepted as a sentence, but also when we assume that unless an utterance contains both a "subject" *and* a "predicate" it is not a sentence. Such an assumption would make us exclude most requests or commands.

[12] Barker, *The Sentence, op. cit.*, p. 4.

The materials examined for this book abound in such expressions as:

> come over soon
> send me a memorandum
> wait a minute

In respect to these expressions it is usually insisted that additional words are "understood." We must supply the "subject" word *you*. If, however, these expressions are to be accepted as fulfilling the requirements of the definition above on the ground that we must *supply words that are not there but "understood,"* then certainly by the same procedure many other expressions must be accepted as sentences. Nothing in the criteria furnished in these definitions gives us any indication of a limit to the number or the kind of words that may be "understood."

Actual expression as heard	Expression with possible words "understood"
Congratulations	I offer you my congratulations
Fire	The building is on fire
Hands up	You put your hands up
Tomorrow	(When are you going) I'm going tomorrow
Down with the King	You let us dethrone (cast down) the King

The following newspaper headlines would also be filled out to make complete sentences with words "understood."

Headline	To be supplied
Wedding Bells for Student and Japanese Bride	ring
New Charge against Doctor ———	is made
Three Fraternities on Probation after Party	are put
Strike Called in Protest to King Leopold	is

By means of supplying words "understood," practically any expression can be made to fit the requirements set up in the definitions. Clearly these definitions as they stand do not furnish all the criteria needed nor all that are actually used in practice by teachers in the schools to determine whether any particular collocation of words is a sentence.

Much labor has thus, over a period of many years, been devoted to the problem of defining the sentence. Collected evidence of this labor appears in the books that have, during the last twenty years, reviewed and criticized the former definitions and attempted to state anew the essential features of the sentence. John Ries, for example, subjects some 140 of the different definitions to much sound and searching criticism and then adds to the number by creating a new one. (The English here is my translation.) [13]

> A sentence is a grammatically constructed smallest unit of speech which expresses its content with respect to this content's relation to reality.

In 1935 Eugen Seidel [14] published his history and criticism of some eighty of the most important definitions, and in 1941 Karl Sundén published his *Linguistic Theory and the Essence of the Sentence.*[15] Sundén also devotes special attention to a critical evaluation of the more recent treatments of the sentence, especially those of Ries, Gardiner, and Jespersen, and then finds the "essence of the sentence" in what he calls its modal function—its stating that the thing meant by the sentence "has reality even if it belonged

---

[13] John Ries, *Was ist ein Satz?* first published at Marburg in 1894, and then revised and published at Prague in 1931 (*Beiträge zur Grundlegung der Syntax*, Heft 3). "*Ein Satz ist eine grammatisch geformte kleinste Redeeinheit, die ihren Inhalt im Hinblick auf sein Verhältnis zur Wirklichkeit zum Ausdruck bringt.*"

[14] Seidel, *op. cit.*

[15] Karl F. Sundén, *Linguistic Theory and the Essence of the Sentence* (Göteborgs högskolas årsskrift) 47 (1941), No. 5.

to the world of the imagination." His conclusion is embodied in his definition:

> A sentence is a portion of speech that is putting forward to the listener a state of things (a thing meant) as having validity, i.e., as being true.[16]

Practically all of this tremendous labor which has concerned itself with defining the sentence as a grammatical unit has approached the problem of analysis *by way of the meaning or thought content.* Most of those who have sought to define the sentence, under whatever term used—λόγος, *oratio, propositio, phrase, thèse, Satz*— have tried to find universal characteristics of meaning content for this speech unit—characteristics that could not only be identified in the utterances of all languages, but would serve also as defining criteria of the sentence in any language. They have assumed that "language is a 'reflection' of thought," and that grammar, which was assumed to be the "laws of language," must therefore represent the laws of human thought. Sometimes it has been explicitly asserted that "the human mind thinks in sentences," "understands in sentences." Therefore, it is argued, the basic characteristics of the sentence, the "essence of the sentence," must be something common in the utterances of all languages. The very fact, however, that the many attempts to grasp the "essence of the sentence" by this type of subtle reasoning and analysis have not given us a satisfactorily acceptable or workable set of criteria to make an acceptable definition (shown by the continual argument and dispute, and the varied attempts to form new definitions) seems to indicate that we must approach the problem from a different point of view.

The more one works with the records of the actual speech of people the more impossible it appears to describe the requirements

[16] *Ibid.,* p. 40.

of English sentences in terms of meaning content. It is true that whenever any relationship is grasped we have the material or content with which a sentence can be made. But this same content can be put into a variety of linguistic forms, some of which can occur alone as separate utterances and some of which always occur as parts of larger expressions. As indicated above, a situation in which a dog is making the noise called *barking* can be grasped either by the linguistic form *the dog is barking*, which can occur as an utterance separated from any other speech, or the same situation can be grasped in the form *the barking dog*, a form which, except as an answer to such a question as "What frightened the burglar away?" occurs only as a part of some larger expression, such as *the barking dog protected the house*. In similar fashion a situation in which a mother provides a home for her boy may be expressed either in the linguistic form *the mother supports him* or in the form *his mother's support*. In both expressions the relationship that has been grasped is the same. The form of the first is that which might appear entirely by itself in a separate utterance; the form of the second might appear as a part of a larger unit such as *his mother's support enabled him to devote himself to music*. A situation in which water is mixed with some solution to weaken it may be grasped in the form *the water diluted the solution*, which might occur as a separate utterance, or in the slightly different form *the water diluted solution*, which would occur only as part of a larger expression such as *the water diluted solution was too weak to be effective*.

In other words, the characteristics which distinguish those expressions which occur alone as separate utterances and those which occur only as parts of larger units are not matters of content or meaning, but matters of form. These formal matters are not the same from language to language. Each language has its distinct patterns of formal arrangements for utterances which occur alone as separate expressions. The one thing in which various languages do agree is the fact that, in all the languages that we know, there are utterances that stand alone, that are separate from other utterances, that occur with silence before and after the utterance. This common fact has been made the basis of some of the definitions of the sentence. Jespersen, for example, framed his definition in this way.

> A sentence is a (relatively) complete and independent human utterance—the completeness and independence being shown by its standing alone or its capability of standing alone, i.e., of being uttered by itself.[17]

Somewhat similar, and earlier, the definition by Meillet furnished the base upon which others have built.

> . . . the sentence can be defined [as follows]: a group of words joined together by grammatical agreements [relating devices] and which, not grammatically dependent upon any other group, are complete in themselves.[18] [The English here is my translation.]

Bloomfield used that part of Meillet's definition which touched formal features.

> A sentence is a construction (or form) which, in the given utterance, is not part of any larger construction.[19]

The following quotation will help to make clear the significance of Bloomfield's definition.

[17] Otto Jespersen, *Philosophy of Grammar* (New York: Henry Holt and Co., 1924), p. 307.

[18] A. Meillet, *Introduction à l'étude comparative des langues indo-européenes* (Paris, 1903), p. 326 (3d ed., 1912, p. 339). ". . . *la phrase peut être définie: un ensemble d'articulations liées entre elles par des rapports grammaticaux et qui, ne dépendent grammaticalement d'aucun autre ensemble, se suffisent à elles-mêmes.*"

[19] Leonard Bloomfield, "A Set of Postulates for the Science of Language," *Language*, 2 (1926), 156. See also Bloomfield's review of Ries's *Was ist ein Satz?* in *Language*, 7 (1931), 204.

In any utterance, a linguistic form appears either as a constituent of some larger form, as does *John* in the utterance *John ran away*, or else as an independent form, not included in any larger (complex) linguistic form, as, for instance, *John* in the exclamation *John!* When a linguistic form occurs as part of a larger form, it is said to be in *included position;* otherwise it is said to be in *absolute position* and to constitute a *sentence.* . . .

An utterance may consist of more than one sentence. This is the case when the utterance contains several linguistic forms which are not by any meaningful, conventional grammatical arrangement (that is, by any construction) united into a larger form, e.g., *How are you? It's a fine day. Are you going to play tennis this afternoon?* Whatever practical connection there may be between these three forms, there is no grammatical arrangement uniting them into one larger form: the utterance consists of three sentences.

It is evident that the sentences in any utterance are marked off by the mere fact that each sentence is an independent linguistic form, not included by virtue of any grammatical construction in any larger linguistic form.[20]

In this book we shall accept as our general definition of the sentence—our starting point—the words of Bloomfield.

> Each sentence is an independent linguistic form, not included by virtue of any grammatical construction in any larger linguistic form.

The basic problem of the practical investigation undertaken here is not solved simply by accepting Bloomfield's definition of a sentence. As one approaches the body of recorded speech which constitutes the material to be analyzed [21] (or any body of re-

---

[20] Leonard Bloomfield, *Language, op. cit.,* p. 170.

[21] See Chapter I, p. 3, for a description of these materials.

corded speech), just how should he proceed to discover the portions of an utterance that are not "parts of any larger construction"? How can he find out the "grammatical constructions" by virtue of which certain linguistic forms are included in larger linguistic forms? What procedure will enable him to decide which linguistic forms can "stand alone as independent utterances"?

Answers to these questions had to be found early in the investigation.[22]

We started first with the term *utterance*. Although the word *utterance* appears frequently in linguistic discussions and has occurred a number of times in this chapter, there has been nothing to indicate how much talk an "utterance" includes. The definition that "an act of speech is an utterance" [23] doesn't furnish any quantitative measure of either "an act of speech" or of "an utterance." Bernard Bloch calls attention to this vagueness but finds it unnecessary for his purpose to give the term more definiteness.

> A single act of speech is an *utterance*. It is true that this definition, like Bloomfield's, leaves the limits of an utterance completely vague, and therefore fails to tell us just how much of speech an utterance is supposed to include. For our purpose, however [phonemic analysis], the length or inclusiveness of utterances can be ignored.[24]

[22] Very few investigators have tried to discover answers to such questions as these. Roy G. Curtis reported the results of his study in a dissertation entitled *An Investigation of Some of the Structures of Independent Utterances in Modern English* (Ann Arbor: University of Michigan, 1947). He studied the spontaneous responses of one thousand native English-speaking informants to a carefully prepared page of printed material consisting of a succession of words in which various types of sequence were "planted," but in which appeared no marks to separate any groups or sequences. He attempted to record the responses of these informants in order to determine which sequences would be reacted to as units that could occur alone in their natural English speech— i.e., units that could, in their own practical conversation, normally occur with silence on their part, before and after the utterance.

[23] Bloomfield, "A Set of Postulates . . ." *op. cit.*, p. 154.

[24] B. Bloch, "A Set of Postulates for Phonemic Analysis," *Language*, 24 (1949), 7.

For the purposes of this investigation, however, which aimed to discover and describe the significant features of "sentences" as they occur in the records of actual conversation, it was necessary to start with some unit of talk that could be marked off with no uncertainty. These units were to be collected from the materials, and then compared and classified.

The recorded conversations provided the suggestion for the first step. The easiest unit in conversation to be marked with certainty was the talk of one person until he ceased, and another began. This unit was given the name "utterance." In this book, then, the two-word phrase *utterance unit* will mean any stretch of speech by one person before which there was silence on his part and after which there was also silence on his part. Utterance units are thus those chunks of talk that are marked off by a shift of speaker. As indicated above, it was necessary to find some way of deciding what portions of speech could "stand alone," what constituted independent or free expressions—free, in that they were not necessarily bound to other expressions to make a single unit. It seemed obvious that in a conversation in which two speakers participate, the stretch of speech of one speaker at one time can be taken as a portion that does stand by itself, unless, of course, that speaker has been so completely interrupted that he stops because of the interruption.[25] The first step, then, in the procedure to determine the linguistic forms that can stand alone as independent utterances

---

[25] These interruptions which stop the speaker can be recognized by certain matters of "external" evidence. Among these are: (1) The speech activities of two or more persons overlap. The records reveal the beginning of the speech of a second speaker while the first is still speaking and sometimes the beginning of the new speaker is so loud that it makes the continued speech of the first speaker difficult or impossible to hear and understand. (2) Certain utterance forms occur only in situations in which there is evidence of such breaking in of a second speaker. (3) Statistically the situations were very few in which it was impossible to hear all of an utterance unit, or rather such an utterance as would fit into the classification groups of Chapter III.

was thus to record the utterance units as marked off by a change of speaker.

These utterance units exhibited great variety both in length and in form. It was a basic assumption of our approach, however, that all the utterances that appeared in the recorded materials were pertinent to the investigation. It was not our task arbitrarily to include some and to exclude others as unworthy of consideration. The great range of actual variety in these utterance units was thus an accepted factor of the problem before us. The following conversation, consisting of sixteen utterance units, shows something of the variety of the units marked off by this first step of our procedure.[26]

1. [A—— I don't know whether you let B—— go out during the week do you suppose he could come over tonight while we go out to dinner]
2. [Well the difficulty is J—— that he got back in his lessons]
3. [Oh|oh]
4. [And in his last report about two weeks ago he was down in two subjects his father hasn't been letting him do anything]
5. [Well that's a good idea]
6. [I'm awfully sorry]
7. [Well that's all right thanks A—— to tell you the truth I don't want awfully badly to go you know what I mean]

[26] It is perhaps unnecessary to remind the reader that the body of material which furnished the basis for this study was living speech mechanically recorded, not writing. Punctuation, therefore, has no part in our descriptive treatment of the sentence. The final chapter, however, dealing with "Practical Applications," does contain some discussion of the punctuation of sentences in written material. Quotations from the materials will use conventional spelling but no punctuation. Sometimes intonation marks will be necessary.

   8. [M⌐hm⌐] [27]
   9. [Well how's the garden]
   10. [Oh it's much worse than yours I imagine the only
       thing that looks decent at all is the strawberries]
   11. [Yes I know but you know they're not going to be
       any good unless they get some sun and dry weather]
   12. [No well there's still time for them isn't there]
   13. [Yes I know]
   14. [I've got strawberries started have you]
   15. [What]
   16. [Some of the berries have started on my plants]

Because the recorded materials were all of practical conversations, not lectures, nor sustained narratives, the utterance units
marked by a shift of speaker were limited in length. Even so, it
could not be assumed that each of these utterance units contained
only one unit that could stand alone. We could not take for granted
that these utterance units contained only a single free utterance,
nor that they were minimum free utterances. We could assume,
however, that each utterance unit if not interrupted must be one
of the following:
   1. A single minimum free utterance.
   2. A single free utterance, but expanded, not minimum.
   3. A sequence of two or more free utterances.
   We start then with the assumption that a sentence (the particular unit of language that is the object of this investigation) is a
single free utterance, minimum or expanded; i.e., that it is "free"
in the sense that it is not included in any larger structure by means
of any grammatical device.
   Our immediate task will be to identify and to classify the single
free utterances, the *sentences*, that appear in our materials. The

---

[27] See Note on Intonation on p. 26 ff.

procedures [28] for that task and the resulting classification constitute the subject matter of the next chapter.

NOTE ON INTONATION

All the sounds of language must inevitably be of some pitch. Languages differ greatly, however, with respect to the use and significance of pitch changes. Speakers of American English employ a variety of pitch sequences, covering especially the ends of phrases or utterances, that fall into a few significant patterns. It is these significant patterns that we refer to when we use here the term "intonation." Here, we are not concerned with those intonation sequences or contours or curves that carry emotional meanings but with the few patterns that provide the basic molds for ordinary English utterances. These are part of the signalling system of English structure, and at times they furnish the minimum distinctive contrast to separate different structural meanings. In general, the discussion in this book strives to center attention upon the signals of structural meaning other than intonation. It will be necessary, however, from time to time to point out the contrastive features of intonation that furnish special structural signals. For this purpose I shall use the following simplified system of marking and notation adapted from the work of Dr. Kenneth L. Pike as summarized in his *Intonation of American English* (Ann Arbor: University of Michigan Press, 1945).

[28] It is not my intention to burden the reader with all the details of each of the procedures used in this investigation. Throughout the book, attention should center primarily upon the description of the results of the study—the characteristics of the sentence units revealed by this examination of a large body of English utterances. Occasionally, however, it has seemed necessary to explain at some length some features of the procedures used, in order that the reader might understand more fully the statements of the results and evaluate their soundness. This more complete statement seemed especially necessary at the beginning to show the methods I used to determine the units to be examined. Sometimes, however, it has seemed unnecessary to do more than to make a brief general statement of the method employed.

1. *Four levels include all the intervals essential for American English:*
   No. 1—extra high (two steps above the usual voice level)
   No. 2—high (one step above the usual voice level)
   No. 3—the usual voice level
   No. 4—low (one step below the usual voice level)

2. *Intonation sequences will be marked by lines or by numbers or by both. They will be referred to by numbers.*

He went to the |o| ffice
(3——————2——————4)

What did you |tell| him
(3——————2——————4)

These are examples of the most frequent intonation curve in American English, the 2–4 pattern, sometimes also indicated as the 3–2–4 pattern.

The lines that represent intonation patterns must not be taken to mean that the voice maintains exactly the same pitch throughout all the syllables included by the line. These lines are schematic and represent only the points on the contour significant for the particular structure being discussed.

The drop from 2 to 4 occurs between syllables of words of more than one syllable but glides through the vowel of a one-syllable word.

on the |black| board   on the |wall|
(3——2——4)   (3——2——4)

Special stress to bring into prominence particular words will shift the emphasis but will not change the pattern of the intonation.

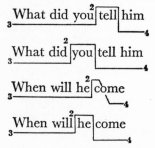

A 2–4 intonation curve usually carries a meaning of finality and is, therefore, the most frequent pattern for the ends of sentences of all kinds—statements, questions, and requests.

A 2–3 intonation curve usually signals a continuation rather than the end of a sentence.

$$_3\overline{\quad\text{Tom has}\quad}\overset{2}{\ulcorner\text{gone}}\searrow_4$$

$$_3\overline{\quad\text{Tom has}\quad}\overset{2}{\ulcorner\text{gone}}\searrow_3 \qquad \text{(but he may come back)}$$

Rising intonations 3–4–2 or 3–2–1 or 3–2 often carry the meaning of unfinished utterance, as in a series.

$$_3\overset{2}{\diagup\text{one}} \quad _3\overset{2}{\diagup\text{two}} \quad _3\overset{2}{\diagup\text{three}} \quad _3\overset{2}{\diagup\text{four}}\searrow_4$$

Rising intonations are also used in some questions:

$$_3\overline{\quad\text{Do you know}\quad}_4\overset{2}{\ulcorner\text{him}} \qquad 3\text{–}4\text{–}2$$

$$_3\overline{\quad\text{Do you}\quad}\overset{2}{\ulcorner\text{know him}}\overset{1}{\urcorner} \qquad 3\text{–}2\text{–}1$$

III. Kinds of Sentences

As indicated above, simply to insist that a *sentence* is a free or independent span of talk marked by the fact that no specific grammatical device makes it a portion of a larger unit, provides little help to an investigator who collects a body of actual conversations and then attempts to discover inductively the formal patterns of the various kinds of utterances that can stand alone. He must have a procedure that does not demand for its starting point information that forms part of the object of the investigation. He must have a body of acceptably identified single free utterances in which he can isolate the minimum free utterances before he can discover the grammatical devices by which minimum utterances are expanded and by which smaller structures are included in larger units. Our definition furnishes only the basic characteristic of the kind of units the grammarian must deal with. We cannot employ that basic characteristic (no specific grammatical device makes it a portion of a larger unit) as a means of isolating a body of free utterances in order to discover the grammatical devices they use. Although units of this kind seem to occur in all the languages we know, the formal patterns of these units in English, the patterns we are seeking to discover and describe, differ, we assume, from those of any other language. The method of approach we use here may be useful for investigators in other languages, but the description of the results here obtained has meaning solely for English.

In the effort to find a workable method of identifying **and** separating the single free utterances from sequences of two **or** more free utterances and to group them into their various kinds in order to discover the particular formal patterns that English uses, it was necessary again to turn aside from the usual procedures and classifications of the conventional grammars. Two kinds of classification usually appear in those grammars, both based upon definitions attempting to state *the characteristic meaning content of each class*.

Typical of the first kind of classification into simple, compound, complex, and compound-complex sentences are the following statements.

> A "simple sentence" is a group of words which expresses a single independent thought.
>
> A "compound sentence" is a group of words which expresses two or more connected and co-ordinate thoughts.
>
> A "complex sentence" is a group of words which expresses two or more unified thoughts, one of which is the main or principal thought having dependent on it one or more subordinate thoughts.[1]

> Sentences are divided according to their structure into classes—simple, compound, and complex. A simple sentence contains but one independent proposition. A compound sentence contains two or more independent propositions. A complex sentence contains one independent proposition and one or more subordinate clauses.[2]

> According to their form sentences are classified as simple, complex, and compound. The first contains one independent clause only, with no dependent clause; the second contains

---

[1] Bertha M. Watts, *Modern Grammar at Work* (Boston: Houghton Mifflin Co., 1944), pp. 404, 405, 407.

[2] George O. Curme, *A Grammar of the English Language* (Boston: D. C. Heath and Co., 1931), III, 161.

in addition one or more dependent clauses; the third contains more than one independent clause. The complex and compound types may combine in the same sentence. . . .

The clause is a syntactical unit consisting of a combination of subject, verb, and complement, or any two of these three. . . . It will easily be seen that the terms sentence and independent clause are closely allied in meaning, and the latter might be dispensed with except that it is often convenient to use in describing the "sentence part" of a sentence.[3]

These definitions provide no practical means of sorting out the single free utterances from other utterances presented in the recorded conversations. To use them at all we must have clear, precise meanings for such terms as "single independent thought," "connected thoughts," "unified thoughts," "subordinate thoughts," "independent proposition," "independent clause," "dependent clause," "subordinate clause," "the 'sentence part' of a sentence." Not only do we not have acceptable precise meanings for these terms, but the very object of our investigation at this point is to discover and describe the objective facts which these terms are designed to cover.

Typical of the second kind of classification are the following quotations:

> According to their idea or content English sentences are classified as declarative, interrogative, imperative, or exclamatory. The first makes a statement, the second asks a question, the third makes a request or command, and the fourth expresses strong emotion.[4]

> The form of the sentence may be: (1) exclamatory, uttering an outcry, or giving expression to a command, desire, often closing with an exclamation point—perhaps the oldest

---

[3] Janet Rankin Aiken, *A New Plan of English Grammar, op. cit.*, pp. 15, 16, 31.
[4] *Ibid.*, p. 15.

form of the sentence; (2) declarative, stating a fact, closing with a period; (3) interrogative, asking a question, closing with an interrogation point.[5]

The imperative, one of the four sentence types, embodies command. . . . The exclamatory sentence expresses strong emotion in the form of an exclamation or cry. . . . The interrogative sentence asks a question. . . . The declarative sentence states a fact.[6]

Again the definitions furnish no practical help in sorting out our utterances. It is not enough to say that a sentence that "asks a question" is an "interrogative sentence," or that a sentence that "gives a command" is an "imperative sentence," or that a sentence that "makes a statement" is a "declarative sentence." No real gain derives from simply attaching technical names to the meanings "asks a question," "gives a command," "makes a statement." We are concerned with discovering just how we know that any particular sentence "asks a question," or "gives a command," or "makes a statement." In other words, how in English are these particular meanings signaled?

There are two important steps in the procedure adopted here in the effort to arrive at a body of single free utterances for examination and to separate them into their different kinds. The basis for this procedure can perhaps be made clear by the use of a general formula to represent the function of language.[7]

Descriptions of all types of animal behavior often employ the terms "stimulus" and "response." The cat which has been without

[5] George O. Curme, *A Grammar of the English Language, op. cit.*, p. 1.

[6] Margaret M. Bryant, *A Functional English Grammar* (Boston: D. C. Heath and Co., 1945), pp. 99–102.

[7] This formula must not be taken as representing any psychological assertions or assumptions whatever. It is strictly schematic and limited to the particular point dealt with here—the representation of certain broad aspects of the functioning of language.

food for some time, stimulated by certain sensations, responds by
seeking food and devouring it. Man, too, stimulated by the sensa-
tion called "hunger," may respond by silently seeking food and
eating it. Or, stimulated by excessive heat of the direct sun, he
may respond by seeking the comparative coolness of a place under
a shade tree or in the water of a river or of a shower. In each
instance, we can describe the behavior by indicating the situation
which provided the stimulus and the practical action which was
the response.

$$S \longrightarrow R$$

In many circumstances when we observe acts of behavior we can
do little more than guess which particular elements of a situation
actually operated as the stimulus. We assume, however, that there
was some stimulus, and in the practical affairs of life assume a connection between regularly recurring acts of behavior and the
presence of certain situations.

In the instances of the cat and of the man indicated above, the
practical action of the response as well as the stimulus which arose
out of the practical situation were both within the same individual.
The same nervous system that received the practical stimulus responded with practical action. With man, however, the process
may be quite different. A man, stimulated by a practical situation
of hunger, may respond, not by seeking food directly and eating
it, but by uttering certain speech sounds, and his wife, or the cook,
or the waiter in a restaurant, will respond practically to the
stimulus of these speech sounds by seeking or preparing food and
bringing it to him. Man has thus learned to use the sound waves
as a means of connection between two nervous systems.[8] When

----

[8] For a more complete discussion of language as the use of sound waves to bridge
the gap between two nervous systems, and of the "meaning" of linguistic forms, see
Leonard Bloomfield's *Language*, Chapters 2 and 9, pp. 21–41, 139–57. The sketch
here is based on Bloomfield's material. See also the chapter, "The Nature of Human
Language," in my forthcoming book, *Toward an Understanding of Language*.

stimulated by some practical situation he may thus respond by setting up certain vibrations in the sound waves ($S \longrightarrow r$), and these vibrations striking the ear of another person become the stimulus for a "directed" practical response on his part ($s \longrightarrow R$). A formula to represent this modified sequence would be

$$S \longrightarrow r \longrightarrow s \longrightarrow R,$$

in which the capital S represents the practical situation that creates the practical stimulus, and the capital R at the end represents the practical response. The small r represents the sounds spoken by the first individual as a substitute for a practical response on his part, and the small s represents these sounds as heard and understood by another individual, providing in him the effective stimulus to the practical response.

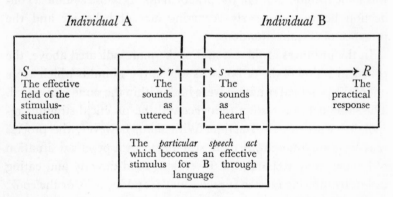

The actual speech act consists of both the r, the sounds uttered by individual A, and the s, the sounds heard by individual B. The "meaning" of any speech signal must consist, then, not only of the practical situation which stimulates the making of the particular speech sounds but also of the practical response which these particular speech sounds (through language) produce in another individual.

One cannot predict the particular speech sounds that A will

utter in any situation or whether he will utter any sounds at all, but, if language is to fulfill its function of providing the means of precise social co-operation, then individual A must be able to predict with considerable accuracy the practical response which particular speech sounds will elicit in individual B. A speaker selects a particular set of speech sounds (a particular *r*) because he knows that it will produce the kind of response he seeks to elicit.[9]

In studying the materials of speech the student can give his attention solely to the *r* of our formula—the sounds as produced by a speaker. He can, for example, examine the articulatory processes by which these sounds are produced, or the acoustic qualities of the sounds in terms of the frequency and the strength of the sound vibrations. If, however, he intends to study a *language as a functioning tool of human society* then he gives his attention to either—

1. The speech sounds in correlation with the situations that usually call them forth, or

2. The speech sounds in correlation with the responses which they elicit.[10]

In the study of the language records of a former time we have usually had to proceed in accord with (1)—that is, examine the details of the language materials as recorded, in relation to the particular situations in which they occurred. The nature of the

---

[9] It is probably valid to insist that any particular speech sounds are "language" in so far as they elicit regular, predictable responses. From this point of view a "linguistic community" consists of those who make the "same" regular and predictable responses to particular speech forms.

[10] See also the following statement from Bloomfield: "Man utters many kinds of vocal noise and makes use of the variety: under certain types of stimuli he produces certain vocal sounds, and his fellows, hearing these same sounds, make the appropriate response. To put it briefly, in human speech, different sounds have different meanings. *To study this co-ordination of certain sounds with certain meanings is to study language.*" [Italics mine.] *Language*, p. 27.

evidence made it necessary to try to arrive at the meanings of language forms by connecting them with recurring elements of the situations in which they were used. The editors of the great Oxford English Dictionary worked in this way.

In the study of living languages, however, it is often possible to proceed in accord with (2). We can observe directly the responses which particular language forms elicit in a speech community. We can proceed on the assumption that if a particular response *regularly* occurs after a speech form or a language pattern then this pattern or form "means" this response. The regularity with which the response follows the utterance of the language pattern becomes the basis for the kind of prediction of a following response that makes the functioning of language possible.[11]

It was this view of language material in relation to the functioning of language that led to the procedures adopted here for the initial sorting and classifying of the utterance units in the mechanically recorded materials that formed the basis for this study. As indicated above, if we were to proceed inductively to find the formal patterns of sentences (single free utterances) in English, we needed to find a workable method of identifying and extracting from the recorded conversations the single free utterances that occurred there—workable in the sense that there should be no uncertainty in the criteria used and that others taking the same set of criteria would arrive at the same results.[12]

The first step in the method used was described in the preceding chapter. We isolated for examination all those stretches of speech that were bounded by a change of speaker, and we called them "utterance units." We assumed that each such utterance unit was

[11] A speech community could thus be defined as all those who make the "same" responses to a set of language patterns.

[12] Only after considerable fruitless experimenting with other approaches to the problem—including the marking of pauses, and of intonation sequences—did I arrive at the procedure here outlined.

one that in English could be spoken by itself—it could stand alone. We did not assume that each of these units, bounded by a change of speaker, constituted a *single* free utterance, but we did assume that (apart from the comparatively few interrupted utterance units which we identified and excluded) each of these chunks of talk must be one of the following:

1. A single *minimum* free utterance.
2. A single free utterance, not minimum but expanded.
3. A sequence of two or more free utterances.

Repeated examination of all these utterance units finally led to a second type of grouping that could be made on a strictly formal basis and thus with a minimum of uncertainty. It was a very simple grouping but it proved to be very useful. All these utterance units marked by a change of speaker could be put into one of the two following classes:

1. Some of the utterance units *began* conversations. No talk preceded them in the particular conversation in which they occurred.[13]

2. All the other utterance units occurred after the conversation had started. They occurred as *responses* to preceding utterance units.

The utterance units of the first group, those that began conversations, I have called "situation utterance units." The utterance units of the second group, those that occurred after the conversation had started, I have called "response utterance units."

Even a very superficial examination of the utterances in the two groups revealed the fact that the "situation utterance units," those that began the conversations, showed less diversity of form than the "response utterance units." Typical of the "situation utterance units" are the following:

---

[13] Most of the conversations were telephone conversations of from five to thirty minutes in length. The repetition of the word *hello* was ignored in gathering the units that began these conversations.

1. I wanted to talk to you about lot number fifty (47) [14]
2. Mr. W—— asked me to ask you if you could come to a meeting in his office tomorrow at nine with Mr. O—— and Mr. B—— (145)
3. Say I just got on Saturday another letter from P—— R—— that has a bearing on the P—— matter (52)
4. When is M—— going up to camp (49)
5. I wonder if I can get an address from you (54)
6. I inquired at your office last week one day about the quonset huts (55)
7. Are you taking orders this morning for funeral flowers (27)
8. I've thought of you a dozen times today it's a wonder your ears haven't been burning up (84)
9. I didn't know whether you called me or not I've been out all evening (88)
10. I wanted to tell P—— about a service on Thursday afternoon the memorial service for —————— (96)
11. I talked to S—— just now and he wants to know how many exactly do we have (111)
12. Mrs. B—— wants you to call her (112)
13. Please excuse this intrusion at your home I just couldn't call on Thursday morning as you asked me to (30)
14. Two things do you happen to have an address or telephone number for L—— and what about those corrections for E—— (97)
15. Do you know if any action was taken in the matter of —————— (117)

---

[14] The numbers in parentheses following the quotations are reference or index numbers to the transcribed material of the conversations which furnished the basic evidence for this study.

16. I forgot when I talked to you just a moment ago to give you C——'s number (121)
17. Listen did you get any shoes (129)
18. Please take these two night letters (146)
19. Just hold on a moment until I answer the doorbell (151)
20. R—— send me two hundred of your cinder blocks tomorrow (244)
21. Would it be possible for me to talk to Dr. F—— just a moment or two (136)
22. I talked to Mr. G—— and he referred me to Dr. A—— and Dr. A—— has approved and is going to call Mr. G—— (138)
23. Will we be able to get into the pool at noon today (43)
24. I was going to talk to you about something but I don't remember what it was (130)
25. A—— I don't know whether you let B—— go out during the week do you suppose he could come over tonight while we go out to dinner (74)
26. My name is C—— D—— (102)

As a matter of fact the few examples just given are not only typical of the "situation utterance units," they represent quite well the range of varieties in these units.[15] From this point, by a long process of comparing each utterance unit with many of the others, *seeking recurrent partials*, it was possible to separate those that consisted of single free utterances from those that consisted of sequences of free utterances. For example, even a very superficial comparison of (5) with (9) above and with (25) leads one to suspect at once that (25) is more than a single free unit. With hundreds of

[15] That is, of the shorter units, for I have not included here examples of long utterance units that began conversations. As a working procedure I assumed that these were not single free utterances.

similar comparisons it was possible to separate all the utterance units that started conversations into two groups: (1) those that were single free utterances and (2) those that were made up of two or more single free units. The basic analysis of the single free utterances that were "situation" rather than "response" utterances was confined to those single free utterances that started conversations and did not include those that occurred after the first single free unit in a stretch of talk made up of several free units. Those single free utterances that were not the first in such a series I have called "sequence" sentences. They differ in form from the first free utterances in a conversation primarily in the fact that they contain sequence signals which tie them to preceding utterances. These sequence signals constitute an important part of English structure and will be discussed in Chapter XI. In other respects these utterances duplicate the forms of the first single free units. In fact, it was this duplication of form that made them recognizable as separate free units. They will, therefore, appear in the discussion as examples without special note of the sequence signals they contain.

With the same process of comparison—seeking recurrent partials—applied to the whole body of single free utterances that had been established, it was possible to arrive at minimum free utterance forms and to find the forms or arrangements by which the minimum free utterances are expanded. The minimum free forms are discussed in connection with basic sentence structure frames in Chapter VIII and the varieties of expansion appear especially in the chapter dealing with "modifiers."

With these single free utterances as a base the greatly diverse utterances in the group of "response utterance units" were examined. Many of this group were found to fit the patterns represented in the group first examined—the "situation utterance units." Many of the "response utterance units," however, differed completely from anything found among the "situation utterance units." [16] Those "response utterance units" that differed from those found among the "situation utterance units" will be discussed later, especially in Chapter VIII.

A third type of grouping derived its method from the formula discussed above. There it was insisted that speech forms mean not only the situations in which they usually occur but also the regular responses which they produce. In connection with our single free utterances—our sentences—we assumed that if certain formal patterns are regularly followed by (correlate regularly with) particular responses on the part of English-speaking hearers, then we can conclude that these formal patterns in our linguistic community (in our language) "mean" these responses—that these formal patterns elicit these responses. We set out, therefore, to group our single free utterances in accord with the responses that followed them. All the evidence that appeared in our records *concerning the nature of the response* was used for this purpose.

This procedure produced the following groups described here in terms of particular features of the responses.[17] It is true that these responses do not occur with 100 per cent frequency,[18] but the regularity of sequence is sufficient to form patterns of response upon which to establish a classification. Upon this basis we find three major groups of utterances in which the evidence of the response was clear in the recorded materials:

I. Those that were immediately and regularly followed by "oral" responses only.

II. Those that were immediately followed by "action" re-

[16] The failure to make this division between "situation utterance units" and "response utterance units" seems to me to account for much of the difficulty grammarians have had in making satisfactory statements concerning English sentences.

[17] Chapter VIII will be devoted to describing the formal structural patterns of the utterances which comprise each of the groups thus identified by the regularity of a particular type of response.

[18] Those utterances for which there appeared no evidence of response in the materials were simply put aside.

sponses, sometimes accompanied by one of a very limited list of oral responses.

III. Those that were accompanied (not necessarily followed) by very brief oral signals of attention interjected at irregular intervals but not interrupting the span of talk.

I. Those single free utterances that are immediately and regularly followed by "oral" responses only

The single free utterances that are characterized by immediate and regular "oral" responses constitute a large group made up of several different kinds. The formal differences in the "oral" responses themselves make it possible to separate this large group of utterances that elicit these "oral" responses into three classes for our description.

A. There are those in which the oral response regularly repeats the preceding utterance. The repetition of the utterance in the response does not always, however, have the same intonation curve. The usual intonation sequence on both utterance and response is the common "falling" contour at the end (3–2–4 or 2–4). These utterances with the oral response repeating the utterance itself [19] occurred, not always, but frequently, at the beginnings of conversations—and often at the end. They are the formulas of greeting and of leave-taking.[20] Although the number of the instances of these utterances with their repeated responses is large, the number of different utterances of this kind is very small. In the recorded

[19] In fact, the repetition of the utterance in the response can probably be used as the formal mark of the greeting when there may be ambiguity. For example, if the utterance *how are you* is followed by the response *how are you* in repetition of the utterance, it is operating as a formula of greeting; if it is followed by the response *fine how are you* it is operating as a question (see section C, p. 45).

[20] In the material following, the single term *greetings* is used as a convenient short name to include not only the formulas of greeting but also those of leave-taking.

conversations the following appeared, listed here in the order of the frequency of their occurrence: [21]

1. At the beginning of conversation.

UTTERANCE	RESPONSE
Hello	Hello
/haɪ/	/haɪ/
Good morning	Good morning
Good afternoon	Good afternoon
Good evening	Good evening

2. At the end of conversation.

Good-by	Good-by
See you later	See you later
See you soon	See you soon

Limited to brief periods of time, two seasonal greetings occurred at the beginnings of the conversations.

Merry Christmas	Merry Christmas
Happy New Year	Happy New Year

Often in these instances the response included only the latter part of the utterance.

Hello Merry Christmas	Merry Christmas
Good morning Happy New Year	Happy New Year

[21] In the materials recorded, there were no examples of *how do you do* and its various reduced forms at the beginning of conversations as a greeting, nor of *good morning, good afternoon, good evening* at the end of conversations in taking leave. *How do you do* and its various reduced forms may, in certain areas, be limited to formal introductions, of which there were none in my recorded materials.

B. There are those in which the oral response consists of one of a very limited list of single words or short word-groups. The utterances themselves that precede and elicit these particular responses usually consist of the names of persons or certain words designating persons. These utterances we have designated as "calls." Only a very few examples of this kind of utterance occurred in the recorded materials. In order to show more of the range of this class of utterances I have added below to the examples taken from the recorded conversations some other instances from notes of other conversations observed directly.

UTTERANCE	RESPONSE
Carol	What
Dad	Yes
Mother	What is it
Say dear	Yes

(From other notes):

UTTERANCE	RESPONSE
1. Robert	Did you call
2. Hey you	What do you want
3. Mr. President	Yes Mr. James
4. Coach	What now
5. Colonel Howard	Just a moment now what is it
6. Steward	Coming sir what is it sir
7. Waiter	Did you want something

In (1), (2), (4), (6), and (7) of the latter instances, as they occurred, the response was accompanied by a movement by the one making the response toward the speaker of the utterance.

It should be noted that the *oral responses* in this group, B, are often of the same form and arrangement as the *utterances* of the next group, C, that elicit a different type of response.

C. *There are those—a very large number—in which the oral response consists of a great variety of forms* other than (*1*) *the repetition of the utterance and* (*2*) *the limited list of words and word-groups that comprise the responses to calls.*[22] These utterances—those that regularly elicit any of this great range of responses—are "questions."

Typical examples taken from the units that "begin conversations" are the following:

UTTERANCE	RESPONSE
Do you remember H—— that worked in ——	Yes yes (205)
Is Mrs. M—— there	No. Mrs. M——'s gone away on vacation (212)
Is Mr. L—— there	I'm sorry he isn't in just now (214)
Have you got moved in	Oh we're all moved in (192)
Will tomorrow night be all right for —	Yes any time tomorrow (189)
What are you going to do for the summer	Oh work (218)
How's your family	Oh everybody's real well (219)
Could you pick me up sometime Saturday morning	Yeah Saturday say between ten and eleven (203)
Do you know whether they've come to take the table top away	I don't know it went downstairs (192)
What was the number of —— on North Ingalls	four—— (206)

[22] This statement is put negatively here and the description of the varieties of these responses reserved for Chapter VIII.

When do you begin out there	Monday (200)
Does B—— have to pay the regular sixty-dollar fee	That's right (99)

Typical examples taken from utterances that appeared after conversations had begun are the following:

UTTERANCE	RESPONSE
I thought I'd go ahead with these is that all right	Yes indeed (207)
Is that going to be too early	No that'll be O.K. (248)
Would Tuesday be possible	Well I think so (225)
Did they say anything about the new one	They didn't know a thing (192)
Go to school did you say	Yeah (217)
Well how are you going to do that you can't do both	I don't know it's going to be difficult (200)
And then when will I move my stuff from here	Friday night if you want to (202)
Where are you now	—— North Ingalls (205)
Where's it going to be	In Detroit (195)
When was that	Monday at eleven (224)
Well what time	Oh any time (219)
How do you spell your name	F—— (215)
That's the amount that *was* deposited	Yes sir (213)
There's no way of getting a substitute	well I don't know (238)
Then you'd have it all ready	I hope so yes (203)
Well now you're sure you won't want it tomorrow	I don't think so I don't need it (203)

Oral responses from a second speaker so regularly follow utterances of this kind—those we call "questions"—that it seems sound to conclude that these utterances *elicit* oral responses—that they are directed to this purpose. "Questions," then, make up the largest group of those utterances that regularly elicit oral responses. The other two groups that elicit oral responses, "calls" and "greetings," not only occur less frequently by comparison with "questions" but they have nothing of the diversity of form (especially in the oral response) that is characteristic of "questions." Together, "questions," "calls," and "greetings" make up the first of the three large classes of utterances that resulted when we grouped them in accord with the kind of response following the utterance.

II. Those single free utterances that are regularly followed by "action" responses

The second of the larger classes of utterances grouped according to the nature of the response is that in which the response is regularly "action" of some kind. These utterances are so regularly followed by an "action" response that they can be said to be directed to eliciting that kind of response. We shall call them "requests."

The following are typical examples of these request utterances with an indication of the actual response for which the materials furnished evidence.

UTTERANCE	RESPONSE
Read that again will you	[Reads aloud a telegram] (239)
Just hold the phone he's on the other wire	[Waits until R—— speaks] (240)
Oh wait a minute	[Waits, silent, until A—— speaks again] (97)
Let me talk to him a minute	[L—— is called to phone] (98)
Let me speak to her please	[She is called to the phone] (110)

Will you see just exactly what his status is

[Clerk checks account and gives the amount owed] (101)

Would you please have Mr. L—— tell her that the Institute is sending her tickets to-day

[Message delivered through Mr. L——] (118)

That'll be O.K. you call the operator

[L—— called the operator immediately] (105)

Please have him call Operator Six when he comes in

[Later F—— called in accord with message delivered] (208)

With utterances of this kind—the request sentences—one of a narrow range of oral responses may accompany the "action" response. It is, however, the regularity of the "action" response that constitutes the pattern here.

UTTERANCE

RESPONSE

Just wire me collect if anything has happened

O.K. [Later the wire is received] (118)

See if you can get a check worked through

All right I'll try [Later call indicates that arrangements have been satisfactorily made] (110)

Let me speak to Miss B—— please

Just a minute [Miss B—— is called to the telephone] (248)

Let us go through the list and then we'll let you know

All right I'll call again in an hour [Calls as promised] (114)

Lets call him ourselves instead of sending B—— over

O.K. that's better [Call made immediately] (105)

Request sentences such as these—utterances regularly eliciting "action" responses—constitute the second large class of utterances grouped in accord with the special type of response they elicit.

III. Those single free utterances in a series that have as responses continued attention, conventionally signalled

The third, and last, of the larger classes of utterances grouped according to the particular kind of response they regularly elicit is that in which the hearer gives continued attention to a series of utterances. Usually the hearer, in some inconspicuous but conventional way, gives the speaker signals of this continued attention. In telephone conversations these signals consist of brief oral sounds interjected at irregular intervals but not interrupting the speaker's span of talk. These brief oral sounds are not predictable, but, in a telephone conversation, if such a sequence of utterances occurs without oral signals of attention on the part of the hearer, the speaker usually interrupts his continuous discourse with such questions as *do you hear me* or *are you (still) there*. In conversations that are not by telephone but face to face, the signals of continued attention are often made not by words but by nods of the head.

The following brief oral signals of attention occurred in the materials. The order of the list represents their relative frequency in our materials.

Yes (most frequently with rising intonation 3–2) [23]

Unh‾|hunh

Yeah (most frequently with rising intonation 3–2)

I see

Good

Oh (usually with rising intonation 3–2)

---

[23] Even when these signals have a falling intonation the descent is usually to 3, not to 4.

> That's right (often with rising intonation 2-3-2)
> Yes I know
> Oh|oh
> Fine
> So (with rising intonation 3-2)
> Oh my goodness
> Oh dear

These oral reactions on the hearer's part do not interfere with the continuous flow of the utterances of the speaker. They simply serve to give something of the hearer's reaction and to signal the fact that he is listening attentively to the speaker. The utterances of the speaker are those of continuous discourse on his part. Sentences having these special characteristics, sentences that are regularly directed to eliciting attention to continuous discourse, we shall call "statements." An example of the utterances of continuous discourse, taken from our recorded materials, follows. The signals of continued attention on the part of the hearer and his reactions are given in parentheses at the places they occurred.

> I wanted to tell you one more thing I've been talking with Mr. D—— in the purchasing department about our typewriter (yes) that order went in March seventh however it seems that we are about eighth on the list (I see) we were up about three but it seems that for that type of typewriter we're about eighth that's for a fourteen-inch carriage with pica type (I see) now he told me that R——'s have in stock the fourteen-inch carriage typewriters with elite type (oh) and elite type varies sometimes it's quite small and sometimes it's almost as large as pica (yes I know) he suggested that we go down and get Mrs. R—— and tell her who we are and that he sent us and try the fourteen-inch typewriters and see if our stencils would work with such type (I see) and if we can use them to get them right away because they have

those in stock and we won't have to wait (that's right) we're
short one typewriter right now as far as having adequate
facilities for the staff is concerned (yes) we're short and we
want to get rid of those rentals (that's right) but they are
expecting within two weeks or so to be receiving—ah—to
start receiving their orders on eleven-inch machines with
pica type (oh) and of course pica type has always been best
for our stencils (yes) but I rather think there might be a
chance that we can work with elite type (well you go over
and try them and see what they're like and do that as soon as
you can so that we'll not miss our chance at these) (121–123)

In these three large classes of sentences, separated by the characteristic responses that regularly followed or attended their
utterance, the last, the sentences of continuous discourse, "statements" exceeded the others in frequency. Of all those that made
up the body of this special material—the ones for which the recorded material furnished clear evidence marking the responses—
"statements" furnished more than 60 per cent of the bulk; "questions," something over 28 per cent; "requests," less than 7 per
cent; "greetings," 4 per cent; and "calls," less than 1 per cent.
All these together constitute the corpus of sentences to be examined
for formal differences. We have assumed that if certain sentences
—single free utterances—are regularly followed by particular responses then these sentences elicit these responses. We have assumed also that if the responses of the different groups are uni-
formly different there must be characteristic formal differences
that mark each group and produce the differing responses—that
the form of a "statement" differs from that of a "request," and
that the form of a "question" differs from both. We assume that
it is possible to discover and describe these differences in form.
Our next chapters will undertake to identify the units of these
forms and the arrangements of these units that constitute the
differences in the various kinds of sentences.

Before we proceed with that particular analysis, however, one other type of free utterance unit needs comment. These utterance units did not appear in any of the mechanically recorded materials examined for this study. I have recorded them from time to time in incidental notes as I heard them—or rather as I overheard them, for they occurred usually when the speaker was alone. The situations in which they appeared were *not* those in which the speaker was using speech forms *in order to elicit particular responses from hearers*. The utterances were not directed to a listener—even to the speaker himself as a hearer. I have called them "noncommunicative utterance units."

Some of these noncommunicative utterances of English, given here in conventional spelling, are the following: *oh* [with both egressive and ingressive air]; *oh, oh; wow; zowie; goodness; damn; damn it; damnation; thunderation; pshaw; my God; gosh; darn; the devil; the deuce*. They are short and usually heavily stressed. Frequently they are uttered without vibration of the vocal cords. The intonation patterns usually end with descending contours, heavy to light stress.

These noncommunicative utterances have some "meaning" in the sense that they are each usually associated with particular situations. They do not elicit regular predictable responses. *Oh; wow; zowie; oh, oh; my God; goodness* are usually uttered in situations in which surprise is an important element. *Ouch* or a strong friction from ingressive air between the upper and lower front teeth are rather definitely limited to situations in which sudden pain is experienced; a prolonged *o—h* or /ˀm/ when the pain continues for a longer time. *Damn; damn it; thunderation; pshaw; oh darn; the devil* usually appear in situations characterized by anger or disgust. A repetition of /a/ with glottal stop preceding each syllable is the laughter that occurs in situations that appear humorous.

All these expressions seem to be spontaneous speech reactions to situations suddenly confronting the speakers. They are, however, in their particular forms, conventional and limited to speakers of English.[24] They may, of course, be overheard by a listener, and the hearer gains some impression of the kind of situation to which the speaker is reacting. In this sense they have "meaning." These forms, with meanings inferred from the situations in which they usually occur, are not used to elicit regular responses from those who hear them.[25] Their purpose is not communicative.[26]

The processes of classification employed here give us the following kinds of sentences or free utterance units.[27]

Communicative utterances

I. Utterances regularly eliciting "oral" responses only:
A. *Greetings.* B. *Calls.* C. *Questions.*

II. Utterances regularly eliciting "action" responses, sometimes accompanied by one of a limited list of oral responses: *requests* or *commands.*

III. Utterances regularly eliciting conventional signals of attention to continuous discourse (sometimes oral signals, but of a limited list, unpredictable in place, and not interrupting the span of talk or utterance unit): *statements.*

Noncommunicative utterances

Utterances characteristic of situations such as surprise, sudden pain, prolonged pain, disgust, anger, laughter, sorrow.

[24] Compare, for example, the expressions used in similar situations by speakers of German, or French, or Chinese, or Aztec. Even where apparently equivalent word forms occur, entirely different values are usually attached.

[25] Some of them, as for example those that occur in situations of pain, may of course be uttered to be overheard and thus arouse sympathy.

[26] Some of these forms are conventionally included in the "exclamations" or "exclamatory sentences." Sometimes they are classed as "interjections." It seems to me very desirable to make a sharp division between the many utterances that have a communicative purpose and the few that have not.

[27] This outline does not include the great diversity of response utterance units indicated above. These will be discussed in Chapter VIII.

IV. Sentence Analysis: Meaning or Form

In the analysis of sentences to be carried out here, just as in our establishing of a practically useful definition of the sentence and in our classifying of the various kinds of sentences, the procedure differs markedly from that usually employed in the schools. Perhaps it will help clarify our discussion to bring into sharp contrast the characteristic features of the conventional approach to the analysis of sentences and those of the approach to be used here.

In the usual approach to the grammatical analysis of sentences one must know the total meaning of the utterance before beginning any analysis. The process of analysis consists almost wholly of giving technical names to portions of this total meaning. For example, given the sentence *the man gave the boy the money*, the conventional grammatical analysis would consist in attaching the name "subject" to the word *man*, the name "predicate" to the word *gave*, the name "indirect object" to the word *boy*, the name "direct object" to the word *money*, and the name "declarative sentence" to the whole utterance. If pressed for the basis upon which these names are given to these words, one would, in accord with the traditional method, say that the word *man* is called "subject" because it "designates the person about whom an assertion is made"; that the word *gave* is called "predicate" because it is "the word that asserts something about the subject"; that the word *boy* is called "indirect object" because it "indicates the person to or for whom the action is done"; and that the word *money* is called "direct object" because it "indicates the thing that receives the action of the verb." [1] The sentence is called a "declarative sentence" because it "makes a statement." The whole procedure begins with the total meaning of the sentence and consists solely in ascribing the technical terms "subject," "predicate," "indirect object," "direct object," and "declarative sentence" to certain parts of that meaning. "Knowing grammar" has thus meant primarily the ability to apply and react to a technical terminology consisting of approximately seventy items.[2] It is this kind of "grammatical knowledge" that is assumed in the usual discussions of the value of "grammar" for an effective practical command of English, or for English composition, or for mastery of foreign language. It is this kind of grammatical analysis, this starting with the total meaning, *and the using of this meaning as the basis for the analysis*—an analysis that makes no advance beyond the ascribing of certain technical terms to parts of the meaning already known— it is this kind of grammatical analysis that modern linguistic science discards as belonging to a prescientific era.

What, then, have we, in contrast, to substitute for this type of grammatical analysis? Let us begin again with the sentence given above, *the man gave the boy the money*. First of all, we need to distinguish sharply at least two kinds of meaning in the total meaning of this utterance. There are, for example, the meanings of the separate words as the dictionary would record them—the lexical

---

[1] These definitions appear in nearly all the school textbooks that contain any "grammar."

[2] See *Report of the Joint Committee on Grammatical Terminology*, reprinted 1918, adopted by the Modern Language Association of America, the National Education Association, and the American Philological Association. See also the thirty items in C. D. Thorpe, *Preparation for College English* (Ann Arbor, 1945), p. 13. Also *English Grammar for Language Students*, by Frank X. Braun (Ann Arbor, 1947).

meanings. The dictionary would tell us something of the kinds of creatures referred to by the words *man* and *boy;* it would tell us the sort of thing the word *money* represents; and it would tell us the kind of action indicated by the word *gave*. Beyond these meanings the dictionary does not go. And yet we get from this sentence a whole range of meanings not expressed in the lexical records of the words themselves. We are told, for example, that the "man" performed the action, not the "boy"; we are told that only one man and only one boy are involved; we are told that the action has already taken place, it is not something in process, not something planned for the future; the information is given to us as a statement of fact, not something that is questioned, nor something that is requested. Such meanings constitute what we shall call the *structural meanings* of the sentence.[3] The total linguistic meaning of any utterance consists of the lexical meanings of the separate words plus such structural meanings. No utterance is intelligible without both lexical meanings and structural meanings. How, then, are these structural meanings conveyed in English from the speaker to a hearer? Structural meanings are not just vague matters of the context, so called; they are fundamental and necessary meanings in every utterance and are signalled by specific and definite devices. It is the devices that signal structural meanings which constitute the grammar of a language. *The grammar of a language consists of the devices that signal structural meanings.*

The contrast between the older traditional procedure of grammatical analysis and the approach used here lies in the fact that the conventional analysis starts from the undifferentiated total meaning of an utterance and raises the question, "What names

---

[3] The borderline between lexical meanings and structural meanings in a language like English that uses "function" words is not always sharp and clear. See the discussion of "function" words in Chapter VI. More important, perhaps, is the fact that meanings which in one language are signalled by patterns of form and arrangement, in another language may depend upon the choice of vocabulary items.

apply to various parts of this meaning?'' whereas our analysis [4] starts from a description of the formal devices that are present and the patterns that make them significant *and arrives at the structural meanings as a result of the analysis.* From a practical point of view we are concerned, too, with the utterances in which clear grammatical signals are not present, and thus *when* and *why* the structural meanings of any utterance become ambiguous.

Does a child of four who has learned to talk English as his native language know the grammar of that language? The answer to this question will depend upon the particular meaning one attaches to the word *know.* If *know* means the ability to make generalizing statements about the devices that signal structural meanings in English, then certainly he does not know the grammar of his language; nor, for that matter, do most adult speakers of English. But how will he react if he hears directed to him such an utterance as *is your mother home?* Will he recognize it as a question and reply with an answer? In other words, has he learned to respond to the particular devices by which English signals the fact that a particular utterance is a question? Or, again, when he hears, in the story that is being read to him, that *the hunters killed the wolf,* will he know that it was the hunters that survived and not the wolf? In so far as he has learned to respond to the signals of such structural meanings as these, he "knows" the grammar of his language. One cannot speak or understand a language without "knowing" its grammar—not consciously, of course, but in the sense of making the proper responses to the devices that signal structural meanings and also of producing the proper signals of his own structural meanings.

One of the earliest steps in learning to talk is this learning to use automatically the patterns of form and arrangement that constitute the devices to signal structural meaning. So thoroughly have they become unconscious habits in very early childhood that the

[4] The word *analysis* here does not mean our procedure for the investigator.

ordinary adult speaker of English finds it extremely difficult not only to describe what he does in these matters but even to realize that there is anything there to be described.[5] One of the basic assumptions of our approach here to the grammatical analysis of sentences is that all the structural signals in English are strictly formal matters that can be described in physical terms of forms, correlations of these forms, and arrangements of order. An example of part of what this basic assumption covers is furnished by a comparison of an Old English sentence with a parallel word-for-word arrangement of the Modern English lexical equivalents.

O. E.	Glædne	giefend	lufað	God
Mdn. E.	Cheerful	giver	loves	God

But the Modern English word for word equivalents of the Old English words do not represent the meaning of the Old English sentence. The lexical meanings are the same but the structural meanings differ. In the Old English sentence the *-ne* on the end of the word *glædne* signals the fact that the *glædne giefend* (the cheerful giver) is the object of God's love. The inflectional ending of the word, not the word order within the sentence, constitutes the structural signal in the Old English sentence. To render this structural meaning in Modern English the positions of the words must be changed to *God loves cheerful giver*. In the sentences

O. E.	Glædne	giefend	lufað	God
Mdn. E.	God	loves	cheerful	giver

the structural meanings are the same, but the formal devices that signal these similar meanings differ.

---

[5] Several months ago even a college professor confronted with the demand to explain how he knew that the utterance *is the teacher here* is a question, could offer no better answer than, "Because it asks for information."

The following comparison will furnish another example.

O. E.	In	ænium	oþerum	mynstres	þingum
Mdn. E.	In	any	other	monastery's	things

As these expressions stand, the structural meaning of the Modern English rendering does not represent the structural meaning of the Old English phrase. In the Modern English expression the word-order arrangement signals the fact that *any* and *other* go with the word *monastery*. In the Old English sentence, however, the *–um* endings on the words *ænium* (*any*) and *oþerum* (*other*) signal the fact that these belong to *þingum* (*things*) which has the same *–um* ending. The Modern English equivalent of the structural meaning of the Old English expression cannot be rendered with the words in the same order as they stand in Old English. To represent the Old English meaning the Modern English words would have to be *in any other things of the monastery*, with *any* and *other* preceding the word *things*, and the word-group *of the monastery* following it. In the Old English example, the endings or the forms of the words are the determining signals indicating the word to which *any* and *other* are to be attached; in the Modern English rendering, the word-order arrangement is the important feature of the structural signal. In each, however, there is a definite formal device to signal this particular structural meaning. The lexical meanings of the words themselves give no clue concerning such a meaning. Some type of formal grammatical device, the endings or forms of the words, the order of the words, or both, must signal the direction of modification. We have thus assumed that the signals of all structural meanings in English are similarly formal matters that can be described in terms of forms, correlations of these forms, and arrangements of order.

Another of the basic assumptions of our approach here to the grammatical analysis of sentences is that the formal signals of structural meanings operate in a system—that is, that the items of form and arrangement have signalling significance only as they are parts of patterns in a structural whole. An illustration may help to explain the significance of this second assumption.

A man stands sixty feet away from a flat object lying on the ground. He throws a ball of a certain size so that it passes directly over the flat object at a height of three feet, and two inches inside the right edge. This act is of practically no significance in itself, but if this throwing occurs within the structural frame of a baseball game, by virtue of the patterns of that game, it gets a special significance—it is a "strike." Again, the man may throw the ball so that it passes over the flat object (the "plate") at a height of only two and a half feet, but three inches inside the left edge. In spite of all the specific differences, because of the patterns of the game, this also has the same significance; it too is a "strike." Again, the thrown ball may pass directly over the center of the plate but at a height of four and a half feet. According to the pattern this may or may not be a "strike." It will depend upon a different kind of contrast, upon whether the "batter" is a tall or a short man. The height of the ball over the plate must be above the knees but not above the shoulders of the batter. Or again, the ball may not pass over the plate at all, but six inches outside the right edge. This, according to the pattern, may be a "ball"; but, by a still different significant contrast, that is, if the batter attempts to hit the ball with his bat and misses, it can also be a "strike." Or again, the batter may strike at the ball and hit it so that it drops to the ground outside the playing "diamond." This is, of course, a "foul"; but if the batter has not already had two "strikes" against him, it is also a "strike." In spite of the very great specific differences from all the others, this "strike" is structurally the "same" as the others. Every one of these throwings by the "pitcher" differs from all the others, and yet, as far as the patterns of the game are concerned, they are the "same." They are all significant as "strikes." The number of specifically different throwings that can fit into the pattern of the "strike" is almost infinite, as is the number of differing actions that can fit into the pattern of an "out." But the number of the patterns themselves in the structural whole of the game of baseball is very limited. The game itself is a system of contrastive patterns that give significance to an infinite variety of specific actions.[6] In similar fashion, a language as a whole consists of a system of contrastive patterns that give significance to an infinite variety of specific acts of speech. It is only these patterns that can give significance to the features of form and arrangement that operate as the devices of structural meaning. It is our task, therefore, not only to describe the items of form and arrangement which constitute the devices that signal structural meanings, but also, and especially, to set forth the contrastive patterns of the system through which these items acquire signalling significance.

What then are the basic items of the patterns of grammatical structure in present-day English?

Sometimes, at street intersections, signs which alternately show the single words *Go* and *Stop* control the traffic. When the word *Go* appears, the traffic facing that sign moves forward. When the word *Stop* appears, that traffic ceases its forward movement. We recognize these single-word utterances as "commands" or "requests." To other single-word utterances such as *Wai⌐ter, Mo⌐ther,*

Boy we respond differently; we recognize these as "calls." Would

an utterance of the single word *Skip* be a "call" like *Wai⌐ter,*

---

[6] Animals other than man can be taught to throw a ball, to catch it, to hit it, and to perform various other specific acts that occur in the game of baseball; but, so far as I can discover, they cannot be taught to "play the game" of baseball—they cannot grasp the system of contrastive patterns that give significance to the specific acts of one who is "playing the game."

$\overline{Mo}$|*ther*, $\overline{B}oy$, or a "command" like $\overline{Go}$, $\overline{Stop}$, $\overline{Walk}$? It could be either; as it stands, with no other clues to the situation in which it is uttered, it is ambiguous. As the nickname for a boy, it would be a call. If no such boy is present, it would be a command. The linguistic difference between single-word utterances such as *Waiter, Mother, Boy, Dad, John* on the one hand and those of *Go, Stop, Walk, Run, Smile* on the other is a matter of the "form-class," the "part of speech," to which the words belong. The ambiguity of single-word utterances like *Skip* (or *Hope* or *Rush*) without further clues arises from the uncertainty concerning the form-class or part of speech to which this word, in this particular utterance, belongs. Some type of structural ambiguity always results in English whenever the form-classes of the words are not clearly marked.

The utterance *ship sails today* (which might appear in a telegram) is ambiguous as it stands because of the absence of clear part-of-speech markers. If a clear part-of-speech marker, *the*, is put before the first word as in "*The* ship sails today" there is no ambiguity; we have a statement. If, however, the same marker is put before the second word as in "Ship *the* sails today" there is also no ambiguity, but the utterance is different; we then have a request. Other clear part-of-speech markers would also resolve the ambiguity, as with the addition of such a marker as the ending *–ed*.

> Ship*ped* sail today
> Ship sail*ed* today

Newspaper headlines very frequently are structurally ambiguous because of the lack of definite part-of-speech or form-class markers. Some typical examples out of many are the following:

1. "Vandenberg Reports Open Forum."

The ambiguity of this heading could be cleared by the use of such markers as *the* or *an*, as:

Vandenberg Reports Open *the* Forum
Vandenberg Reports *an* Open Forum

2. "Unfavorable Surveyor Reports Delayed Michigan Settlement." The ambiguity of this heading would be cleared by the use of such markers as *have* or *a*:

Unfavorable Surveyor Reports *Have* Delayed Michigan Settlement
Unfavorable Surveyor Reports *a* Delayed Michigan Settlement

3. "Briton to Be Tried for Missing Jewish Youth's Murder." Such a marker as *a* would clear the ambiguity here:

Briton to Be Tried for *a* Missing Jewish Youth's Murder
Briton to Be Tried for Missing *a* Jewish Youth's Murder

4. "Marshall Calls on Congress to Help Prostrate Europe." Here again the markers *a* or *–ed* would clear the ambiguity:

Marshall Calls on Congress to Help Prostrat*ed* Europe
Marshall Calls on Congress to Help *a* Prostrate Europe

Or the marker *to* would make unmistakable the other meaning.

Marshall Calls on Congress to Help *to* Prostrate Europe

As we examine the utterances of English, we shall find that unless certain large form-classes or parts of speech have their characteristic markers the structural meanings of the utterance will be ambiguous.

We have assumed in our approach here that the signals of all structural meanings are formal matters that can be described in terms of form and arrangement. We have assumed, too, that these items operate in a system, that they have signalling significance only as they are parts of patterns in a structural whole. In our attempt to describe the contrastive patterns of the system through which the structural meanings of English are signalled we find that the basic items to be distinguished are certain large form-classes of the words, the lexical units. *An English sentence then is not a group of words as words but rather a structure made up of form-classes or parts of speech.* In order to know the structural meanings signalled by the formal arrangements of our sentences *one need not know the lexical meanings of the words but he must know* [7] *the form-classes to which the words belong.* Our description of the patterns of devices to signal structural meanings will, therefore, be in terms of the selection of these large form-classes or parts of speech and the formal arrangements in which they occur.

[7] "Know" in the sense of "respond to."

V. Parts of Speech

A number of examples given in the preceding chapter were used to demonstrate the fact that, in English, some type of structural ambiguity results whenever an utterance consists of certain important form-classes or parts of speech without clear markers. The markers that distinguish these important parts of speech in English are therefore of primary importance in our description of the patterns of the devices that signal structural meanings—a description which will be made in terms of the selection of these parts of speech and the formal arrangements in which they occur. What parts of speech, then, can we—or, rather, must we—recognize in English for a basic description of our utterances, and what are the special markers of these parts of speech?

All the conventional school grammars deal extensively with the "parts of speech," usually given as eight in number, and explained in definitions that have become traditional. It has often been assumed that these eight parts of speech—noun, pronoun, adjective, verb, adverb, preposition, conjunction, interjection—are basic classifications that can be applied to the "words" of all languages [1] and that the traditional definitions furnish an adequate set of criteria by which to make the classifications.

As a matter of fact our common school grammars of English have not always used eight parts of speech. Some have named ten,

[1] "The distinctions between the various parts of speech . . . are distinctions in thought, not merely in words." John Stuart Mill, *Rectorial Address at St. Andrews*, 1867.

making the "article" and the "participle" separate classes.[2] Some have included the "adjective" under the name "noun" and have given as subclasses of "nouns" the "noun substantive" and the "noun adjective."[3] Others have insisted that "interjections" are not "parts of speech" but "sentence words." Some of the early Greek grammarians recognized only three parts of speech, ὄνομα (names), ῥῆμα (sayings), and σύνδεσμοι (joinings or linkings). The Latin grammarian, Varro, distinguished four parts of speech: (1) words with cases (nouns), (2) words with tenses (verbs), (3) words with both cases and tenses (participles), (4) words with neither cases nor tenses (particles). The current conventional classification of words into the particular eight parts of speech now common seems to have begun with Joseph Priestley and to have been generally accepted in the grammars since 1850.[4] We cannot assume without question that the eight parts of speech thus inherited from the past will be the most satisfactory or the essential classification of the form-classes of present-day English, but will instead examine anew the functioning units in our collection of utterances, with a view to establishing the minimum number of different groups needed for a basic description of the signals of the most important structural meanings.

---

[2] See Goold Brown, *The Grammar of English Grammars* (10th ed., New York, 1868), pp. 220–23.

[3] "How mony partyse of speche ben þer? Viii. Wych viii? Nowne, pronowne, verbe, aduerbe, partycypull', coniunccion, preposicion, and interieccion. . . . How mony maner of nownys ben' there? Ii. Wyche ii? Nowne substantyfe & nowne adiectyfe." From Douce Ms. 103 (fifteenth century). Text printed in *PMLA*, 50 (1935), 1012–32.

"Nouns are distinguished into two sorts, called noun substantives and noun adjectives." William Ward, *A Practical Grammar of the English Language* (London, 1765), p. 324.

[4] "I shall adopt the usual distribution of words into eight classes. . . . All the innovations I have made hath been to throw out the *Participle*, and substitute the *Adjective*, as more evidently a part of speech." Joseph Priestley, *Rudiments of English Grammar* (London, 1769; 1st ed., 1761), p. 3.

Unfortunately we cannot use as the starting point of our examination the traditional definitions of the parts of speech. What is a "noun," for example? The usual definition is that "a noun is the name of a person, place, or thing." But *blue* is the "name" of a color, as is *yellow* or *red*, and yet, in the expressions *a blue tie, a yellow rose, a red dress* we do not call *blue* and *yellow* and *red* "nouns." We do call *red* a noun in the sentence *this red is the shade I want. Run* is the "name" of an action, as is *jump* or *arrive. Up* is the "name" of a direction, as is *down* or *across.* In spite of the fact that these words are all "names" and thus fit the definition given for a noun they are not called nouns in such expressions as "We *ran* home," "They were looking *up* into the sky," "The acid made the fiber *red.*" The definition as it stands—that "A noun is a name"—does not furnish all the criteria necessary to exclude from this group many words which our grammars in actual practice classify in other parts of speech.

In the expressions *a blue tie, a yellow rose, a red dress,* the words *blue, yellow,* and *red,* in spite of the fact that according to their meanings they are "names" of colors, are called "adjectives," because the adjective is defined as "A word that modifies a noun or a pronoun." A large part of the difficulty here lies in the fact that the two definitions—the definition of the noun and the definition of the adjective—are not parallel. The one for the noun, that "a noun is a name," attempts to classify these words according to their *lexical meanings;* the one for the adjective, that "an adjective is a word that modifies a noun or a pronoun," attempts to classify the words according to their *function in a particular sentence.* The basis of definition slides from meaning to function. For the purposes of adequate classification, the definitions of the various classes must consider the same kind of criteria.

Even with the usual definition of an adjective the criteria are not always consistently applied. Many grammars will not classify *boy's* as an adjective in *the boy's hat,* nor *his* as an adjective in *his hat*, in spite of the fact that both these words, *boy's* and *his*, "modify" the word *hat*, and thus fit the definition. *Boy's* is usually called "noun in the possessive case," and *his*, a "possessive pronoun" or a "pronoun in the possessive case." Here again, criteria that are not included in the definition—in this case certain formal characteristics—are used in practice to exclude from the classification items that fit the definition.

The common definition for a pronoun presents even more difficulty. "A pronoun is a word used instead of a noun." But just what kind of substitution is to be called "pronoun" in the following examples? In the sentence *John and James brought their letters of recommendation* there should be no question that *John* and *James*, as the names for two persons, are nouns. In the following series of words "substituted for these two nouns" just which are to be called pronouns and why?

> John and James
> The two boys
> The undersigned
> A few
> The two
> Two   brought their letters of recommenda-
> A couple   tion
> Several
> Some
> Both
> These
> They

A slightly different kind of series, substituted for the noun *Wednesday* in the sentence *Wednesday is the time to see him*, presents the same problem. Which of the following substitutes are "pronouns"?

Wednesday ⎫
Tomorrow ⎪
Today ⎪
Next week ⎪
Later ⎬ is the time to see him
Now ⎪
When ⎪
This ⎪
That ⎪
It ⎭

Obviously even in the usual procedure of classifying words into "parts of speech"—noun, adjective, pronoun—the criteria indicated in the definitions, that "names" are nouns, that "modifiers of nouns" are adjectives, and that "substitutes for nouns" are pronouns, do not include all that is actually used, and these definitions, therefore, cannot provide the basis for our approach here. We cannot use "lexical" meaning as the basis for the definition of some classes, "function in the sentence" for others, and "formal characteristics" for still others. We must find, as the basis for our grouping into parts of speech, a set of criteria that can be consistently applied.

Two problems then confront us:

1. We have concluded above that the structural signals of English consist of arrangements, not of words as words, but of words as parts of speech. We should be able, then, to express our descriptions of the patterns that signal structural meanings in terms of formulas with the various parts of speech as the units. Our first problem, then, is to discover just how many different kinds of these functioning units the formulas for English require, and precisely what they are.

2. We have insisted that unless these functioning units, these parts of speech, are clearly marked, are identifiable in an utter-

ance, some type of structural ambiguity will result. The ambiguity of the following utterances, for example, arises because of the uncertainty of the kind of functioning unit of each of the italic words:

> *Ship sails* today
> *Time flies*
> The dogs looked *longer* than the cat
> Avoid infection by *killing* germs

The conventional definitions do not provide the necessary criteria. Our second problem is to discover just what the criteria are that the users of the language actually employ to identify the necessary various form-class units when they give and receive the signals of structural meaning.

You will remember Alice's experience with the poem of the Jabberwocky: [5]

> Twas brillig, and the slithy toves
>   Did gyre and gimble in the wabe;
> All mimsy were the borogoves,
>   And the mome raths outgrabe. . . .
>
> "Somehow [she said], it seems to fill my head with ideas —only I don't exactly know what they are!"

What are the "ideas" she gets and how are they stimulated? All the words that one expects to have clearly definable meaning content are nonsense, but any speaker of English will recognize at once the frames in which these words appear.

> Twas ——, and the ——y ——s
>   Did —— and —— in the ——;
> All ——y were the ——s,
>   And the —— ——s ——.

[5] For the suggestion of this type of use of nonsense words I am indebted to Prof. Aileen Traver Kitchin. I had used algebraic symbols for words but not with the success she has attained with "Jabberwocky" material.

The "ideas" which the verse stimulates are without doubt the structural meanings for which the framework contains the signals. Most of these nonsense words have clearly marked functions in frames that constitute familiar structural patterns. These "ideas" seem vague to the ordinary speaker because in the practical use of language he is accustomed to dealing only with total meanings to which lexical content contributes the elements of which he is conscious.

For the Jabberwocky verse certain familiar words of the frame in which the nonsense appeared furnished important clues to the structures; but such clues are often unnecessary. One need not know the lexical meaning of any word in the following:

1. Woggles ugged diggles
2. Uggs woggled diggs
3. Woggs diggled uggles

If we assume that these utterances are using the structural signals of English, then at once we know a great deal about these sequences. We would know that *woggles* and *uggs* and *woggs* are "thing" words of some kind; that in each case there is more than one of these "things," and that they at some time in the past performed certain "actions"; and that these actions were directed toward other "things," *diggles*, *diggs*, and *uggles*.

As speakers of English, given the three utterances above, we should not hesitate to make such new utterances as the following:

4. A woggle ugged a diggle
5. An ugg woggles diggs
6. A diggled woggle ugged a woggled diggle

We would know that *woggles* and *uggs* and *woggs* are "thing" words, in sentences 1, 2, 3, because they are treated as English treats "thing" words—by the "positions" they occupy in the utterances and the forms they have, in contrast with other positions and forms. We would know that *ugged* and *woggled* and *diggled* are "action" words in these same sentences because they are treated as English treats "action" words—by the "positions" they occupy and the forms they have, in contrast with the positions and forms of the other "words."

We would make the new utterances 4, 5, 6 with confidence because in these we simply proceed to continue to treat the various units of the utterances in accord with the formal devices which constitute the grammar of English. For all of this it has not been necessary to know the meaning of a single word. As native speakers of English we have learned to use certain formal clues by which we identify the various kinds of units in our structures. The process is wholly unconscious unless some failure attracts attention;— just as unconscious as our responses to sight clues with the muscular adjustments of balancing when we walk.

The game of baseball, again, may provide a more satisfactory illustration. Like any other game that results in "winners," baseball consists of a system of contrastive patterns which give significance to an infinite variety of specific actions. The "strike" is one of the basic patterns. One cannot really play baseball without being able to recognize and deal with a "strike" immediately, unconsciously, as a conditioned reflex. One cannot define a strike with any simple statement that will furnish much help to a beginner. It is true that all strikes are the "same" in baseball. But that "sameness" is not physical identity; it is not even physical likeness with an area of tolerance. All strikes are alike in baseball only in the sense that they have the same functional significance. We cannot then hope to find in strikes physical boundaries of an objective likeness common to all. We can only enumerate the very diverse kinds of contrasts that constitute the criteria for determining whether any particular throwing by a pitcher is to be assigned to the pattern of a strike for the batter, i.e.:

1. Did the ball pass over the plate or not?

2. If the ball passed over the plate was it, in height, between the shoulders and the knees of the particular batter?

3. If the ball passed outside or inside the plate, or was higher than the shoulders or lower than the knees of the particular batter then "at bat," did the batter attempt to hit it with his bat and miss?

4. If the batter hit the ball and it fell to the ground outside the playing "diamond" did the batter have less than two strikes against him?

5. If the batter hit the ball very slightly so that the ball did not rise above the level of his head, and if the batter already had two strikes against him, did the catcher catch and hold the ball?

A part of speech in English, like the strike in baseball, is a functioning pattern. It cannot be defined by means of a simple statement. There is no single characteristic that all the examples of one part of speech must have in the utterances of English. All the instances of one part of speech are the "same" only in the sense that in the structural patterns of English each has the same functional significance.

This does not mean that in analyzing our sentences we must first determine the function of a word and then assign it the name of one of the parts of speech. Each part of speech like the strike in baseball is marked off from other parts of speech by a set of formal contrasts which we learn to use unconsciously as we learn our language. The patterns of our parts of speech as functioning units are complex just as the patterns of the game of baseball are complex. But in spite of the complexity of the structure of the game of baseball and the variety of the criteria by which the different specific actions are assigned to significant patterns, boys ten years of age learn not only to play the game skillfully, but also to apply consciously, as well as to discuss vigorously, the intricate criteria by which widely differing actions have the same structural significance.

As indicated above, if we are native speakers of English, we have learned to use and react to the contrasts that mark our functioning parts of speech. As speakers we are not accustomed to describe them and we find it difficult to know exactly what they are. If we have studied the conventional grammar of the schools we find it doubly difficult because the channelling of our thinking by the traditional materials leads away from the descriptive approach.

In Chapter VII we shall enumerate and describe the various contrasts which we have found to mark the parts of speech in English. In the rest of this chapter we shall sketch the procedure used here in the attempt to discover inductively from the recorded materials what these various contrasts were.

We concluded above that the signals of structural meaning in English consisted primarily of patterns of arrangement of classes of words which we have called form-classes, or parts of speech. We have assumed here that all words that could occupy the same "set of positions" in the patterns of English single free utterances must belong to the same part of speech. We assumed then that if we took first our minimum free utterances as test frames we could find all the words from our materials that would fit into each significant position without a change of the structural meaning. It was not necessary for us to define the structural meaning nor to indicate the structural significance of any particular "position"; we simply had to make certain whether with each substitution, the structural meaning was the same as that of our first example or different from it.[6] After using the minimum free

---

[6] The use of the technique of substitution in investigation always demands control of certain features of "meaning." The investigator must, in some way, either through an informant or by using his own knowledge, control enough of a particular kind of meaning to determine whether the frame is the "same" or "different" after any substitution is made. In the substitution process used here a knowledge of the lexical

utterances we tested the resulting lists in the "positions" that
appeared in the single free utterances that were not minimum but
expanded in various ways.[7]

The minimum free utterance test frames that formed the basis
of our examination were the following:

Frame A

> The concert was good (always)

Frame B

> The clerk remembered the tax (suddenly)

Frame C

> The team went there

We started with the minimum free utterance *the concert was good*
as our first test frame and set out to find in our materials all the
words that could be substituted for the word *concert* with no change
of structural meaning. The words of this list we called Class 1
words.[8] When we repeated this process for each of the significant

---

meanings of the words is unnecessary; a control of the structural meaning of each
frame used is essential. See also my discussion in *Meaning and Linguistic Analysis*. Of
course, the object of our search here is not the meaning but the strictly formal features
which make a difference in the "meaning."

For a brief statement of some of the problems in the process of substitution see
Zellig Harris, "From Morpheme to Utterance," *Language* XXII (1946) 161–65.

[7] The necessity of testing "same" or "different" in "expanded" structures will
appear from the following illustration from another problem. In the minimum structures *the boy laughed at the man* and *the boy called up the man*, the expressions *laughed at*
and *called up* seem structurally alike. The first however can be expanded with *vigorously*
between *laughed* and *at*, as, *the boy laughed vigorously at the man;* the second cannot. The
second can be shifted to *the boy called the man up;* the first could not appear with this
order.

[8] I include here not the complete list of all the words from our materials but only
a hundred examples of the various forms that occurred. The order of the words in the
list here follows the order in which they occurred in the materials. These words are
to be taken *only in the particular lexical meaning* they have in the recorded utterances
from which they were gathered. Whenever some question seems probable concerning

positions in all the structural frames we found in our materials, we had a large number of examples of each of the parts of speech we must recognize for present-day English.

WORDS OF CLASS 1 [9]

Frame A

    The *concert* was good
        food
        coffee
        taste
        container
        difference
        privacy
        family
        company [guests]

that meaning a brief gloss is given in brackets. There are often other lexical meanings of these words that do not fit in the particular frame used. We were not attempting to classify words *in isolation* but examples of words from actual utterances in which the selection of a particular lexical meaning is identified. These words in their particular meanings were grouped into classes by testing them in the frames used here. As they stand in the lists they are always to be considered as belonging in their special "position" in the frames that have been used to test them. All the examples in the lists are taken from the recorded materials and thus appeared there in "positions" that formed part of the testing.

[9] A hundred examples from the total list follow: *meal, water, sugar, list, time, cooker, charcoal, stuff, temperature, trouble, heating* [of a house], *eating* [at a particular boarding-house], *combination, business* [of a particular corporation], *thing, variation, thought, moisture, green* [of a particular shade], *boiling* [as a process of sterilization], *home, delivery, intrusion, reference* [name for recommendation], *possibility, examination* [set of questions], *afternoon* [as a time for meeting], *convenience, expense, course, positive* [photographic print], *sixth, upstairs* [of a new house], *introduction* [of a book], *assembly* [meeting], *lounge* [room in a residence hall], *building* [edifice], *fun, abstract* [of title to a property], *deed* [document showing ownership], *summer* [season], *commissioner* [public officer], *direction* [administration], *teaching* [process of instruction], *supervisor, picture, hose* [for garden], *spray* [mixture for treating plants], *construction* [of a house], *memo-*

The process of substitution in one position in our first frame provided a large list of items that for English structure are the same kind of functioning unit—our first class. Mindful of the diversity of the "strike," we did not assume that this particular frame would provide for all of Class 1, nor that it was a complete test. Such words as *meals*, *reports*, and *lessons* required an adjustment in certain word forms. These words without the "s" endings [10] did fit the frame as it stood.

> The *meal* was good
> *report*
> *lesson*

But with the "s" ending another word, *were*, occurred in similar minimum utterances instead of *was*.

> The *meals* were good
> *reports*
> *lessons*

The adjusted frame provided for many more words in our list and also for one subgrouping of the words in Class 1.

> The ——— was good
> ———s were

___

randum, annoyance, inquiry [method of examination], width [dimension], length, specification [giving of details], floor, weather, fall [season], luncheon, reason [particular basis for an action], difficulty, history [subject of study], dance [particular pattern of steps], arrangement, management [administrative direction], catering [providing food], location, shape, report [certificate of school grades], idea, sun [sunshine], corn, use, kind, husband, note, street, appointment [engagement for meeting], English [language used], permanent [hair-curling], garage [auto service shop], price, shingling [roofing material installed], painting [process], machinery, name, cutter, wife, foot, care, washing [process], laundry [soiled clothes for washing or clothes that have been washed], place, service [of church], office [place of work], institute, training [process of teaching], woman, facility [a mechanical convenience].

[10] The expression "'s' ending," means, of course, the sounds [s], [z], or [ɪz], which constitute inflectional signs of a plural number.

Many of the words with these "s" endings appeared in the materials in situations similar to those of our frame but without the preceding word *the*. Our frame then could be adjusted as follows:

CLASS
1
(The) ——— is/was good
———s   are/were

Coffee is good
Sugar is good
Reports were good

The word *the*, although it accompanied all the words of our original list, and, when present, served as one of the markers of Class 1, is not a necessary accompaniment of all Class 1 words. We can thus take the adjusted frame and find the words which do not use the marker *the*, but which must also be included in Class 1. As we shall see later there are other subdivisions within this general class and some other kinds of words that must be included; but, for the present, we can insist that we have here a body of words that belong to the same part of speech by virtue of the fact that they can all fill this particular position in this minimum free utterance. They are all Class 1 words.

The words of our list also fitted into other positions in other minimum and expanded free utterances. The various "positions" in which a part of speech can stand in our sentences constitute its functions or uses.[11] All the words of this particular list could appear in the positions indicated in the following minimum frames:

---

[11] This point will be developed later in Chapters VIII, IX, X, and XI.

Frame B

> The *clerk* [12] remembered the *tax*
> > *husband*   *food*
> > *supervisor*   *coffee*
> > *woman*   *container*
> >   *difference*
> >   *family*

Frame C

> The *team* went there
> > *husband*
> > *woman*
> > *supervisor*

It is not enough for our purpose to say that a Class 1 word is any word that can fill certain positions in the structure of our sentences, even if we enumerate all these positions. We want to know what the special characteristics of these words are that make them recognizably different from the words used in other positions. To discover these characteristics we need to explore these other positions and form comparable lists of words that can fill these positions.[13] Significant formal characteristics of each class will appear then in the contrasts of one class with another. Before proceeding further with Class 1 words, therefore, we need a general view of the other major parts of speech in present-day English.

---

[12] Although structurally any Class 1 word may be used in this position, only certain subgroups (those for which *he* or *she* can be a substitute) would commonly occur with (i.e., be lexically compatible with) such a Class 2 word as *remembered*.

[13] It is probably unnecessary to point out that the "positions" used here are absolute order positions *only in the minimum free utterances*. In general they are significant structural positions. Ultimately the proof of the identity of particular positions in expanded structures rests upon the facts of "same" or "different" responses by native speakers. These are observed responses, not those elicited by direct question concerning "same" or "different."

WORDS OF CLASS 2

Again we proceed with the process of substitution. To be consistent we use the same test frames we have already tried for Class 1 words, but seek substitutions in another "position." The words that fit this position we have called Class 2 words.

Frame A

	CLASS 1	CLASS 2	
(The)	———	*is/was*	good
	——s	*are/were*	

seems/seemed
seem
sounds/sounded
sound
feels/felt
feel
becomes/became
become

The particular words from our materials that could fit into this position of this particular frame were very few.

For the next frame, however, a great many more appeared.[14]

---

[14] A hundred examples from the total list are the following:

1. Those that fitted into the frame without any correlation with the presence or absence of an "s" ending on the Class 1 word: *felt, arranged, ironed, worked, dried, included, started, applied, asked, needed, deposited, collected, mentioned, cleared, delivered, removed, decided, billed, reimbursed, worked* [operated], *made, isolated, turned, pleased, painted, bought, planned, consulted, called, thanked, wore, appreciated, touched, complicated, reported, contracted* [shortened], *knocked, handled, assumed, inconvenienced, lost, burned, sold, ordered, addressed, finished, invited, forgot, tested, produced.*

2. Those that fitted into the frame with a correlation of an "s" or no "s" ending on

Frame B

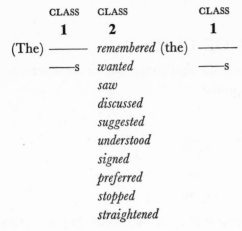

CLASS 1	CLASS 2	CLASS 1
(The) ———	*remembered* (the)	———
———s	*wanted*	———s
	saw	
	discussed	
	suggested	
	understood	
	signed	
	preferred	
	stopped	
	straightened	

Frame C

CLASS 1	CLASS 2	
(The) ———	*went*	there
———s	*came*	
	ran	
	started	
	moved	
	walked	
	lived	
	worked	
	met	
	talked	

All the words on this list can occupy the same structural position in our test frames. The separation of the test frames is signif-

___
the Class 1 word: *sees, tells, knows, has, makes, gets, includes, believes, owes, wants, means, decides, follows, offers, leaves, shields, accept, change, try, guess, know, see, allow, specify, borrow, use, work, help, find, watch, apply, recommend, embarrass, convince, imagine, settle, purchase, forward* [send on], *order, like, expect, bring, separate, run* [operate], *mow, correct, give, doubt.*

icant only for subgroupings of these words. They are all Class 2 words.

WORDS OF CLASS 3

For Class 3 words we again take our original sentences and explore another position:

Frame A

	CLASS 1	CLASS 2	CLASS 3
(The) ———	is/was	*good*
———s	are/were	

Here we are concerned with all the words that are structurally like *good*. Because we found that the absolute order position of *good* in this frame permitted the overlapping of several kinds of structural units as shown by confusion in the decisions of "same" and "different" from informants, we used a double position for the test of Class 3 words. To be accepted as belonging to Class 3 a word had to be one that could fit both in the position after the Class 2 word and also between *the* and the Class 1 word.

	CLASS 3	CLASS 1	CLASS 2	CLASS 3
(The)	*good*	———	is/was	*good*
		———s	are/were	
	large			*large*
	necessary			*necessary*
	foreign			*foreign*
	new			*new*
	empty			*empty*
	hard			*hard*
	best			*best*
	lower			*lower*

All of the words of this list [15] belong in a single part-of-speech class. They can all be substituted in these significant positions in our test frame—they are all Class 3.

WORDS OF CLASS 4

For the next large class of words we shall take those that can be substituted in the position following the three already explored.

Frame A

	CLASS 3	CLASS 1	CLASS 2	CLASS 3	CLASS 4
(The)	——	——	is/was	——	*there*
		——s	are/were		*here*
					always
					then
					sometimes
					suddenly
					soon
					now
					generally
					lately

[15] A hundred examples of the words from the total list of this group are the following: *English, educational, general, eighth, elite, small, regular, usable, short, fine, long, ready, great, good, straight, particular, last, personal, first, right* [correct], *supplementary, big, earlier, final, quick, greater, better, oral, low, glad, principal, high, free, whole, little, public, shut, pink, sure, essential, clear, anxious, separate, red, commercial, vigorous, complete, singular, important, permanent, intimate, vivid, real, full, awful, nice, later, convenient, busy, drunk, excellent, difficult, probable, outstanding, technical, easy, confident, open, strong, sufficient, outside, higher, clean, kind, weak, hot, tentative, slightest, physical, serious, close, religious, possible, international, different, broad, white, hostile, welcome, ordinary, afraid, domestic, wide, heavy, young, valuable, least, lost, younger, unsightly.*

Frame B

	CLASS 1	CLASS 2		CLASS 1	CLASS 4
(The)	———	remembered	(the)	———	*clearly*
	———s				*sufficiently*
					especially
					repeatedly
					soon
					then
					suddenly
					later
					always

Frame C

	CLASS 1	CLASS 2	CLASS 4	
(The)	———	went	*there*	*upstairs*
			back	*away*
			out	*rapidly*
			up	*eagerly*
			down	*confidently*
			upward(s)	*singly*
			forward(s)	*safely*

We have called all the words of this list [16] Class 4 words although the need for making subgroups in this class becomes immediately

[16] Other examples of words that fit these positions of our frames are the following: *usually, often, frequently, seldom, downward, over, under, through, across, easily, tentatively, suspiciously, awhile, last, next, brokenly, religiously, inconveniently, personally, principally, technically, artistically, conveniently, confidently, completely, definitely, directly, absolutely, cheaply, luxuriously, surely, closely, perfectly, somewhere, anywhere, everywhere, longer, privately, sadly, idly, crazily, openly, recently, finally, meanwhile, hourly, annually, once, twice, again, vigorously, first, increasingly.*

apparent when we attempt to explore the other positions in which the Class 4 words can operate. Although there is considerable overlapping in the positions the words of our list can occupy, there are also positions in which large groups naturally fit, from which other groups are excluded. Here it will be sufficient to point out the three subgroups that show themselves when we attempt to use several of these words together. If two or more of these words belong to the same subgroup then a formal connecting word such as *and* or *but* appears between them. But if the two or more words belong to different subgroups then no such word occurs.

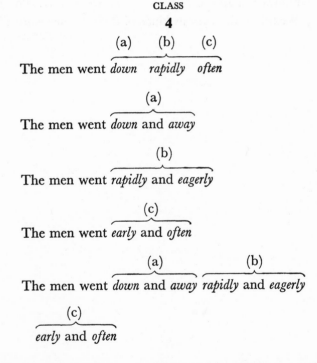

CLASS

4

(a)   (b)   (c)

The men went *down   rapidly   often*

(a)

The men went *down* and *away*

(b)

The men went *rapidly* and *eagerly*

(c)

The men went *early* and *often*

(a)   (b)

The men went *down* and *away   rapidly* and *eagerly*

(c)

early and *often*

For the present, however, we shall consider all these words as belonging to a single large form-class or part of speech—Class 4.

The full lists of the words that comprise these four parts of speech contain a large part of the vocabulary items of our recorded materials. If each "word" is counted every time it occurs, then these four parts of speech contain approximately 67 per cent of the total instances of the vocabulary items. If, however, each "word" is counted only once and repeated instances of the same word ignored, then, in the material of 1,000 different words, the percentage of the total vocabulary in these four parts of speech is over 93 per cent. In other words our utterances consist primarily of arrangements of these four parts of speech. These utterances contain also, however, a body of other words, comparatively few in actual number of items, but used very frequently. The next chapter will explore the various kinds of these "other words."

VI. Function Words

The four parts of speech, arrived at by the processes sketched in the preceding chapter, make up the bulk of the "words" in our utterances. We have given them no names except the numbers, Class 1, Class 2, Class 3, Class 4. The reader, familiar with the conventional grammar, will probably attempt or has already attempted to equate these class numbers with the usual names, "nouns," "verbs," "adjectives," and "adverbs," and has assumed that the numbers are simply somewhat confusing new names for the old classes. If he does, he will certainly find increasing difficulty in the following chapters. It is true that many of the functioning units grouped in Class 1 would be called "nouns" by those who customarily use the traditional terms; and many of those in Class 2 would be called "verbs"; many of those in Class 3 would be called "adjectives"; and many of those in Class 4 would be called "adverbs." The two sets of names, however, do not coincide in either what is included or what is excluded.[1] More important still, perhaps, it is impossible to make a satisfactory comparative analysis of the precise differences in what the old and the new terms cover because the conventional grammars vary tremendously in what they include under each of the old terms. In the use of the numbers for the four functioning units or parts of speech set up here there should be no uncertainty for one who will forget the old terms and follow strictly the procedures of this approach.

Chapter VII will continue the discussion of these four parts of speech and attempt to make clear the special marks by which

[1] See especially Chapter X.

each class can be identified in the structural signals of our utterances and thus the range of those included under each class number. Here, we need to gather into groups the "words" that we have not included in those four classes. We have headed this chapter "Function Words" but we do not intend to start with a definition of that term. We shall proceed simply to gather examples of the various kinds of words that operate in "positions" other than those explored in the preceding chapter, giving identifying letters to each of the different groups as we go; and then, after we have all the examples before us, we shall attempt to discuss them as a whole and consider the term *function words*.[2]

The frames used to test the "words" thus far were taken from the minimum free utterances extracted from the "situation" utterance units (not the "response" utterance units) of the recorded materials. The important fact here is that the four parts of speech indicated above account for practically *all the positions* in these minimum free utterances. In the sentence frames used for testing, only the one position occupied by the word *the* has not been explored; and, as shown in the modified frame structure, this position is optional rather than essential in the "minimum" free utterances. All the other kinds of words we shall find, therefore, belong then in "expanded" free utterances.

We begin then with the test frames used above and explore positions that the expanded free utterances show are possible in these test frames.

GROUP A

In the first test frame we want all the words for the position in which the word *the* occurs.

---

[2] The reader must not assume that with the term "function words" I am simply following those grammarians who have attempted to make a distinction between "content" words and "empty" words.

GROUP	CLASS	CLASS	CLASS
A	**1**	**2**	**3**
(*The*)	concert	was	good

GROUP			CLASS	CLASS	CLASS	CLASS
A			**1**	**2**	**3**	**4**
(*The*)			——	is/was	——	——
the	*a/an*	*every*	——s	are/were		
no	*my*	*our*				
your	*her*	*his*				
their	*each*	*all*				
both	*some*	*any*				
few	*more*	*most*				
much	*many*	*its*				
John's	*this/these*	*that/those*				
one	*two*	*three*				
four	*five*	*eighteen*				
twenty	*thirty-one*	(etc., to in-				
		clude *ninety-nine*)				

The fact that some of these "words" (*one, all, both, two, three, four, that, those, this, these, each, few, many, much, more, most, some, any, its, John's*) may also appear in the positions of Class 1 words does not concern us here; nor does the fact that *all* and *both* may occur before *the*. Group A consists of all the words that can occupy the position of *the* in this particular test frame. The words in this position all occur with Class 1 words and only with Class 1 words in our structures. Structurally, when they appear in this "position," they serve as markers of Class 1 words. Sometimes they are called "determiners." [3]

[3] See below (end of Chapter VII) for the "rank" of the words of this group as markers of a form-class.

GROUP B

For Group B we want the words for the position in which the word *may* occurs in the following sentence frame.

GROUP A	CLASS 1	GROUP B	CLASS 2	CLASS 3
The	concert	(*may*)	be	good

GROUP A	CLASS 1	GROUP B	CLASS 2	CLASS 3	CLASS 4
——	——	(*may*)	(be)	——	——
		might			
		can			
		could			
		will			
		would			
		should			
		must			
		has	(been)		
		has to	(be)		

GROUP A	CLASS 1	GROUP B	CLASS 2
The	——	——	moved
		had	
		was	
		got	

GROUP A	CLASS 1	GROUP B	CLASS 2
The	——	——	moving
		was	
		got	
		kept	

GROUP	CLASS	GROUP	CLASS
A	1	B	2
The	——	——	move
		had to	
		did	

Words of Group B all go with Class 2 words and only with Class 2 words. Structurally, when they appear in this position, they serve as markers of Class 2 words and also, in special formulas, they signal some other meanings which probably should be included as structural.[4] That there are several distinct subgroups of these words seems to be proved by their distinctive positions when used together.

GROUP	CLASS	GROUP			CLASS	CLASS
A	1	B			2	3
		(a)	(b)	(c)		
The	students	*may*	*have*	*had to*	be	good
		might				
		would				
		must				

GROUP	CLASS	GROUP				CLASS
A	1	B				2
		(a)	(b)	(c)	(d)	
The	students	*may*	*have*	*had to*	be	moving
		might			get	
		would			keep	
		must, etc.				
					be	moved
					get	moved

---

[4] See, for example, C. C. Fries, "*Have* as a Function-Word," *Language Learning*, I (1948), 4–8. The structural meanings of the function words of this group are not

GROUP C

For Group C we have but one word here, *not*. This *not* differs from the *not* included in Group E below.

GROUP	CLASS	GROUP	GROUP	CLASS	CLASS
A	**1**	**B**	**C**	**2**	**3**
The	concert	may	*not*	be	good

GROUP	CLASS	CLASS	GROUP	CLASS
A	**1**	**2**	**C**	**3**
The	concert	was	*not*	good

GROUP D

For Group D we need to gather all the words that can occur in the position of *very* immediately before a Class 3 word in the following sentence frame.

GROUP	CLASS	GROUP	GROUP	CLASS	GROUP	CLASS	CLASS
A	**1**	**B**	**C**	**2**	**D**	**3**	**4**
The	concert	may	not	be	*very*	good	then

quite, awfully,
really, awful,
real, any,
pretty, too,
fairly, more,
rather, most

Additional words of this kind occurred before a Class 3 word when that Class 3 word was one of those with an inflectional ending like *harder*.

---

discussed in this book. Certain uses of function words are touched on in various parts of the following discussions, but a systematic treatment of function words is reserved for a later publication.

GROUP A	CLASS 1	GROUP B	CLASS 2	GROUP D	CLASS 3
———	———	———	———	*still*	better
				even	
				much	
				some	
				no	

All these words of Group D are attached to Class 3 words, and in spite of differences between them, and without any connection with their lexical meanings in other positions, all signal some degree or quantity of the "quality" for which the Class 3 word stands.[5] Most of these same words also fill a similar position for Class 4 words. With Class 4 words, also, some words appear that are not in the list for those in the position before Class 3 words.

GROUP A	CLASS 1	CLASS 2	CLASS 4		
			(a)	(b)	(c)
The	men	went	down	rapidly	later

GROUP A	CLASS 1	CLASS 2	GROUP D	CLASS 4(a)	GROUP D	CLASS 4(b)	GROUP D	CLASS 4(c)
———	———	———	*(a)way*	down	*very*	rapidly	*much*	later
			really		*quite*		*still*	
			more		*pretty*		*even*	
			less		*rather*		*no*	
			more or less[6]		*awfully*		*right*	now
			almost		*mighty*		*just*	now
			right		*more*			
					too			

[5] Here also belong those degree words that are sometimes considered "profanity" —*darn, damn, damned.*

[6] As we shall see later, a number of these words belong here only when the sequence in which they occur has a particular intonation pattern.

Although all these words can be put in one large group of "degree" words because of the particular positions they occupy before Class 3 and Class 4 words, the fact that some of them can be used together with distinct positions in relation to each other provides a basis for some subgrouping. Examples of such distinct positions are the following:

GROUP D			CLASS 3
(a)	(b)	(c)	
very much	*too*		small
	rather	(*too*)	small
	just	*too*	small
	any	*more*	important
very much	*more*		important
very much	*too*		much

GROUP E

For Group E we want those words that can stand in the various positions occupied by *and* in the following sentence frame.

GROUP A	CLASS 1	GROUP E	GROUP A	CLASS 1	CLASS 2	GROUP E	CLASS 2
The	concerts	*and*	the	lectures	are	*and*	were

CLASS 3	GROUP E	CLASS 3	CLASS 4	GROUP E	CLASS 4
interesting	*and*	profitable	now	*and*	earlier

Only a very few words make up this group: *and, or, not, nor, but, rather than.*

All the words of this group stand only between words of the same part-of-speech class or subgroup, but the two words between which they stand may be of any one of the four classes. Group E words are signals of "leveling," of connecting two units with the "same" structural function. At times certain other words may appear before the first members of the two which are joined by the words of Group E. These two then belong together.

> *both* the concerts *and* the lectures (Class 1)
> *either* are *or* were (Class 2)
> *neither* interesting *nor* profitable (Class 3)
> *not* now *but* [7] earlier (Class 4)

GROUP F

For Group F we take the words that can stand in the various positions occupied by the word *at* in the following sentence frame.

GROUP	CLASS	GROUP	GROUP	CLASS	CLASS	GROUP	GROUP	CLASS
A	**1**	**F**	**A**	**1**	**2**	**F**	**A**	**1**
The	concerts	*at*	the	school	are	*at*	the	top

GROUP	CLASS	GROUP	GROUP	CLASS	CLASS	CLASS	GROUP	GROUP	CLASS
A	**1**	**F**	**A**	**1**	**2**	**3**	**F**	**A**	**1**
The	dress	*at*	the	end	is	dirty	*at*	the	bottom

---

[7] *But*, alone, often stands between two Class 3 words (*his parents are poor* but *honest*) or Class 4 words (*P— and F— can work anywhere* but *here*) but it does not often appear between two Class 1 or Class 2 words except in such expressions as the following:

all
anybody
everybody
nobody   } *but*   Peter
everyone   he/him
no one

all
everything
anything   } *but* the table
nothing

They seldom go out *but* they fight

GROUP	CLASS	GROUP	GROUP	CLASS	CLASS	CLASS	GROUP	GROUP	CLASS
A	1	F	A	1	2	3	F	A	1
		at							

by, for, from, in,
of, on, to, with,
over, up, across,
after

The words of Group F are followed by Class 1 words [8] but may be preceded by words of Class 1, Class 2, or Class 3.

GROUP G

For Group G we have but one word, but this word appears in various forms: *do, does, did*. In these forms the word is like the vocabulary item *do* with the meaning of "make," "accomplish," "perform," "be appropriate." In the positions here examined, however, *do* is not the word with these meanings and can be clearly separated from it by the use of both words in the same test frame.[9]

GROUP	GROUP	CLASS	CLASS	GROUP	CLASS	CLASS
G	A	1	2	A	1	4(b)
Do	the	boys	do	their	work	promptly
Did			correct			
			return			
			examine			

[8] Possible exceptions are *at large, in short, at least, at best*. The uses of *to* followed by a Class 2 word will be treated in the publication referred to in footnote 4 above. The uses of these words in combinations such as *call up the man, run down the child*, are not discussed in this book. They are being studied by Edward Anthony of the English Language Institute.

[9] That there are other words with the same shape (homonyms) which occur in other "positions" with other meanings is of no significance for our treatment of the function-word positions.

In this position the *do* always stands before a free utterance form with the word-order arrangement of a statement sentence in which a Class 2 word other than *is/are, was/were* is used. The result of the use of this word *do* before such an utterance is to make it a question sentence.

The same forms *do, does, did* occur in another position with no meaning other than that of the position itself. Here it appears before the Group C word *not*, the negative.

GROUP	CLASS	GROUP	GROUP	CLASS	GROUP	CLASS	CLASS
A	**1**	**G**	**C**	**2**	**A**	**1**	**4**
The	boys	*do*	not	do	their	work	promptly
				correct			
				return			
				examine			

GROUP	GROUP	GROUP	CLASS	CLASS	GROUP	CLASS	CLASS
G	**C**	**A**	**1**	**2**	**A**	**1**	**4**
Do-	n't	the	boys	do	their	work	promptly

GROUP H

For Group H we have one word, *there*. It seems to appear in a very limited number of sentence frames, and in two positions that are functions of Class 1 words. This word is not a Class 1 substitute, for the Class 1 word (or a substitute) with its usual correlations always appears in the sentence also. This word has the same shape as the Class 4 word *there* except for the fact that it is always unstressed.

GROUP	CLASS	GROUP	CLASS	GROUP	GROUP	CLASS
H	**2**	**A**	**1**	**F**	**A**	**1**
There	is	a	man	at	the	door
There	are		men	at	the	door

GROUP	CLASS	GROUP	CLASS	CLASS
H	2	1		4
There	is	a	man	there
There	are		men	there

CLASS	GROUP	GROUP	CLASS	CLASS
2	H	A	1	4
Is	*there*	a	man	there
Are	*there*		men	there

GROUP	CLASS	GROUP	CLASS	
H	2	A	1	
There	comes	a	time	(when we must decide)

But with *come* the reversed order *comes there a time* does not occur.

GROUP	CLASS	GROUP	CLASS	CLASS
H	2	A	1	4
There	appears to be	no	student	there
There	appear to be	no	students	there

GROUP I

For Group I there are the words used in the position of *when* in the following sentences:

GROUP	CLASS	GROUP	CLASS	CLASS
I	2	A	1	2
When	was	the	concert	good
Why				
Where				
How				

GROUP	GROUP	GROUP	CLASS	CLASS
I	**G**	**A**	**1**	**3**
When	did	the	student	call
Why				
Where				
How				
Who				
Which				
What				

All these words occur also as single-word utterances in "response" sentence units.

In the positions shown above, in single free utterance units, they operate as signals of question sentences. Some of them (*who, which, what*) occur also in the positions of Class 1 words. In the positions of Class 1 words their signal of "question sentence" supercedes that of the form-class arrangement (see Chapter VIII).

GROUP	CLASS
I	**2**
(also Class 1)	
Who	came
Which	
What	

GROUP J

In Group J we include those words that stand in the position of *after* in the following sentence.[10]

---

[10] See the discussion in Chapter XI of "sequence" sentences and "included" sentences. Certain of the words there called "sequence signals" must be included among the function words. Here I have not made them a separate group but tentatively considered them a special division of Group J.

GROUP	CLASS	CLASS	CLASS	GROUP	GROUP	CLASS	CLASS	CLASS
A	**1**	**2**	**3**	**J**	**A**	**3**	**1**	**2**
The	orchestra	was	good	*after*	the	new	director	came

when	*so*
whenever	*nevertheless*
because	*therefore*
although	*and*
since	*but*
before	

The important fact concerning the position of these words is that they all stand before groups of words having the characteristic arrangements of parts of speech that occur in single free utterance units.

The words of Group J are thus the functioning units by means of which sentence units are included in larger structures. The words of this group fall into several subdivisions in accord with the positions which the included sentence unit may occupy. The following examples illustrate the chief subdivisions.

(a) The included sentence as the first unit

> *When* the new director came the orchestra was **good**
> *After*
> *Before*
> *Because*

(b) The included sentence after the other unit

> The orchestra was good *whenever* the new director came
> *after*
> *because*
>
> The students were uncertain *whether* the new director had come

(c) The included sentence within the structural arrangement of the other unit

The orchestra *which* the new director organized was good
           that

The place *where* he lived was near a swamp (819)
The time *when* he is least busy is Friday afternoon (830)

GROUP K

For Group K there are four words that occurred very frequently at the beginnings of "response" utterance units. These "response" utterance units were very frequently but not exclusively answers to questions. These words also occurred at the beginnings of other sentences that continued rather than introduced conversations. They are the words *well, oh, now, why* (always [waɪ], never with aspiration [hwaɪ]).

Well that's more helpful (256)
Well I've called the meeting for four o'clock (260)
Well can I make connections to get over to P—— by nine o'clock (261)
Well I think you better come over and look at it (269)
Well do it your own way (278)

Oh I have another suit (276)
Oh that would be wonderful (273)
Oh do you have records for the square dance (271)
Oh what day does it come up (269)
Oh distribute them to the students (280)

Now that would mean that they were limited in the use of their property (264)
Now I just wish you both could see it (267)

Now what group could afford it (265)
Now if people will get on the job it can be voted down
   tonight (266)

Why it would be nice if you would (270)
Why we'll just go after it (262)
Why just say you can't afford it (289)
Why when do you think (294)
Why it's largely the report of our conference with the
   dean (226)

These words *well, oh, now, why* as they appear in the materials, introducing response utterances, seem to operate without any difference of meaning and to have no more significant relation to the rest of the sentence than to provide a starting syllable. The sentences to which they are attached are not of any single kind. *Now*, in this use, clearly distinct from *now* of Class 4, appeared very frequently in such expressions as *now look here, now see here.*

Now look here we mustn't ignore them (465)
Now see here what does it all amount to (541)

GROUP L

In this same position of introducing response utterances occur also the two words *yes* and *no*. These two words differ from the preceding in two respects: (1) They have a meaning of affirmation and negation which is usually supported by the utterance they introduce.

Yes we're on our way now (320)
Yes I know (86)

No he's not here now (236)
No they don't arrive until eight (242)

(2) Each of these two words often constitutes the whole of a response utterance.

GROUP M

Probably we should include as a separate kind, or Group M, the three words that appeared at the beginnings of "situation" utterance units as attention-getting signals: *look, say, listen.*

> *Say* I just got on Saturday another letter from P——
> R—— (52)
> *Listen* did you get any shoes (129)
> *Look* I want to ask you two questions (210)

GROUP N

In Group N there appears only the one word *please* which occurs with request sentences, most frequently at the beginning. It operates as a "polite" formula attached to the request.

> *Please* take these two letters (146)

GROUP O

Like *please* in that it occurs in a position with request sentences, but differing from *please* in its structural signal is the form *lets.* This form *lets* operates as a device which makes a request sentence into a request or proposal that includes the speaker. It differs from the phrase *let us* in its use, and the historical fact that "it is a contraction of *let us*" is not significant. Compare, for example, the difference in response to the following sentences:

> Let us go through the list and then we'll let you know (114)
> Let us look up the account and call you back (280)

Lets do the invitations right away (308)
Lets call him ourselves instead of sending B—— over (105)

The use of *us* with *lets* occurs rather frequently.

Lets us take the elite type and not wait for the others (124)

Altogether then we have, in this chapter entitled "Function Words," set off fifteen separate groups. The procedure employed has been the same as that used in the preceding chapter, where we set up four separate classes, there called "Parts of Speech." In both we took from our materials single free utterances as test frames and, by the process of substitution, tried to find the words which, with the marks they had in their original utterances, could be used in the test frames without a change in the structural meaning. For the decision of "same" or "different" we had to depend on the responses of native speakers of the language.

Although each of the fifteen groups set up here differs quite markedly from every other group, they all have certain characteristics in common—characteristics which make them different from the four classes of words identified previously.

1. In the mere matter of number of items the fifteen groups differ sharply from the four classes. The four classes together contain thousands of separate items. There was no difficulty whatever in selecting from our long lists a hundred different items of each of the four classes as examples. On the other hand, the total number of the separate items from our materials making up the fifteen groups amounted to only 154.

Although the separate items are few they occur very frequently —so frequently indeed that these 154 items, some of them repeated in every utterance, make up about one-third of the total bulk of the materials. A very different picture is presented when one counts each separate item only once. The table below shows the percentages of each of the four classes and the total of the fifteen groups for the first, second, third, and fourth hundred separate words, for the total of a five-hundred-word count, and for a total of a thousand-word count. In these figures each item is counted only once; repetitions of the items are ignored.

Items counted	Class 1	Class 2	Class 3	Class 4	Total of Classes 1, 2, 3, 4	Total of all fifteen groups of function words
First hundred	30%	19%	7%	10%	66%	34%
Second hundred continuous	34%	20%	17%	11%	82%	18%
Third hundred continuous	32%	25%	25%	8%	90%	10%
Fourth hundred continuous	39%	25%	16%	13%	93%	7%
Total 500	35%	23%	17%	11%	86%	14%
Total 1000	39%	25%	17%	12%	93%	7%

In the first hundred items counted, it makes very little difference whether one counts all the instances or only the separate items. The function words amount to about a third of the total. In the next hundred, however, if one goes on counting only new items and not those that are repetitions of those counted in the first hundred, the proportion of function words decreases sharply. By the end of the fourth hundred approximately half of all the function words found in the complete materials have appeared and new items are added very slowly. For a thousand-word conversation (i.e., one that employs a thousand different words), 93 per cent of the words would belong to Classes 1, 2, 3, and 4, and only 7 per cent to the fifteen groups of function words.

2. It was pointed out above, but it needs repeating here, that the four classes first identified account for all the significant positions of our minimum free utterances. In fact, Classes 1 and 2 alone appear in many minimum free utterances. On the other hand the

words of our fifteen groups of function words appear most frequently in expanded single free utterances. As we shall see later, it is arrangements of Class 1 and Class 2 words that form the basic signals of our sentences. Only "response" utterances, not "situation" utterances, can have words from the fifteen groups of function words alone—without words from the four classes.

3. In the four large classes, the lexical meanings of the separate words are rather clearly separable from the structural meanings of the arrangements in which these words appear. In the words of our fifteen groups it is usually difficult if not impossible to indicate a lexical meaning apart from the structural meaning which these words signal. It is not especially difficult to identify and describe, for practical purposes, the actual experiences to which we apply such words as *horse, dog, scorpion, tree, window;* or *run, swim, spin, sink, talk;* or *young, hard, false, dirty, true;* or *now, often, rapidly, smoothly.* It is, however, a different problem, and a more difficult one, to identify and describe actual experiences apart from the structural signals in our utterances, to which we can apply the words *the, shall, and, do* (in *do the boys come home early*), *there* (in *there's a man at the door*), *who* (in *who came*). It is true that, within some of the groups, the differences between the items can be described apart from the structure—as, for example, some of the differences between *in, on, at.* But that kind of description for these words presents many problems [11] not encountered in descriptions for words of Classes 1, 2, 3, and 4.

4. More important than these other differences, and the basis for separating the words of these fifteen groups from the others and for calling them "function words," is the fact that in order to respond to certain structural signals *one must know these words as items.*

[11] See the descriptions or definitions in the Oxford Dictionary for the words of our fifteen groups as compared with those of the words of the four classes. For *at, by, for, from, in, of, on, to, with,* the average number of separate meanings given is $36\frac{1}{2}$.

The following illustrations may help to make clear the significicance of that assertion.

> *The man* came
> *The boys* came
> *They* came
> *Many* came

These are all statements, and that fact is signalled by the arrangement of the Class 1 and Class 2 words. The particular meanings of the separate words are unnecessary for the signalling of this structural meaning. Nonsense words would do as well. *Woggles came* would also be a statement.[12] But with one of our function words *who* or *which* or *what* the situation changes:

> *The man* came
> *The boys* came
> *They* came
> *Many* came
> *Woggles* came
>
> *Who* came

The expression *who came* signals a question, not because of a different arrangement, but solely because the signal of question is in the word *who* as a word. In the other sentences one does not need to know the meanings of the words themselves, in fact the word may be entirely unfamiliar. If it has the marks of a Class 1 word, the structural signal of a statement is clear. But in the sentence *who came* one must be able to recognize this special word *who* and he must know that this word in itself in that position signals a

---

[12] With a nonsense word and no special distinctive intonation this arrangement would always be responded to as a statement.

question—a sentence directed to eliciting an oral response. It is these words, which must be learned as separate items signalling particular structural meanings, that I have called "function words."

In such sentences as the following we must know the words in italics as items and the different structural meanings they signal. There is, so far as I can see, no other way to identify the particular structural meaning.

> The boy *was* given the money
> The boy *had* given the money

A nonsense word in this position would make it impossible to determine whether the "boy" was the "performer"—the giver of the money—or the "receiver."

> The boy *vab* given the money

The same is true for the words in italics in the following sentences:

> The boys *and* the leaders were invited
> The boys *of* the leaders were invited

To identify the structural relation of *the leaders* one must know the words *and* and *of* as words. A nonsense word here would remove the structural signal.

> The boys *taf* the leaders were invited

The separate function words we use are comparatively few. In all the materials examined here there were only 154 in all. These must be learned as separate items. In some cases they are items belonging to a list, and the whole list signals the same structural meaning. But there are no formal contrasts by which we can identify the words of these lists. They must be remembered as items.[13]

For the four classes that contain most of our vocabulary, identification rests upon a different basis. The lists for each of these four classes are almost unending. Fortunately the words of these classes have a variety of formal markers which provide the means of recognition of the class even when the meaning of the word itself is unknown. The next chapter will describe these various marks of identification.

[13] That words of the same shape have other uses is not significant in the discussion of this chapter. Here we are concerned solely with these words in the function-word "positions."

VII. Parts of Speech:
Formal Characteristics

In the preceding two chapters the point of view has been that of the investigator who, having gathered a mass of recorded conversations, is trying to classify the words of these materials in functioning units—in parts of speech. In that attempt we have assumed that all words that could occupy the same "set of positions" in our utterances belong to the same part of speech. We have therefore taken from our materials certain single free utterances to be used as test frames for the units of our materials. From the point of view of the investigator, we sought to find a large body of units that could with some confidence be grouped together and labeled a single part of speech. We assumed that when we had explored each of the positions in the single free utterances—the sentences—identified in our materials, we would have such a body of items for each of the parts of speech which English uses. With this procedure we found four major parts of speech and fifteen kinds of units which we have called "function words."

Now we must raise a different question. How does the user of our language recognize each of these functioning units in the stream of speech? We have insisted that unless he does recognize the differing functioning units, the separate parts of speech, he cannot respond to (or give) the necessary signals of structural meaning. This recognition, however, for the users of the language, need not be in any way a conscious recognition. We mean by "recognition" here an automatic conditioned response that, in general, the naïve native speaker cannot usually analyze or describe. He must, nevertheless, respond accurately to these differing functioning units or he cannot understand the language or communicate in it. What precisely are the identifying features that operate for these practical users of the language?

For all the fifteen groups of function words we have insisted that the words must be learned and reacted to as *words*. I have called them "function words" because I have been able to find no general identifying characteristics by which to recognize the groups of these words. So far as I can see, all these words have to be recognized as special items, and, in most cases, items that belong to a particular list. In each, the structural signal comes only through the word itself as a special item. Fortunately, although there are fifteen groups, the number of separate items is comparatively small—in the great mass of materials examined here, only 154 in all.

On the other hand, the four form-classes, each of which contains hundreds of separate items, do have identifying characteristics. For these four form-classes or parts of speech we can make nonsense words and produce utterances in which the structural meanings are perfectly clear—that is, those structural meanings that depend upon arrangements of Class 1, Class 2, Class 3, and Class 4 words.

The vapy koobs dasaked the citar molently

The identifying characteristics of these four parts of speech are the subject of this chapter. Our procedure for finding these identifying characteristics was a study of the contrasts between the forms of the items in our lists for each of the four classes *in the frames by which they were tested*. This examination gave us not only contrasts in the forms themselves but also contrasts in *the formal marks of the various "positions"* in which each of the classes could appear. Our identifying characteristics, therefore, are of both kinds. We are not concerned here with classifying words in isolation but solely with these items as they occur in live utterances carrying on conversations—with the practical functioning of language.

In many instances, in more than teachers usually believe, it is possible to point to contrastive identifying forms of the words themselves, as in *goodness, departure,* of Class 1; *soften, befriend,* of Class 2; *misty, boyish,* of Class 3; *rapidly,* of Class 4. Contrasts of form such as *goodness* taken against *good, departure* against *depart, soften* against *soft, befriend* against *friend, misty* against *mist, boyish* against *boy,* and *rapidly* against *rapid* furnish many of the clues that speakers of English actually use in responding to the structural signals. Evidence for this use comes from the responses to utterances in which forms present minimum contrasts.

> This exercise is *fun*
> This exercise is *funny*

> The hinges worked *loose* after being oiled
> The hinges worked *loosely* after being oiled

Although such an utterance as *ship sails today* is ambiguous because of the lack of clear marks by which to identify the parts of speech of the first two words, the forms of these words themselves could be such as to make the recognition of the form-classes unmistakable and thus produce an utterance entirely unambiguous.

> Ship*ed* sails today
> Ship sail*ed* today

But these significant formal contrasts in the shapes of the words themselves are not only supplemented by but often superceded by the formal characteristics of the particular positions the words of these four classes occupy as they occur in live utterances. We shall first list the chief formal contrasts that furnish the criteria of the four word-classes to which users of the language respond and then comment upon the "rank" of these criteria.

CLASS 1 WORDS

A comparative survey of all the words of our lists reveals the following important formal identifying contrasts for the words of Class 1 in our utterances.

(a) **Regular patterns of contrast of form between Class 1 words and the words of the other classes (some of these patterns include many separate words, others only a few items)**

1. Class 1 contrasting with Class 2

	CLASS 1	CLASS 2	CLASS 1	CLASS 2
(1)	arrival	arrive	dismissal	dismiss
	refusal	refuse	reversal	reverse
	denial	deny	approval	approve
	acquittal	acquit		
(2)	departure	depart	closure	close [z]
	failure	fail	enclosure	enclose
	erasure	erase		
(3)	delivery	deliver	recovery	recover
	discovery	discover	flattery	flatter
(4)	acceptance	accept	appearance	appear
	acquaintance	acquaint	attendance	attend
	admittance	admit	performance	perform
	annoyance	annoy	remembrance	remember

	CLASS 1	CLASS 2	CLASS 1	CLASS 2
(5)	accompaniment	accompany	agreement	agree
	accomplishment	accomplish	employment	employ
	achievement	achieve	nourishment	nourish
	adjournment	adjourn	punishment	punish
	advertisement	advertise	payment	pay
	amusement	amuse		
(6)	deformity	deform	perplexity	perplex
	disability	disable		
(7)	collision	collide	elision	elide
	decision	decide	division	divide
	derision	deride		
(8)	appendage	append	drainage	drain
	breakage	break	leakage	leak
(9)	defense	defend	pretense	pretend
	offense	offend		
(10)	catcher	catch	maker	make
	helper	help	reader	read
	hinderer	hinder	teacher	teach
	knitter	knit	writer	write
(11)	applicant	apply	claimant	claim
	assistant	assist	servant	serve
	disinfectant	disinfect	superintendent	superintend
(12)	advice [s]	advise [z]	abuse [s]	abuse [z]
	house [s]	house [z]	device [s]	devise [z]
	use [s]	use [z]		
(13)	súbject	subjéct	óbject	objéct

CLASS 1	CLASS 2	CLASS 1	CLASS 2
(14)[1] eating	eat	boiling	boil
teaching	teach	walking	walk
painting	paint		

Some miscellaneous contrasts between Class 1 and Class 2 words are the following:

deceit	deceive
receipt	receive
complaint	complain
bequest	bequeath
gift	give
blood	bleed
behavior	behave

2. Class 1 contrasting with Class 3

CLASS 1	CLASS 3	CLASS 1	CLASS 3
(1) bigness	big	iciness	icy
blackness	black	kindness	kind
closeness	close [s]	sickness	sick
goodness	good	slipperiness	slippery
happiness	happy	thickness	thick

[1] These occur in a limited list of positions. They differ in some important structural ways from other Class 1 words that contrast in form with Class 2 words.

His *eating* rapidly and *dashing* off at once has become very annoying
Any *painting* of this house is a waste of time
His *teaching* of mathematics developed his accuracy

CLASS 1	CLASS 3	CLASS 1	CLASS 3
(2) activity	active	sincerity	sincere [2]
complexity	complex	fertility	fertile
equality	equal	regularity	regular
falsity	false		
purity	pure		
(3) truth	true	width	wide
warmth	warm	strength	strong
depth	deep	length	long
breadth	broad		
(4) idealism	ideal	realism	real
truism	true	dualism	dual

Some miscellaneous contrasts between Class 1 and Class 3 are the following:

supremacy	supreme	bravery	brave
justice	just	wisdom	wise
importance	important	freedom	free
violence	violent	anxiety	anxious
independence	independent	necessity	necessary
absence	absent	clarity	clear

(b) All compounds of which the last unit is *one*, or *body*, or *thing*, or *self/selves*

[2] In these words quite noticeably, and in other words less noticeably, there are phonetic differences which have been ignored here in the attempt to center attention upon the major feature of each contrasting pattern. A complete description should indicate all these differences. Here, the purpose is neither exhaustive enumeration nor complete description. Enough samples have probably been given to show something of the extent of such contrasting patterns. These contrastive patterns are of course matters of sound not of spelling.

–one	*–body*	*–thing*	*–self/selves*
someone	somebody	something	myself
anyone	anybody	anything	yourself
everyone	everybody	everything	himself
	nobody	nothing	herself
			itself
			ourselves
			yourselves
			themselves

(c) **The "s" ending correlating with the "meaning" of more than one item of whatever the word represents—in contrast with the absence of an "s" ending, correlating with the "meaning" of only one item of what the word stands for**

boys	boy
desks	desk
thighs	thigh

(d) **A few other formal identifying contrasts of the forms of particular Class 1 words which have the same type of correlation as the contrast of "s" ending with the absence of "s" ending**

men	man	children	child
feet	foot	oxen	ox
teeth	tooth	women	woman [3]
mice	mouse		

(e) **The "s" ending correlating with the "meanings" of "possession," "ownership," "related to," etc.**

In shape, the words with this ending are like those with the "s" endings listed in (c) above. Although alike in the living language

---

[3] Here again the important contrast is not the spelling difference, but the difference in sound [wɪmən—wumən].

of speech, in writing, a graphic mark—the apostrophe—differentiates the forms. In the matter of the "s" ending correlating with the number (whether one or more than one) of the items of whatever is represented by the word to which the "s" ending is attached, there were the exceptional forms listed in (d) above. For this "s" ending correlating with the "meanings" of "possession," "ownership," "related to," etc., there are no such exceptions: *man's, men's, mouse's, woman's, child's, children's, ox's, oxen's.*

1. The *boy's* hats are on the table
   The *boys'* hats are on the table
2. A *boy's* hat is on the table
3. A *boy's* is on the table
4. *John's* is on the table
5. The *teacher's* teachers or the *teachers'* teachers [ðe tičərz tičərz]

In the living language the words with this "s" ending (e) are differentiated from those with the "s" ending of (c) by position as in (1), (2), and (5) and by correlations of form as in (3) and (4).

(f) In utterances, all words marked by one of the "determiners" (the function words of Group A)

The, a/an, every, no, my, our, your, her, his, their, and the following when they are in a position that is not in itself a position for a Class 1 word: *this/these, that/those, each, some, any, much,* etc. These markers identify the functioning form-class of those words that have the same shape in two or more parts of speech. In any utterance the italic words in the expressions, the *jump,* the *walk,* the *catch,* the *make,* the *break,* the *fall,* would all be Class 1. In similar fashion the italic words would also be Class 1 in the following:

> The *poor* and the *rich,* the very *lowest* and the very *highest*
> are . . .

(g) In utterances, the words used with the function words listed in Group F

Most frequently these Class 1 words have other markers as well; but such expressions as the following are frequent: *at school, in class, by air, by telephone, by committee, to church, after tea, on leave, in sight, in prison.*

(h) In utterances, positions for Class 1 words in structures identified by the recognition of the other form-classes of which the structures are composed

In the following newspaper heading the part of speech of the word *fares* is identified by its position in a structure in which the word *cheap* has by its formal characteristics been recognized as a Class 3 word.

Bus Fares Cheap in Emergency

The word *fares*, in this particular position with *cheap* as a Class 3 word, must be a Class 1 word. In the following heading, however, the conclusion would be different.

Bus Fares Badly in Emergency

In this structure, with *badly* recognized as a Class 4 word, the word *fares* could not be a Class 1 word.

The indirect clues of position in identified structures such as these seem to be the only way to recognize the "substitutes" in this part of speech. Of course, the list of these substitutes is short and the units are probably also learned as separate items belonging in this list.

Only in the words of this list of substitutes and only in six of the words of the list are there differences in form for certain differing positions of Class 1 words.

he	him
she	her
they	them
who	whom
I	me
we	us

In all other Class 1 words or Class 1 "substitutes" no differences of form mark the words in different positions.

Others of the list of substitutes are the following: *it, its, mine, ours, yours, hers, theirs, none, others, lots, this/these, that/those, another, each, both, many, much, several, few, some, any, all, which, what, who, whichever, whatever.*

Especially useful for our structural description is a classification of all Class 1 words into three groups in accord with the following correlation forms:

CLASS 1 WORDS	CORRELATION FORMS [4]
1. Mother, father, son, daughter, clown, waiter, maid, woman, teacher, cook, librarian, parent, etc.	*he* or *she*
2. (*a*) Child, dog, beast, cat, kitten, lamb, cow, bull, doe, buck, deer, pig, hen, rooster, mare, enemy, coward, etc.	*he/she* or *it*
(*b*) Group, committee, nation, government, club, class, gang, herd, crew, enemy, family, crowd, etc.	*they* or *it*

[4] In English, certain names have the correlating form *he*, others the correlating form *she*. *John, Peter, James, Thomas, Robert, Charles, George, Frank, Edward*, have *he*; and the following have *she*: *Emily, Elizabeth, Margaret, Patricia, Joanne, Roberta, Charlotte, Grace*. The following may have either *he* or *she*: *Carol*, and such diminutives as *Frankie, Bobby, Georgie*. In this book I have not dealt with proper names.

3. Book, tree, paper, ink, leaf,   *it*
bud, chair, seat, shop, rook,
money, water, coffee, sugar, etc.

It will be found that every word of Class 1 can be put into these subordinate groups in accord with its correlation with a particular one of the "substitute" words *he, she, it.*[5] This grouping is not only important as an identifying characteristic but also for the distinguishing of certain structural meanings which will be discussed in Chapter IX. With certain words the correlation is constant—words like *man, boy, son, uncle, father, brother, king, duke, count, actor* (profession), *butler, master, waiter, lad*—with the substitute *he;* or *woman, girl, daughter, aunt, mother, sister, queen, duchess, countess, actress, maid, mistress, waitress, lass, lady, wife, niece*—with the substitute *she;* or *tree, desk, window, chart, money, paper, coffee, poverty, leisure*—with the substitute *it.* With other words the correlation may be either *he* or *she*—the words *parent, relative* (kinship term), *cousin, ancestor, teacher, typist, artist, pianist, librarian, professor, president, chairman, thief, coward, cook, clown, dancer, poet.*

With a considerable number of words the correlation is at times either *he* or *she* and at others *it,* as with *child, dog, cat,*[6] *rooster, hen, cow, bull, duck, ram, ewe, lamb, puppy, ox, beast, brute, buck, doe, pig, hog, rabbit, rat, bird, turkey, stallion, mare, ship.* With some the correlation is at times *they* (for the singular form) and at others *it,* as with *family, crowd, gang, crew, club, class.*

Every word of Class 1 has also one of the two following substitute forms with which it correlates: *who, which.* With this correlation the form which marks the distinction between one or more

---

[5] There are a few words, such as *scissors, trousers, pants, pliers, oats, clothes, glasses* (worn to improve vision), that use only *they* as the correlating substitute.

[6] Even for such distinctive pairs of words as *rooster—hen, bull—cow, ram—ewe, buck—doe, stallion—mare,* I have recorded many instances of the substitute *it* rather than *he* or *she.*

than one item makes no difference: "the *man who* came"; "the *men who* came"; "the *package which* came." Class 1 words therefore, in accord with this correlation, fall into somewhat different groups.

CLASS I WORDS	CORRELATION FORMS
1. mother, father, woman, man, son, daughter, king, queen, duke, lady, etc.	*who*
2. child, parent, cook, clown, enemy, waiter, friend, butler, etc.	*who/which*
3. dog, beast, kitten, cat, lamb, ram, stallion, ewe, mare, rooster, hen, money, water, coffee, cup, etc.	*which*

The sets of contrasting features given here constitute most of the identifying characteristics by which the users of the language recognize Class 1 words. The full range of the "positions" that these Class 1 words can occupy also make part of their distinctive features, but the discussion of these "positions" will more conveniently enter the materials of the next chapters, especially Chapter IX. We need here to summarize the contrasting formal features of the words of the other parts of speech: Class 2, Class 3, and Class 4.

CLASS 2 WORDS

The comparative survey of all the words of our lists reveals the following important formal identifying contrasts for the words of Class 2 in our utterances.

(a) Regular patterns of contrasts of form between Class 2 words and the words of the other classes

1. Class 2 contrasting with Class 1 [7]

	CLASS 2	CLASS 1	CLASS 2	CLASS 1
(1)	befriend	friend	besiege	siege
	behead	head	bewitch	witch
(2)	enjoy	joy	entrain	train
	enrage	rage	entrance	trance
	enrapture	rapture	empower	power
(3)	colonize	colony	burglarize	burglar
	idolize	idol	agonize	agony
(4)	beautify	beauty	dignify	dignity
	glorify	glory	personify	person [8]

Some miscellaneous contrasts between Class 2 and Class 1 are the following:

CLASS 2	CLASS 1	CLASS 2	CLASS 1
strive	strife	clothe	cloth
bathe	bath	lengthen	length
believe	belief	heighten	height
relieve	relief	frighten	fright
grieve	grief	acknowledge	knowledge
prove	proof	unearth	earth

[7] In the lists given above for Class 1 words the Class 2 word is taken as the base with the Class 1 word as the derived contrasting form. Here the Class 1 word is taken as the base.

[8] See footnote 2 above.

2. *Class 2 contrasting with Class 3*

CLASS 2	CLASS 3	CLASS 2	CLASS 3
(1) brighten	bright	ripen	ripe
cheapen	cheap	soften	soft
darken	dark	shorten	short
deepen	deep	stiffen	stiff
freshen	fresh	thicken	thick
harden	hard	weaken	weak
(2) enable	able	enrich	rich
endear	dear	embitter	bitter
enlarge	large		
(3) equalize	equal	solemnize	solemn
liberalize	liberal	civilize	civil

(b) The "dental suffix," [d], [t], or [ɪd], correlating usually
with the setting in a past time of whatever the Class 2
word represents, in contrast with the absence of this
"dental suffix," correlating usually with the setting in
a present or "general" time of whatever the Class 2
word stands for

considered	consider	discussed	discuss
turned	turn	started	start
stopped	stop	recommended	recommend

(c) A few other contrasts of the forms of particular words in
which these contrasting forms have the same kind of
correlation as that indicated above in (b)

rode	ride	sang	sing
rose	rise	tore	tear
wrote	write	knew	know
froze	freeze	was/were	is/are

(d) **In utterances the "s" ending, [z], [s], or [ɪz], correlating in general with a lack of "s" ending on the Class 1 words in the "first" position of our test frame**

CLASS 1	CLASS 2	
Your husband (no *s*)	know*s*	the work of the Institute (90)
These formula*s*	appear (no *s*)	very frequently (241)

(e) **In utterances, the words used with the function words of Group B**

The Class 2 words with some of these function words have the "simple," the base form of the Class 2 word; with others they have the form with the "dental suffix," or special forms like *written, ridden, frozen, known;* and with others the form with the *–ing* suffix.

	GROUP B	CLASS 2	
The concert	*may*	*be*	good
The students	*should*	*go*	on this trip
The class	*had*	*moved*	to Room 120
The test	*was*	*given*	yesterday
The classwork	*is*	*going*	well
The students	*got*	*talking*	Spanish before we could warn them

(f) **In utterances, positions for Class 2 words in structures identified by the recognition of the other form-classes of which the structures are composed**

Bus Fares Badly in Emergency

In this structure, with *badly* recognized as a Class 4 word, *fares,* in the position it occupies in this utterance, must be a Class 2 word.

If by some marker the word *ship* in the utterance *ship sails today* can be identified as a Class 1 word, as *the ship* or *a ship*, then in this particular structure *sails* must be a Class 2 word.

The distinctive "positions" of Class 2 words in recognized structures provide some of the clues by which to identify the units in utterances that belong to this part of speech.

CLASS 3 WORDS

A survey of all the words of our lists reveals the following important formal contrasts for the words of Class 3 in English utterances.

(a) Regular patterns of contrasts of form between Class 3 words and the words of other form-classes [9]

1. Class 3 contrasting with Class 1

	CLASS 3	CLASS 1	CLASS 3	CLASS 1
(1)	baggy	bag	rainy	rain
	cloudy	cloud	snowy	snow
	dirty	dirt	streaky	streak
	dusty	dust	messy	mess
	funny	fun	nervy	nerve
	hairy	hair		
(2)	beastly	beast	shapely	shape
	friendly	friend	manly	man
	costly	cost	beggarly	beggar
	lovely	love	maidenly	maiden
	timely	time	princely	prince

[9] In the lists given above for Class 1 words and for Class 2 words contrasting with Class 3 words, the Class 3 word is taken as the base and the other as the derived contrasting form.

CLASS 3	CLASS 1	CLASS 3	CLASS 1
(3) bookish	book	foolish	fool
childish	child	feverish	fever
mannish	man	clannish	clan
freakish	freak	selfish	self
sheepish	sheep	snobbish	snob
(4) accidental	accident	ornamental	ornament
brutal	brute	personal	person
coastal	coast	regional	region
causal	cause	seasonal	season
emotional	emotion	sensational	sensation
optional	option		
(5) famous	fame	joyous	joy
porous	pore	nervous	nerve
pompous	pomp	mountainous	mountain
cavernous	cavern	spacious	space
odorous	odor	gracious	grace
vaporous	vapor	religious	religion
virtuous	virtue		
(6) angelic	angel	historic	history
cubic	cube	dogmatic	dogma
metric	meter	syntactic	syntax
sulphuric	sulphur	athletic	athlete
volcanic	volcano	rhythmic	rhythm
(7) nebular	nebula	globular	globe
spectacular	spectacle	consular	consul
molecular	molecule	polar	pole
muscular	muscle		

•

CLASS 3	CLASS 1	CLASS 3	CLASS 1
(8) visionary	vision	momentary	moment
fragmentary	fragment	documentary	document
rudimentary	rudiment	complimentary	compliment
(9) peaceful	peace [10]	successful	success
healthful	health	thoughtful	thought
plentiful	plenty	deceitful	deceit
beautiful	beauty	lawful	law
wrathful	wrath	joyful	joy
faithful	faith	sorrowful	sorrow
powerful	power		
(10) faithless	faith	noiseless	noise
powerless	power	sleeveless	sleeve
thoughtless	thought	seedless	seed
lawless	law	needless	need
ageless	age	fatherless	father
nameless	name	fruitless	fruit
homeless	home	faultless	fault
(11) lifelike	life	warlike	war
workmanlike	workman	ladylike	lady
(12) collegiate	college	affectionate	affection
fortunate	fortune	compassionate	compassion
(13) wooden	wood	woolen	wool
earthen	earth	silken	silk
golden	gold		

[10] A very few Class 3 words with this suffix –ful have a Class 2 word as the base of the contrast: forgetful—forget, resentful—resent, fretful—fret, wakeful—wake.

CLASS 3	CLASS 1	CLASS 3	CLASS 1
(14) skilled	skill	wretched	wretch
ragged	rag	wooded	wood

Some miscellaneous contrasts between Class 3 and Class 1 are the following:

asinine	ass	suburban	suburb
crystalline	crystal		

2. *Class 3 contrasting with Class 2*

CLASS 3	CLASS 2	CLASS 3	CLASS 2
(1) confident	confide [11]	recurrent'	recur
observant	observe	pleasant	please
excellent	excel	coherent	cohere
urgent	urge	prevalent	prevail
expectant	expect	existent	exist
(2) creative	create	instructive	instruct
selective	select	obstructive	obstruct
collective	collect	preventive	prevent
excessive	exceed	prohibitive	prohibit
imitative	imitate	possessive	possess
(3) allowable	allow	explainable	explain
defendable	defend	commendable	commend
readable	read	receivable	receive
perishable	perish	payable	pay
agreeable	agree	resistible	resist

[11] As a contrastive pattern the materials provided a rather limited number of examples, in comparison with the number of Class 3 words of similar shape for which no Class 2 base exists today. Typical examples are *ardent, brilliant, constant, decent, distant, evident, extravagant, flippant, impudent, innocent, prudent, recent, repugnant, silent.*

CLASS 3	CLASS 2	CLASS 3	CLASS 2
(4) meddlesome	meddle	irksome	irk
venturesome	venture	winsome	win
loathsome	loathe	tiresome	tire
(5) congratulatory	congratulate	promissory	promise
regulatory	regulate	conciliatory	conciliate
prohibitory	prohibit		
(6) molten	melt	swollen	swell
shrunken	shrink		

CLASS 3	CLASS 2
(7) separate [sɛpərət]	separate [sɛpəret]
associate [–ət]	associate [–et]
desolate [–ət]	desolate [–et]
moderate [–ət]	moderate [–et]
degenerate [–ət]	degenerate [–et]

(b) The endings –er and –est correlating with the "meaning" of amount or degree of the "quality" which is the referent of the word

Of the patterns of contrast listed for Class 3 words, these endings –er and –est occur only with those given in (a), 1 (1), as, dirtier, funnier, dirtiest, funniest. In general they appear on the Class 3 words that form the base for patterns of contrast with such Class 1 words as kindness, thickness, truth, and warmth, and such Class 2 words, as brighten, ripen, enrich, and enlarge.

| bigger | biggest | (big) | brighter | brightest | (bright) |
| kinder | kindest | (kind) | deeper | deepest | (deep) |

thicker	thickest	(thick)	riper	ripest	(ripe)
truer	truest	(true)	dearer	dearest	(dear)
warmer	warmest	(warm)	larger	largest	(large)
longer	longest	(long)	richer	richest	(rich)

The overlapping use of these endings on Class 4 words, and the situation in which structural ambiguities may result from this overlapping use, will be discussed below in connection with the forms of Class 4 words.

(c) In utterances, the words used with the function words of Group D, very frequently the function words *more* and *most*

Here again there is some overlapping of Class 3 and Class 4 words, for many of the words of Group D also occur with Class 4 words. No structural ambiguities arise from the overlapping use, however, for the Class 4 words, as these occur with these particular function words, have other formal marks to distinguish them from Class 3 words.[12] In general they appear with the words of all the patterns of contrast listed for Class 3 words above, except 1 (1), which usually has the endings –*er* and –*est*.

more friendly	*most* friendly
more timely	*most* timely
more childish	*most* childish
more brutal	*most* brutal
more famous	*most* famous
more athletic	*most* athletic
more muscular	*most* muscular
more fragmentary	*most* fragmentary
more peaceful	*most* peaceful
more lawless	*most* lawless

[12] See page 133.

more warlike	*most* warlike
more fortunate	*most* fortunate
more silken	*most* silken
more skilled	*most* skilled
more asinine	*most* asinine
more coherent	*most* coherent
more possessive	*most* possessive
more readable	*most* readable
more tiresome	*most* tiresome
more moderate	*most* moderate
more swollen	*most* swollen
more conciliatory	*most* conciliatory

More important as a marker, however, is the use of these function words with those Class 3 words that form the base of a significant contrast of form with Class 4 words.

more rapid	*most* rapid	*more* furtive	*most* furtive
more idle	*most* idle	*more* fragrant	*most* fragrant
more acute	*most* acute	*more* recent	*most* recent
more polite	*most* polite		

The three sets of contrasting features given above constitute most of the identifying characteristics by which the users of the language recognize Class 3 words. The full range of the "positions" that these Class 3 words can occupy is also part of their distinctive features, but the discussion of these "positions" will more conveniently enter the materials of later chapters, especially Chapters X and XII.

CLASS 4 WORDS

A survey of the words of our lists reveals the following important formal contrasts for the words of Class 4 in English utterances.

(a) Regular patterns of contrast of form with other word-classes

1. Class 4 contrasting with Class 3

	CLASS 4	CLASS 3	CLASS 4	CLASS 3
(1)	noisily	noisy [13]	socially	social
	wearily	weary	rhythmicly	rhythmic
	happily	happy	separately	separate
	politely	polite	tiresomely	tiresome
	candidly	candid	confidently	confident
	gladly	glad	brightly	bright
	hopefully	hopeful	idly	idle
	cheerfully	cheerful	sadly	sad
	smilingly	smiling	frequently	frequent
	privately	private	immediately	immediate
	openly	open	finally	final
	normally	normal	annually	annual
(2)	abroad	broad	aloud	loud
	along	long	around	round

2. Class 4 contrasting with Class 1

	CLASS 4	CLASS 1	CLASS 4	CLASS 1
(1)	away	way	ahead	head
	aboard	board	afoot	foot
	abreast	breast	apart	part
	aground	ground	across	cross

[13] This contrastive pattern contains many items and is most important in the signalling of structural meanings.

CLASS 4	CLASS 1	CLASS 4	CLASS 1
(2) daily	day [14]	monthly	month
hourly	hour	yearly	year
weekly	week	nightly	night
(3) seaward	sea [15]	windward	wind
homeward	home	leeward	lee

(b) Compounds with *where, time, way*

anywhere(s)   nowhere(s)
somewhere(s)   everywhere(s)

sometime(s)   meantime(s)

sideway(s)   crossway(s)

(c) In utterances, "positions" for Class 4 words in structures identified by the recognition of the other form-classes of which the structures are composed

As indicated in Chapter V above, Class 4 words occur most characteristically in a position following Class 2 words. Other word-classes also follow Class 2 words, but they can be identified

---

[14] This is a very limited list. For all except these few words the –*ly* [lɪ] suffix on Class 1 words is a marker of the Class 3 word. (See (a), 1(2) of Class 3 words above.) These six words, here, function both as Class 3 words and as Class 4 words, with other clues, primarily "position," as the means of distinguishing between the classes. Another which functions in similar fashion but without a contrastive base is *early*.

[15] The pattern of Class 4 words ending in –*ward* contains other items but the contrast is not always one in which the base is another form-class—*afterward, upward, outward, downward, inward*. Others of the pattern are *forward, backward*. Some examples of extensions of the pattern occurred in the materials—*officeward, classward*. Alternate forms with an "s" ending occur rather frequently—*forwards, backwards, homewards, downwards*.

in a variety of ways. Class 1 words in these positions will be dealt with in Chapter IX. Here the distinguishing of Class 4 from Class 3 words is most important. Both Class 3 and Class 4 words occur in a significant position following Class 2 words. The Class 2 words thus followed by Class 3 words constitute a limited list. Most frequent are the forms of *be* (*am, is, are, was, were*), *become, seem*. Other very common Class 2 words on the list are *appear, look, sound, feel, taste, smell*. Less frequent but by no means unusual are the following.

bang (shut)	The shutter *bangs shut* constantly
blow (open)	The door *blew open* just a minute ago
blush (red)	The student *blushed red* when her name was called
break (loose) (even)	The boats *broke loose* from the dock
come (high)	Such clothes *come high* but we must have them
(clean)	The wash *comes clean* with little or no rubbing
continue (cold) (hot) (mild) (warm)	The weather will *continue cold* throughout the next few days
fall (sick)	G—— *fell sick* just before we started to pack for the moving
fly (open) (shut)	The door *flew shut* with a bang and the noise frightened him
force (open) (shut)	The lock jammed when the door banged and it had to be *forced open*
get (well) (sick)	They all *got well* again within three hours

	(late)	It *got* so *late* before we reached it that we decided not to go
grow	(old)	They try to *grow old* gracefully
	(tall)	
go	(blue)	His lips *went blue* and his face *grew pale*
hold	(true)	This rule *holds true* in more than four-fifths of the instances
keep	(thin)	She *keeps thin* by vigorous dieting
	(young)	
lie	(flat)	This paper just will not *lie flat*
lay	(open)	In that case we make a long incision and *lay open* the whole muscle
loom	(large)	Little inconsequential items often *loom large* to invalids
make	(good)	He is somewhat of a problem now but I'm sure he will *make good* as a research man
prove	(true)	
	(false)	Most of his accusations *proved false*
remain	(loyal)	We're certain that most of the group will *remain loyal*
	(ignorant)	
rest	(easy)	He can now *rest easy* in the knowledge that he has done all he could
ring	(true)	He bounced every one of the coins to see if it would *ring true*
	(false)	
run	(dry)	After the long dry season many of the wells *ran dry*
	(slow)	
shine	(clear)	After all the argument several facts *shine clear*
show	(red)	The petals *show red* underneath
sit	(still)	B—— just couldn't *sit still* that long
	(straight)	
	(tight)	

stand	(straight) (still) (firm)	Their posture is stiff and they never *stand straight*
stay	(clean) (bright) (strong)	After being waxed the surfaces *stay clean* for a long time
turn	(red) (green) (black)	The leaves *turn red* in October
wear	(thin)	The soles of shoes worn in that kind of work *wear thin* very rapidly
work	(loose)	The material was poor and the hinges *worked loose* in a very short time

With this limited list of Class 2 words other than *be, become, seem,* but including *appear, look, sound, feel, taste, smell,* the Class 4 words are usually marked by forms contrasting with Class 3 words.

See, for example, the following contrasting pairs of sentences:

The hinges *worked loosely* after being oiled
The hinges *worked loose* after being oiled

The train *appeared slowly*
The train *appeared slow*

The workman *forced* the door *openly*
The workman *forced* the door *open*

The great *clock* ran *slowly*
The great *clock* ran *slow*

The boys *looked eagerly*
The boys *looked eager*

Wherever in these positions after the Class 2 words of this list the Class 4 word does not have such a distinctive form, then structural ambiguity results unless other clues provide for a clear identification of the form-class.

> The watch ran *fast*

In this sentence the word *fast* can be either a Class 3 or a Class 4 word. As a Class 3 word, the structure would make the meaning of the utterance *the watch gained in time so that it indicated a time in advance of the accurate hour*. As a Class 4 word, the structure would make the meaning of the utterance simply that *the ticking was rapid* without any assertion or even implication concerning the accuracy of the time indicated by the watch.

A very few Class 4 words use the endings *–er* and *–est* in utterances expressing a comparison: *fast, slow, hard, late, long, soon, early, near, straight.* With words of this kind that can also be Class 3 words, in positions after the Class 2 words of the special list, the structural meaning will be ambiguous unless other clues resolve the ambiguity.

> The dog looked *longer* than the cat
> The new train appeared *faster*
> The hinges worked *looser* after being oiled
> The boy looked *better* than his companion
> The second man looked *harder* than the first

In all these instances in which the actual form of the Class 4 word is the same as that of a Class 3 word, structural ambiguity may result whenever the word appears after one of the Class 2 words of the restricted list above. This structural ambiguity, however, occurs only with minimum structures and therefore very rarely in actual live conversations. Usually with the more expanded structures of our conversations the identification of the Class 4 word (or the Class 3 word) is accomplished by the recognition of other parts of the total structure which are compatible with only one of these two classes in the particular position—which otherwise could have either. Structures with these same words, if only slightly extended as in the following sentences, have no structural ambiguity because the form-class of the italicized words can be ascertained by the necessities of the "position" created by the fuller structures:

> The dog looked at the strange animal *longer* than the cat (Class 4)
> The hinges worked *looser* and without noise after being oiled (Class 4)

(d) In utterances, "positions" for Class 4 words of special lists

The words of these lists that occurred in the materials examined are the following:

there	under	straight [17]	now	never	late
here	in	fast	soon	ever	already
down [16]	out	slow	next	once	yet
below	through	hard	again	twice	before
above	back	long	often	since	first
on	far	thus	seldom	early	last
over	near	then			

· In spite of the warning in the early part of this chapter that we are not seeking to classify words in isolation, the fact that for each

[16] Some of the words of this list have the same shape as those of Group F of the function words. The "positions" in which they occur, however, are different.

[17] Some of the words of this list have the same shape as certain Class 3 words, but the "positions" differ.

of the four parts of speech we have given certain formal contrast of shape for individual words may lead the reader to forget that we are here concerned solely with words *as functioning units in the structures of our utterances*. We have insisted that the first requisite for grasping the structural signals in English utterances is a recognition of the four parts of speech which in various arrangements constitute these structural signals. In English, although the formal contrasts of the words themselves are often particularly helpful in thus identifying the four parts of speech, these contrasts do not constitute the whole of the evidence for identification and in some instances they are not the most important evidence. We must know just what kind of a functioning unit a word is *in the immediate utterance*, and sometimes the various criteria do not all point in the same direction. Some of the formal contrasts listed for the parts of speech above outrank others.

A return to the illustration from baseball may help to clarify this matter. If the batter hits the ball so that it falls to the ground outside the playing diamond, it is called a "foul" ball, in distinction from a "fair" ball, which is one that falls to the ground inside the playing diamond. The formal criteria for distinguishing a foul ball from a fair ball are quite sharp. There is no limit to the number of "foul" balls the batter can hit in one time at bat. If, however, at the time the batter hits a particular "foul," he has less than two strikes against him, then in that situation, for that play, the "foul" functions as a "strike." In other words, in that particular "position," the kind of hit which would ordinarily function simply as a "foul," becomes, in accord with the outranking criteria of the "position," a different functioning unit. A "foul strike" is first a "foul," but the "foul" by virtue of its occurrence in the circumstances of a batter with less than two strikes against him becomes a "strike" with all the structural meaning for baseball of any other kind of strike. In the sentence *The poorest are always with us* the word *poorest* has the formal char-

acteristics of a Class 3 word but the marker *the* in this position
supercedes the word form and thus in this utterance *poorest* as a
functioning unit is Class 1. This does not mean that we are determining function by the meaning against the formal characteristics of the word, but simply that certain formal matters outrank
others in determining the class of a function unit in any particular utterance. In general, "position" markers in any particular
sentence supercede morphological or form markers.[18] The more
detailed exploration of "positions," or the structures in which the
various parts of speech function, will enter the materials of the
next three chapters.

[18] We are concerned here with form-classes or parts of speech as functioning units
in structure—that is, with syntactic form-classes, not morphological form-classes. Our
words with *particular markings within an utterance* become the significant members of
structural patterns, each of which signals a structural meaning. The *significant markings
within an utterance* consist of relative positions, accompanying function words, contrastive patterns of the shapes or forms of the words themselves, corresponding forms
of other words, substitute forms with which the words themselves correlate—that is,
those that are substitutable for the particular utterance.

VIII. Structural Patterns of Sentences

The fact that some utterances evoke responses essentially different from those of others has furnished the basis for the general classification of utterances described in Chapter III. Using the differing responses as criteria it was possible to put all the single free utterances of our materials into a small number of groups having certain particular features of their responses in common.

We have assumed that if certain utterances are all regularly followed by a particular type of response then there must be something in the formal arrangement of these utterances that elicits this type of response.[1] If, for example, some utterances are immediately and regularly followed by "action" responses and others by "oral" responses then there must be some basic contrastive difference in the formal arrangements of these two groups of utterances. It is these contrastive differences in the formal arrangements of the various groups of utterances that constitute the basic structural patterns of English sentences. It is these contrastive differences in the formal arrangements of the various groups of utterances that signal, as one structural meaning, the kind of utterance, and serve to stimulate the particular responses that regularly follow each kind of utterance. As indicated above, the child, in beginning to speak his native language, learns very early to re-

---

[1] Of course, not in language in general but in a particular language in the linguistic community that uses this language.

spond to these contrastive differences—which signal that such an utterance as *is your mother home* is a "question" seeking an oral response, that another, *give John the ball* is a "request" seeking "action," and that another, *John is sick and cannot come over to play today*, is a "statement" to which the appropriate response is attention until the utterance ceases.

To describe the patterns of the contrastive differences that signal these various types of utterances is the purpose of this chapter. It is sometimes assumed that distinctive intonation curves serve to identify each of the types of sentences—that the voice rises at the ends of "questions" and falls at the ends of "statements," and that "commands" have a special "tone of voice." As Dr. Pike points out,[2] such a simple correlation between primary intonation contours and the chief types of sentences does not exist. It is true that every sentence structural pattern always includes one of the significant intonation contours. Throughout this book the discussion attempts to center attention upon the devices and patterns of structure other than intonation. One cannot, however, have utterances without their intonation contours. We can, nevertheless, find contrastive patterns of form and arrangement of other structural items *within the same primary intonation contours*. In this chapter, therefore, I shall attempt to describe the distinctive contrasts of pattern that mark the various kinds of sentences, not apart from, but within the various primary intonation contours. In all instances in which contrasts of form and arrangement are described, it is to be assumed, unless specifically stated otherwise, that the essential intonation contours are of the same patterns. The descriptions here of the basic structural patterns of sentences will be primarily in terms of the selection of the parts of speech set forth in the preceding chapters and of the distinctive formal arrangements of these parts of speech.

[2] Kenneth L. Pike, *The Intonation of American English* (Ann Arbor: University of Michigan Press, 1945), p. 163.

I

In the great mass of the utterances of our materials the kind of sentence, whether question, or request, or statement, is signalled by special contrastive patterns in the arrangement of only two of these parts of speech—Class 1 and Class 2 words.

A comparison of the following sentences will serve to bring out certain basic features of the contrastive arrangements of these two form-classes.

(A)	(B)
1. The leader is here [3]	1. The leaders are here
2. Is the leader here	2. Are the leaders here

As speakers of English, we respond to the first sentence of each group, *the leader is here* and *the leaders are here*, as statements of fact, not questions seeking information, nor requests for action. We respond to the second sentence in each group as questions.

The first and the second sentences in group (A), the statement and the question, contain exactly the same words, but in a slightly different order. The first and the second sentences in group (B), also a statement and a question, contain exactly the same words, but in slightly different order. In addition, a comparison of the sentences of group (A) with those of group (B) will reveal the fact that in the first and second sentences there is a correlation of the forms of the Class 1 and Class 2 words. In group (A) the Class 1 word *leader*, without an "s" ending, is used with the Class 2 word

---

[3] End punctuation is omitted here in the hope that the omission of these graphic signs will help stress the fact that all examples are to be grasped orally. We are concerned only with speech signals, not with written signs. For each of these sentences, also, we assume the same 2–4 intonation contour at the end. This intonation pattern is very common even in questions of the "yes" and "no" variety. It is the usual falling contour that occurs at the end of most of our expressions:

     The door is │o│ pen   Is the door │o│ pen

is. In group (B) the Class 1 word *leaders*, with an "s" ending, is used with the Class 2 word *are*. In other words, in these two sentences the Class 1 words are "tied" to the Class 2 words by a certain concordance of forms: "The leader *is* here" as compared with "The leaders *are* here," and "*Is* the leader here" as compared with "*Are* the leaders here."

The following additional sentences, to which we respond as requests, must now be added to the two groups for comparison.

(*A*)	(*B*)
3. Be the leader here	3. Be the leaders here

These sentences differ significantly from those compared above in the fact that the same form of the Class 2 word, *be*, is used whether the following Class 1 word has an "s" ending or not.

In other words the basic contrastive patterns for these three kinds of sentences in Modern English can be expressed by the following formulas:

1. Class 1 $\longleftrightarrow$ Class 2 ("tied" by a certain correspondence or concordance of forms) signals a *statement*.

2. Class 2 $\longleftrightarrow$ Class 1 ("tied") signals a *question*.

3. Class 2 (in the simple unchanging form of this part of speech; alone, or followed by a Class 1 word *not* "tied" by a correspondence or correlation of forms) signals a *request*.

That these patterns of form and arrangement do constitute in Modern English the signals of the kind of utterance is supported also by the fact that ambiguity with respect to the kind of utterance results in those infrequent situations (of minimum utterances) in which the details of both form and order happen to be the same for two different kinds of utterance.

The special contrast in the selection of parts of speech between a sentence signalling a statement and one signalling a request appears especially clear in the ambiguous examples used above in Chapter IV. As they stand, the words *ship sails today* could be either a statement or a request, because no markers are present in this utterance by which to determine the part of speech, the functioning class, to which the words *ship* and *sails* are to be assigned. The formal arrangement, as it stands, fits both that of statement and that of request. These words *ship sails* could be Class 1 ⟷ Class 2 "tied" by the concordance of no "s" on a singular Class 1 word *ship* with an "s" on a following Class 2 word *sails*—the pattern of a statement. The word *ship* could also be of Class 2 in the simple unchanging form of that part of speech, followed by a Class 1 word, *sails*, in the plural—the pattern of a request. The marker *the* with the word *ship*, as in *the ship sails today*, would make the arrangement unambiguously a statement. The same marker *the* with the word *sails* would make the arrangement unambiguously a request. The signalling of the kind of sentence in each case is a matter not of the meanings of the words, nor of a vague "context," but solely of the contrastive patterns of the arrangement of the Class 1 and Class 2 words.

In the following sentences the signals are clear.

1. The *man has* paid
2. *Has* the *man* paid
3. *Have* the *man* paid

The first is Class 1 ⟷ Class 2 (tied), signalling a statement.
The second is Class 2 ⟷ Class 1 (tied), signalling a question.
The third is Class 2 (*not* tied to the Class 1 word following), signalling a request.

With the plural *men*, however, the situation is different.

The men have paid

Have the men⌐paid

The men have paid is clearly a statement with Class 1 ⟷ Class 2 (tied). But the form *have* is both the corresponding form for a plural Class 1 word (*men* in contrast with *man*) and also the simple unchanging form. As a result, the utterance *have the men paid* is ambiguous.[4] As it stands (with the common 2–4 intonation curve) it can be either a question or a request. Ambiguity concerning the kind of utterance will necessarily arise wherever the details of both form and order happen to be the same for two different kinds of utterance.

Other examples of similar ambiguity are the following:

Have the boys come
Have the boys run a race

Usually, however, formal differences prevent such ambiguities.

Have they paid
Have them paid

Have they come
Have them come

Have they run a race
Have them run a race

Have the men done the work
Have the men do the work

Have the boys walked
Have the boys walk

---

[4] Of course it is entirely possible to make the sentence *Have the men paid* an unmistakable question by the intonation pattern of a rising contour. But a falling 2–4 contour does not furnish an unmistakable sign of a request, for many clear questions of this kind (made clear by the other formal arrangements) occur with falling 2–4 intonation.

> Have the workers been prompt
> Have the workers be prompt

Basic formulas for the sentence patterns of present-day English can then be set up as the following:

> Class 1 ⟷ Class 2 = statement
> Class 2 ⟷ Class 1 = question
> Class 2 (Class 1) = request

II

Although the basic structural arrangements to signal these particular kinds of sentences—questions, requests, and statements —are these simple formulas, there are in present-day English some complications to be described and some special situations to be listed to make the analysis here complete enough to be fully useful.

(a) Sentences in which the arrangement Class 2 ⟷ Class 1 signalling a question is attained by means other than a simple "reversal"

1. In present-day English, the special Class 2 word be *in its various forms* am, is, are, was, were *is the only word of this part of speech that always operates in a simple contrast or reversal* [5] *to signal a question.*

"*Were* the *teachers* there" with the usual 2–4 intonation signals a question in contrast with "The *teachers were* there" with the same intonation. For all other Class 2 words the function word *do* is employed to obtain the reversal that signals a question. For example "*Does he* go to the school here" (217) signals a question in contrast with "*He goes* to the school here." [6] The word *does* is

---

[5] It is of course arbitrary to assume that the order of the statement is basic and that of the question a "reversal." The order of the question might just as well have been taken as basic and then the order of the statement called a "reversal."

[6] The contrast is not with *He* does go *to the school here* which is used only in statements of contradiction (explicit or implicit).

the bearer of the formal concordance characteristics of the Class 2 word as contrasted with a "*Do* they go to school here." In such a sentence as "*Did* she meet him overseas" (217) the word *did* carries the tense form of the Class 2 word as contrasted with "She *met* him overseas." This word *do* with its various forms *does, did* in this use has no meaning apart from the fact that it fills the position of the Class 2 word in this contrastive pattern of the question sentence. This *does* has no lexical meaning whatever, nor does it convey any special "attitude" toward the action represented by the word *go*, as would such words as *can, must, might*, or *should*. This particular use of *do* as a function word to fill the contrastive pattern of question sentences began in Early Modern English (fifteenth-century) and only gradually displaced the simple reversal formerly used with other verbs than *be*, as in the following examples:

> *Comes he* with good report (Shakspere)
> *Had they* no money (Digby Plays)
> *Desire ye* ought else (Coventry Mysteries)
> *See ye* not where she stands in her doors (*Gammer Gurton's Needle*)
> *Came Christe* to make the worlde moare blynde (Tyndale)

In present-day English one Class 2 word other than *be*, the word *have* (in its various forms), still appears in simple reversal, but in much restricted use.

The arrangement "*Have* you this particular style in stock" appears as well as the more frequent "*Do* you have this particular style in stock." The preterit form *had* appears even less frequently in simple reversal than the present form *have*. Such expressions as the following from the sixteenth century are not likely to occur in present-day English.

> *Had* ever *man* such a frende (*Ralph Roister Doister*)
> *Had you* no need of food

The following are the usual forms of present-day English:

> Did man ever have such a friend
> Didn't you have any need of food

2. *Although the reversal of the relative significant positions of the Class 1 and Class 2 words to signal questions is accomplished very frequently by the use of the function word* do *to fill the pattern, this* do *is not usually used when such "attitude" signalling words as* may, can, must, might, could, would, should *appear with the Class 2 word.*

Nor is *do* used when *will, shall,* as expressions of future, and *have* as an expression of completed action, are added to the Class 2 word. In all these instances these words themselves are used to accomplish the reversal, as in the following:

> *Would Tuesday* be possible (225)
> *Can you* come over soon (526)
> *Should we* organize another section (430)
> *Could we* call you tonight (66)
> *Shall I* introduce him or will he be introduced by somebody else (270)
> *Will you* talk to Miss M—— about it and let me know (273)
> *May I* speak with —— please (274)
> *Must I* always do what B—— wants

This use of the function words with Class 2 words to make the contrastive arrangement to signal questions is limited, except for the forms of the word *be*, to those of the particular list given above —that is, to those of subgroups (a) and (b) in the function words of Group B.[7]

[7] See Chapter VI, Group B.

GROUP **A**	CLASS **1**	GROUP **B**				CLASS **2**
		(a)	*(b)*	*(c)*	*(d)*	
The	students	*may*	*have*	*had to*	*get*	moving
		might			*keep*	
		would				
		must				
		should, etc.			*get*	moved

The function words in subgroups (c) and (d) use the regular question arrangement making function word *do*.

> *Does* he *have* to go tonight (451)
> *Does* she usually *have* her brother figure out her income tax (342)
> *Did* they *get* married in Canada (426)
> *Didn't* they *get* going before eight (271)

(b) Sentences with the basic contrastive Class 1 ⟷ Class 2 arrangement which are not statements

1. Sometimes one of a small group of function words (those of Group I, Chapter VI) provides the distinctive signal of a question.

In the following examples the arrangement of the Class 1 and Class 2 words is clearly that of a statement.

CLASS **1**	CLASS **2**
The man	came
He	came
The others	came
Another	came
These books	came

In the sentence, "*Who* came," the arrangement of the form-classes is exactly the same as that of the five examples above, but the structural meaning is different. *Who came*, in spite of the arrangement which usually signals a statement, is a question—the kind of utterance that regularly elicits a particular kind of oral response. The arrangement signal is superceded by the function-word signal, *who*. Examples of the special function words that thus signal questions are the following:

> *Who* will be responsible for sending out the notices (199)
> *Which* of these came with your subscription (184)
> *Which* will be more convenient (98)
> *What* has to be included in that (94)
> *Whose* car made those tracks (266)
> *What* books are available (186)
> *How many* services were advertised (198)
> The number over there is *what* (93)

In each of these sentences it is not the order and form of the Class 1 and Class 2 words that signal the fact that the utterances are questions, but solely the particular words *who, which, what, how many*—words which are interrogative function words. It should be noted here, however, that these words operate as interrogative function words only in structures that are free utterances; that is, those that have one of the intonation curves that contrast with the 3–2–3 pattern that signals a continuation.

(Question)   Which will be more con│ven│ient

(Statement)   Which will be more con│ven│ient remains
            to be seen

The following pairs of sentences will illustrate this contrast in structural meaning.

(Question)   Who will be responsible for send-
                ing out the ⌐no⌐tices

(Statement)   Who will be responsible for send-
                ing out the ⌐no⌐tices we don't know

(Question)   What has to be in⌐clu⌐ded in that

(Statement)   What has to be in⌐clu⌐ded in that is not
                specified

(Question)   How many services were ⌐ad⌐vertised

(Statement)   How many services were ⌐ad⌐vertised is now
                a matter of dispute

These words *who, which, what, how many,* together with the words *when, where, why,* also appear before the arrangements of Class 1 and Class 2 words, that are in themselves questions:

	CLASS 2	CLASS 1	
Who	are	they	leaving it for (280)
Which	will	they	be likely to take (281)
What	did	you	do the night before (275)
How	will	they	go (276)
When	will	he	return (101)
Where	does	he	come from (102)
Why	are	they	reducing the price now (260)

Here these words *who, which, what, how, when, where, why* are not the sole signal of the question utterance; the order of the rest of the sentence to which they are attached provides the question signal. This conclusion seems to be supported by the fact that in all the instances of this sort in which these words introduce similar expressions that are not questions the order arrangement is that of statement rather than that which is basic for questions. The intonation difference is the same as that described above.

Compare for example the pairs of sentences following.

Question			Statement		
CLASS	CLASS		CLASS	CLASS	
2	**1**		**1**	**2**	
Who	*are*	*they* leaving it for	Who	*they are*	leaving it for we don't know
Which	*will they*	be likely to do	Which	*they will*	be likely to do is anyone's guess
What	*did you*	do the night before	What	*you did*	the night before caused the trouble
How	*will they*	go	How	*they will*	go they didn't say
When	*will he*	return	When	*he will*	return is the important question
Where	*does he*	come from	Where	*he comes*	from no one knows
Why	*are they*	reducing the price	Why	*they are*	reducing the price does not matter

Each of these words, however, *who, which, what, how, when, where, why*, often constitutes the whole of a response utterance, and then the single word signals a question. In these instances, it is the function word itself that gives the signal of the question, not the intonation pattern. Both rising and falling pitch sequences occur with these single words; both are questions. The situations, however, in which the rising intonation occurs differ clearly from those in which the falling intonation occurs. The rising pitch sequence occurs in those situations in which the question seeks *a repetition of a portion of the utterance* immediately preceding. The falling pitch sequence occurs in those situations in which the question seeks *additional information.* Compare, for example, in some detail, the following pairs of quotations that contain the same function words.

Mr. B—— thinks we ought to get the money in hand first and then go after —— —— —— ——

Who

Mr. B—— (262)

We'd like to have someone to say a word at the beginning to welcome the group

Who

We thought you or Dr. —— might do it (270)

We thought the house over on Miller the best we have looked at so far

Which

The one over on Miller Road (263)

We went out this morning and looked at that housing project

Which

The one over near the high-school athletic field (255)

Do they have a car

What

I said do they have a car (256)

There may be arrangements just a little outside of the city that are possible

What

Oh, a lake cottage that could be insulated (268)

They will send her the tickets and instructions through
  the Express Company

How

Through the American Express office in Detroit (119)

She is to leave there on June eighth

How

By bus (119)

I'll do my best to contact you tomorrow before we leave
  for the lake again

When

Tomorrow before we leave (256)

And the Institute of International Education is sending the
  tickets for him

When

On Monday (119)

There's a little house out in Dexter that is available

Where

Out in Dexter about eight miles west (256)

We're sending that to her in a letter

Where

Why we thought she was still in ⸺ (119)

We thought that house was completely out of the picture
  because of the condition

Why⌐

Because it needs so many alterations before they can move
  in (262)

No that can't be right

Why‿

Well the dates don't agree (97)

2. In some situations, very few in the materials examined here, a repetition of a whole or a part of a statement sentence is uttered by another speaker, usually immediately after the statement has been made.

This repetition contains the same word-order pattern as the statement of which it is a partial echo, but, by means of a contrast of the intonation or pitch sequence at the end, it becomes a question.

R—— usually wrote his│own│ speeches

He wrote his│own speeches (630)

He had difficulty with R—— and published it him│self

He published it him│ self (436)

F—— has lost interest for the work is too│hard│ for him

The work is too│hard for him (478)

Not all rising intonations signal questions and not all questions have rising intonation; but an echo of a statement utterance, an echo which has a rising sentence ending curve, becomes a question by the special intonation contrast thus set up.[8]

Sometimes there is no utterance of which the sentence with a rising intonation is an echo. The following example, with the words *you* and *want*, represents the common form of this type of question.

> You want to go to the movies (728)
> I can't tonight

(c) Sentences with the basic contrastive Class 2 ⟷ Class 1 arrangement which are not questions

There are some special situations in which utterances with the word-order arrangement which usually signals a question, Class 2 ⟷ Class 1, are not questions, but statements. These sentences, however, have special features that mark them and set them apart from those in which the word-order arrangement regularly signals a question. There are five kinds.

1. One type of sentence in which the "reversal" of the Class 1 and Class 2 words does not signal a question is that in which one of a very few Class 4 words appears initially.[9]

---

[8] This type of intonation contrast also occurs when the echo utterance ends in a question function word.

> It's a question of his paying the last part of his bill
> It's a question of what (98)

[9] Such sentences as *Away ran John with all his might* and *Up jumped the angry senator and* . . . may be possible, but they do not occur in any materials I have collected. I have seen them written in stories, especially in stories written for children, but I have never heard them in practical conversations. Like the others discussed here they all have a Class 4 word before the Class 2 ⟷ Class 1 arrangement, and they fit an older pattern of English of which the live remnants are indicated in this discussion.

CLASS	CLASS	CLASS	
4	**2**	**1**	
Seldom	is	she	ready on time (851)
Rarely	do	we	eat before seven (1146)
Here	are	the typewriters	now (230)
Not once	did	we	find the papers disturbed (691)
Not often	does	he	come home before six (732)
Never	have	we	had any reason to question her honesty (288)
Not always	have	they	been so inarticulate (941)

Most of the instances that occur with this type of "reversal" have Class 4 words with negatives. Without the negatives the Class 4 words are followed by the usual arrangement of Class 1 and Class 2 words.

> *Once*   we found the papers disturbed
> *Often*   he comes home before six

The Class 4 words given in the quotations above are not always followed by the "reversal" shown there. Examples are the following:

> *Here*   he   comes   now (470)
> *Here*   he   is   just coming in (170)
> *Rarely* we   leave   before Thursday (1031)

The second member of a sentence consisting of two statements in the negative sometimes has the same kind of "reversal."

> That letter does not show his attitude as clearly *as do the words* he used in the meeting (85)
> The motion was not clear to start with *nor did the amendments* make it any more understandable (735)

2. The most frequent type of sentence in which the "reversal" of the Class 1 and Class 2 words does not signal a question is that in which the function word there *occurs initially.*

This word *there* is not the Class 4 word with a "place" meaning, for the two words pattern very differently in English structures and can both be used in the same minimum sentence.

	CLASS 2	⟷	CLASS 1	
There	is	a	guard	there
There	are		guards	there

The two words can even appear side by side at the opening of a sentence. The first *there* is always the Class 4 word, and many other Class 4 words can occur in this position.

CLASS 4	FUNCTION WORD	CLASS 2		CLASS 1
There	*there*	are	few	children of your boy's age (439)
There	*there*	is	no city	sewer (441)
Here	*there*	is		one (441)
Upstairs	*there*	are	two	baths (520)

In such sentences as these the first *there*, the Class 4 word, receives a marked stress; the function word *there* is never a stressed word in the sentence.

There, the function word, has a very limited range of use. It occurs primarily with the forms of *be*, very seldom with any other Class 2 words. Practically the only other Class 2 word [10] used with

---

[10] This was the only word that appeared in the sentences that start conversations. In "sequence utterances" with sequence phrases at the beginning there occurred such words as the following—but examples were extremely scarce.

> In addition *there remain* all the problems of housing and meals (834)
> As a result *there existed* much feeling between them (315)
> In the end *there were created* two other similar committees (430)

this function word *there* is the word *come* in the expression *there comes a time*.

> *There comes a time* when it is useless to struggle (1062)
> *There comes a time* when patience ceases to be a virtue (840)

There, function word, with such a Class 2 word as *breathe*, as in the line "*Breathes there* a man with soul so dead," does not occur in any records I have of present-day conversations. With *there*, function word, the Class 1 word following the *is, are, was, were* practically always has a determiner such as *a, no, two, every, some, few, many*, but very seldom one such as the following: *the, this, that, my*. Compare the following pairs of examples: [11]

(Function word)	*There* is a man that often goes through our back lot (1138)
(Class 4)	*There* is the man that often goes through our back lot
(Function word)	*There* is a can that I've looked for many times (1202)
(Class 4)	*There* is the can that I've looked for many times

That this *there*, function word, is only a structure filling word, patterning quite differently from the Class 4 words that appear with the Class 2 ⟷ Class 1 arrangements seems to be supported by the fact that it becomes the unit "reversed" when questions are formed of these expressions.

[11] Of course *there*, function word, might occur in a sentence with a Class 1 word having one of these determiners if the situation is the special one in which an enumeration is going forward, or a listing of items, e.g., *then there is the boy who delivers the groceries and there is the postman and the paper boy.*

There is much more chance over there
Is there much more chance over there (256)

There are two nursery schools here
Are there two nursery schools here (256)

On the other hand the *there* (Class 4) in questions never appears in this position:

(Class 4)   *There* are the books that I want
Are the books *there* that I want (208)

The "reversal" Class 2 $\longleftrightarrow$ Class 1 which does not signal a question occurred many times in the conversations recorded for this study.

3. Another type of sentence in which the Class 2 $\longleftrightarrow$ Class 1 arrangement does not signal a question occurs less frequently,[12] but here again there are formal features to distinguish this arrangement from that of questions.

The following are examples:

Should they come tomorrow it would be difficult to find them
room (709)
Were they all here we should have a quorum

In these, the intonation curve at the end of the particular structural unit in which the "reversal" occurs marks the nonquestion. The nonquestion ends with a 3–2–3 nonfinal intonation; the question, with either the common 3–2–4 pitch sequence or a rising 3–2 sequence.

[12] More examples of this kind of structure occurred in the letters examined for the *American English Grammar* than in the conversations studied here.

We have asked her to call at our office but she has not yet done so (8144)
Should she do so we shall inquire concerning her son's support

(Nonquestion)   Should they come to mo rrow it would

. . .

(Question)   Should they come to mo rrow

(Question)   Should they come to morrow

(Nonquestion)   Were they all here we should have a
quorum

(Question)   Were they all here

(Question)   Were they all here

In the instances above, the intonation curve provides the only formal clue to distinguish a nonquestion from a question. With sentences in which the singular form of the Class 1 word appears, however, another formal feature distinguishes the nonquestion from the question.

(Nonquestion)   *Were he* here we could proceed
(Question)   *Was he* here

4. *Intonation alone marks another type of Class 2 ⟷ Class 1 arrangement as a nonquestion.*

In these, the contrastive high pitch extends over several syllables before the final drop and the vowels are often considerably lengthened.

Nonquestion

Was he mad

Was he mad

Question

Was he mad

Was he mad

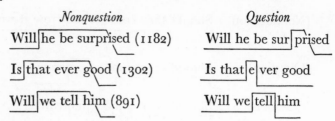

Nonquestion	*Question*
Will he be surprised (1182)	Will he be sur prised
Is that ever good (1302)	Is that e ver good
Will we tell him (891)	Will we tell him

5. Polite formulas that precede request sentences often have the Class 2 ⟷ Class 1 arrangement that usually signals a question.

These polite formulas with the form of questions are sometimes mistaken and responded to as questions, with oral responses rather than with actions, and then the request is repeated or the distinguishing word *please* is used. Sometimes the uncertainty concerning the nature of the utterance shows itself in such a question as "Are you asking me or telling me?" The word *please* provides a clear mark of the request.

Polite formula		*Request*
CLASS	CLASS	
2	**1**	
Will	*you* (please)	take down this message for him (567)
Would	*you* (please)	read and grade as many of the bluebooks as you can before Monday noon (498)

III

The sentence patterns thus far discussed here are primarily those that can occur in the utterances that start conversations, in "situation utterance units." Some of the examples have come from the "sequence utterances," but these have, with few exceptions, been sentence patterns like those that appeared at the start of conversations. They did contain certain sequence signals which have been ignored in these discussions but will be dealt with later in Chapter XI. The few exceptions have been the echoes and the single-word questions noted in the section immediately preceding. In addition, there remain the "response utterance units" that differed completely from any sentence patterns found among the "situation utterance units"—from those sentences found at the beginnings of conversations. Among these, the oral responses elicited by questions—the "answers" to questions—constitute almost the whole of the material.

Answers to questions may consist of practically any linguistic form of the language. These answers constitute "complete" utterance units in that they stand alone. They are marked off by a change of speaker. Although they are independent in the sense that they are not included in a larger structure by means of any grammatical device, their own structural arrangements have significance with reference to the questions that elicited them. In other words, the question itself is part of the frame in which the answer as an utterance operates.

In attempting to classify "situation utterance units" above we grouped them in accord with the responses they elicited regularly. Here we can classify the answers to questions in accord with certain features of the questions to which they are responses.

(a) **For all questions in which the signal of the question is the "reversal" of the basic Class 1 and Class 2 words, the answer usually contains the forms *yes* or *no*.**

A few alternative but equivalent forms occur, like *certainly, probably, decidedly, absolutely, surely;* or *certainly not, decidedly not, absolutely not, surely not.* The *yes* or *no* may be supplemented by one of these alternative forms or by such a word as *indeed.* Most frequently the supplementary material consists of a short statement utterance using substitute forms, as *yes it is, no it isn't, yes I certainly*

166 THE STRUCTURE OF ENGLISH

will, no he mustn't. Answers of this kind occur with all "reversal" questions, no matter how the "reversal" is accomplished, whether by simple "reversal" as in the case of questions with *be* forms, or by *do,* or by such function words as *can, must, should, have,* etc. Such answers are not used, however, with questions which employ the function words of Group I: *who, which, what, whose, how, when, where, why.* Examples of the answers that are elicited by "reversal" questions are the following:

ANSWER	QUESTION THAT ELICITED THE ANSWER
No he's not right now	*Is Mr. L—— there* (244)
No nothing at all	*Is* there *anything* very important coming up Monday (225)
Yes but not completely	*Did I* report back to you the other day (240)
Yes I hope so	*Do you* think you could make it next summer (238)
O.K. I'll do that	*Will you* write him about that too (234)
Certainly not	*Would that* make any difference to you (250)
Probably	*Do you* think we could make the change (825)
Oh no	*Is it* catching (88)
Yes right away	*Could you* bring it over tonight (804)
Yes it is they're closed	*Is it* too late now (83)
No not tonight	*Will you* have any time tonight (82)

In questions of this sort a negative function word does not make a negative situation. The negative appears in those situations in which an affirmative seems to be expected. The question *don't you like to dance* assumes an affirmative situation, in contrast with the question without the negative, *do you like to dance*, which is entirely without commitment concerning any expected situation. In present-day English the form of these questions whether with a negative function word or not, makes no difference in the answer. Answers to all of these questions address themselves to the fact, not to the negative or non-negative form of the question.

ANSWER	QUESTION THAT ELICITED THE ANSWER
Yes it was	*Wasn't* your *price* eight hundred and fifty (79)
Yes for a little while	*Didn't it* work at all (82)
No where	*Didn't I* tell you where (88)
Certainly	*Can't we* get them excused a bit early (87)
No I'm afraid not	*Won't it* be possible to change (89)
Well I can	*Wouldn't you* like to come alone (90)
Maybe	*Couldn't we* do it tomorrow (90)
Yes but he wants help	*Doesn't he* know where to take it (249)
No not yet	*Don't you* think we had better call Dr. H—— (623)

(b) For questions with the function words *who, which, what, whose, how, where, when, why*, the answers may consist of practically any linguistic form of the single form-class fitting the particular type of question.

1. For questions that use the function words who, whose, which, what (*except* what, *or more rarely* which, *with* do *as a Class 2 word*) *the answers usually contain a Class 1 word alone or a Class 1 word with* be, *or* do, *or with any of the functon words in* (a), (b), *or* (c) *of Group B.*

ANSWER	QUESTION THAT ELICITED THE ANSWER
Nothing at all	*What* is there for him for the rest of the year (226)
Those unsightly wires	*What* annoys you so much back there (243)
Dr. H—— and his wife	*Who* are you expecting (808)
My husband and B——	*Who* did you say just came in (824)
The same one we had before	*Which* room did they give us (674)
Oh a much better one	*What'*ll we get in exchange (526)
The one for Miss L——	*What* service is that (86)
B—— did	*Who* took those last sets of books to the post office (249)
Ours I think	*Whose* is the little table in the storeroom on the second floor (630)

2. For questions with what *(or more rarely* which) *with* do *as the Class 2 word the answers frequently consist of any other Class 2 word (other than* be) *alone or with following "objects" or "modifiers."*

ANSWER	QUESTION THAT ELICITED THE ANSWER
Oh just sitting here drinking coffee and talking about their childhood days	*What* have A—— and R—— been *doing* all evening (86)
Throw them out	*What* shall we *do* with the stuff in the old files (469)
Try to get leave for a year	*Which* did he finally decide to *do* (481)

| Get in touch with Dr. H—— | *What* do you think we ought to *do* now (630) |
| Come alone | *What*'ll I *do* if they can't arrange it (645) |

The answers to questions of this kind furnish perhaps the clearest demonstration of the need for considering the structure of the answer in connection with that of the question that elicited it. Taken alone the answer in (481) above, *try to get leave for a year*, has the structural arrangement of a request. It is only when one views the question itself as an essential part of the frame in which the answer as an utterance operates that he has sufficient material to respond accurately to the structural signal. Answers to questions of this kind are clearly separable from request forms whenever the question contains signals of a past time. They overlap with request signals and are ambiguous whenever the question contains signals of a future time, as in (645). One who overhears only one end of a telephone conversation will frequently be misled by responding to the structural signals of answers alone without knowing the questions to which they are responses, and, more important still, without knowing whether the utterance is preceded by a question and is thus a "response utterance."

3. For questions with how *and* what *in a limited type of arrangements such as the following the answers may be any Class 3 word, alone or with the expansions possible with that form-class.*

CLASS 1

How does (did)	——	look (appear, feel, smell, taste, sound)
How was	——	
How did	——	turn out
What is (was)	——	like

ANSWER	QUESTION THAT ELICITED THE ANSWER
Very nice really	*How* is *it* out there (634)
Oh fair	*How* are *you* (235)
Simply wonderful	*What* was the *weather like* in P—— R—— (811)
Pretty good	*How* does it *look* after all that work (870)
Excellent it was one of the best we've had	*How* did the *banquet turn out* (617)

4. For questions using how *with* many, much, far, long, *etc., the answers may be simply single words of number, amount, measure, etc., or these words with possible expansions.*

ANSWER	QUESTION THAT ELICITED THE ANSWER
About a hundred and eighty	*How many* were there this time (617)
Frankly very little	*How much* interest is there in it (727)
Ninety-five cents each	*How much* will they charge (520)
About two miles	*How far* is it from the campus (238)
Just fifteen feet	*How long* a boat is it (685)

5. For questions with the function words when, where, *and* how (manner), *the answers may consist solely of a Class 4 word of the same subgroup, or of word-groups with the function words of Group F or Group J.*

ANSWER	QUESTION THAT ELICITED THE ANSWER
Tomorrow	*When* do they have to have the reservations at the office (88)
Right now	*When* could you see me (630)
Thursday afternoon	*When* is the service (86)
Oh quite late	*When* did he get home (380)
After he has his dinner	*When* would be the best time to call him (847)
Home	*Where* is your brief case now (382)
Down to State Street	*Where* did you take him (85)
At ——— North Ingalls	*Where* are you now (228)

6. *For questions with the function words* why *and* how (*means*) *the answers usually consist not of single words but of word-groups with the function words of Group F or Group J.*

ANSWER	QUESTION THAT ELICITED THE ANSWER
Mostly because the salary really isn't very good	*Why* did he decide against the ——— offer (247)
Because we're awfully short of help right now	*Why* can't we do both sets together (249)
Because of the talk he's working on for tonight	*Why* didn't he come in today (660)
Because of a change in his schedule	*Why* did he drop out (462)
Only by quitting everything else	*How* can you get them out in time (431)
By bus	*How* do they expect them to go (233)

Unlike the questions signalled by a "reversal," in which a negative function word signals an expected affirmative situation, a negative in questions with these function words *who, which, what, whose, how, when, where, why* produces a negative situation as it does in statements. The answers to these questions, therefore, do not, in their form, disregard the negative in the questions.

As one attempts to survey and describe the structural patterns of English sentences he cannot escape the necessity of separating sharply the utterances that are used to stimulate various types of responses from those utterances that are themselves the oral responses regularly elicited by certain structural arrangements. The structural meanings in answers to questions cannot be grasped from the formal arrangements in the answer utterances alone. The question itself, the preceding utterance that elicits the answer response, is an essential part of the linguistic frame through which the answer response signals its structural meanings. For one who is listening in on a conversation it is necessary to hear the question itself if he is to understand the structural meanings in the answer response.

For the other free utterance units in English, sentences other than answers to questions, the structural signals are in the formal arrangements of the functioning units within the sentence itself. For these, the signals of the kind of sentence are, basically, contrasting arrangements of Class 1 and Class 2 words. Intonation contrasts are a part of these signals, but they do not often furnish the sole distinguishing feature of the kind of sentence. Certain function words, however, do play an important part in signalling the kind of utterances we call questions.

IX. Structural Meanings: "Subjects" and "Objects"

For all those who have studied "grammar" in the schools the terms *subject* and *object* are very familiar. The conventional "analysis" of a sentence usually began with pointing out the word or words that functioned as "subject," and many of the sentences analyzed contained various types of "objects." Ability to find the "subject" constituted the first step in knowing grammar. But the textbooks of English grammar have been extremely vague in their statements of just what kind of a functioning unit the "subject" is, and also of the criteria for determining which of several substantives in a sentence is the "subject." The following familiar definition appears in most of the textbooks.

> The subject of a sentence is that word or group of words of which something is said or asserted.[1]

No difficulty arises in applying this definition to such sentences as the following:

> The wind blew violently
> All the young children shouted and ran away

[1] Most of the definitions quoted here are taken from Frank X. Braun, *English Grammar for Language Students* (Ann Arbor, 1947), a very convenient compendium of the conventional statements.

With sentences like these, our students can at once point to the words *wind* and *children* as representing those things "about which something is said or asserted." They remain unconvinced, however, that the sentence *the man gave the boy the money* does *not* "say something" about *the boy* and *the money*, as well as about *the man*. And certainly with such a sentence as *what killed the cat* many of us would consider it very arbitrary to insist that *cat* is *not* "the word of which something is said or asserted." This common definition of "subject" does not seem to furnish the criteria, certainly not all the criteria, which are used in determining the "subject" of a sentence.

The situation becomes worse rather than better when one brings to bear upon the problem the definitions usually offered for the various types of "objects." For the "indirect object," the conventional definition is usually, "The person or thing indirectly affected by the action of the verb," and for the "direct object," "The person or thing directly affected by the action of the verb." [2] Following these definitions, directions are given on "How to find the direct object and the indirect object." [3]

Ex.: "His father gave the beggar a dime." . . .

1. To find the *subject*, ask: Who gave?—his father.
2. To find the *direct object*, ask: His father gave what?—a dime.
3. To find the *indirect object*, ask: His father gave to whom?—to the beggar.

If, however, the sentence of the example appeared in a different form, but representing the same situation, the suggested procedure would certainly not produce the desired results: *the beggar was given a dime by his father*. In this sentence, although *father* still repre-

[2] Braun, *op. cit.*, pp. 7, 9.   [3] *Ibid.*, p. 21.

sents the one who "gave," it is certainly not the "subject," and, although *beggar* still answers correctly the question "His father gave to whom?" it is not the "indirect object," but the "subject."

In the matter of "subjects" and "objects," just as in the attempts to define the "sentence" and the "parts of speech," the conventional grammar has approached the problem by seeking criteria of meaning content rather than of form. It is the usual process of starting with the total meaning of an utterance and then assigning technical names—"subject," "direct object," "indirect object"— to portions of that meaning. In contrast with that approach we have tried here first to find formal characteristics by which to identify each functioning unit and structure, and then have raised the question as to just what meanings these formally identified structures signal. In this chapter we are specifically concerned with the various structures in which Class 1 words are functioning units and with the precise meanings which these structures convey.

I. "SUBJECT"

First of all, it is necessary to insist that such terms as "subject," "indirect object," "direct object" have no relation to the actual facts of a situation in the real world. As grammatical terms they are simply names for particular formal structures within an utterance. Let us assume, for example, a situation in which are involved a man, a boy, some money, an act of giving, the man the giver, the boy the receiver, the time of the transaction yesterday. With a real situation composed of these factors and a statement to be made containing them all, it is impossible to predict which elements would be grasped in the linguistic expression as "subject" or "indirect object" or "direct object." Any one of the units *man, boy, money, give, yesterday* could appear in the linguistic structure as "subject."

The *man* gave the boy the money yesterday

The *boy* was given the money by the man yesterday

The *money* was given the boy by the man yesterday

The *giving* of the money to the boy by the man occurred
yesterday

Yesterday was the time of the giving of the money to the
boy by the man

"Subject" then is a formal linguistic structural matter; it is a particular construction for a Class 1 word; it is not a matter of the meaning of the word with reference to a real situation. It is true that the structural meaning of many "subjects" is "performer," but the meaning of performer is signalled by many other devices, and there are many "subjects" which have other meanings than that of performer. In the preceding chapter we have insisted that the kind of sentence, whether question, or request, or statement, is signalled by special contrastive patterns in the arrangement of Class 1 and Class 2 words. The basic contrastive pattern of a question, for example, consists of Class 2 ⟷ Class 1 "tied" by a certain correspondence or concordance of form; and of a statement, Class 1 ⟷ Class 2 "tied." The "subject" of a sentence, then, is simply the Class 1 word (or words) that is tied with a Class 2 word to form the basic pattern of the sentence. "Subject" is the technical name for the Class 1 word that is thus structurally bound with a Class 2 word. Only Class 1 words bound with Class 2 words in such a structure are "subjects."

This morning the *workmen were* here before seven

Does the *foreman* of the steel workers expect them to finish
today

In English utterances the Class 1 words that are "subjects,"
that is, the Class 1 words that are thus connected in structure with

a Class 2 word to form the basic construction of the sentence, are identified and distinguished from other Class 1 words which may be in the sentence not only by the concordance of form, when that is present in the Class 2 word, but also by certain other contrasts in the formal arrangements of the Class 1 and Class 2 words. These contrasts not only identify the "subject" but also the other structural relationships into which Class 1 words enter and, therefore, can best be described in detail after these other structures are discussed.

We have insisted above that the actual relation of things in the real situation does not determine the grammatical relations of the words representing these things in an English sentence. The performer of an act in the real situation remains the performer, of course, in the linguistic utterance, but the expression of this meaning of performer may be accomplished by any one of a number of linguistic devices.

> The *men built* that tool house very slowly
> The tool house was *built by the men* very slowly
> *Their building* of the tool house was very slow

It is true that very often the "meaning" of the "subject" of the sentence is "performer," but one cannot approach a sentence assuming that whatever Class 1 word represents the "performer" is for that reason the subject. The meaning of "performer" is expressed by Class 1 words not in the "subject" construction, and "performer" is only one of the various meanings of "subject." "Subjects" represent at least five different meanings:

> The *dean* approved all our recommendations (521) [Subject is performer]
> One *difficulty* is the size of the trees (253) [Subject is that which is identified]

The *abstract* is very bulky (200) [Subject is that which is described]

The *requisition* was sent over a week ago (540) [Subject is that which undergoes the action]

Mr. W—— was given the complete file on —— (552) [Subject is that "to or for" which the action is performed]

Although the "subject" structure may in various sentences carry any one of these five meanings, the formal arrangements of any particular sentence will determine which of these meanings the "subject" signals.

(a) The subject signals "performer" whenever the Class 2 word with which it is bound is not one of a special list,[4] or one of the forms of *be* or *get* as function words with the so-called "past participles."

In these situations the "subject" is "performer" not only in the usual practical meanings of this word but as is usually the case with the "meanings" of linguistic structures it is "performer" in the broadest possible sense. The structural meaning of "performer" in this kind of "subject" includes *everything that is linguistically grasped in the pattern of performer*. The following examples show something of the range of this meaning of "performer."

The *dean approved* all our recommendations (521)

The *car turned* the corner on two wheels (921)

The *chair tipped* over (435)

A beautiful *cloth covers* the table (802)

The *accident occurred* yesterday morning (628)

---

[4] The most frequent recurring Class 2 word of this list (see pp. 135–37) is of course *be* in its various forms. The others are those that are frequently followed by Class 3 words. Sometimes ambiguities arise when a Class 3 word is not present, as in *the dog's nose smells*. A Class 3 or a Class 4 word following the Class 2 *smells* would resolve the ambiguity: *the dog's nose smells bad*, or *the dog's nose smells keenly*.

Easter comes in March this year (428)

All the *children like* swimming and boating (823)

What*'s* that *stuff doing* on the table anyway (1208)

The *material* you sent *won't do* at all (509)

His *toys have* no business on the stairway (441)

Some *bread toasts* better than others (841)

The *sentence reads* very smoothly now (1319)

With that goo the *cream whips* very easily (853)

The *examination takes* a full two hours (646)

(b) The subject signals "that which is identified" whenever the Class 2 word with which it is bound is one of a special narrow (2b) list (the forms of *be* most frequently) and this Class 2 word is followed by a Class 1 word having the same referent as the Class 1 word which is "subject."

Mrs. W—— was P——'s *teacher* for three years (728)

Mrs. B—— seems the head *person* over there now (451)

The best *bargain* is the brick *bungalow* out on —— (246)

My *husband* is the *director* of the —— (120)

The *salary* is three *hundred* a month (88)

The *luncheon* today was a very special *one* (49)

Their *car* was a total *loss* (921)

The only *thing* he had pressing was his last *swim* at the pool (56)

(c) The subject signals "that which is described" whenever the Class 2 word with which it is bound is one of the special (2b) list (the forms of *be* most frequently) and this Class 2 word is followed by a Class 3 word.

The farewell *dinner* will be *huge* this time (68)

My *husband's afraid* he won't get out in time (90)

Those *wires* back there are really *unsightly* (243)

Maybe next *summer* will be *better* (238)

(d) The subject signals either "that which undergoes the action" or "that to or for which the action is performed" whenever the Class 2 word to which the subject is bound is the function word *be* (in its various forms) or *get*, with the so-called past participle.

Lots of tools can *be furnished* him right here (83)

All the *ladies were given* orchids (547)

O——— *was elected* sheriff (582)

The *laundry was taken* off the line just a minute ago (85)

Here again, formal characteristics can distinguish the subject which signals "that which undergoes the action" from that which signals "that to or for which the action is performed." It was pointed out in Chapter VII that all Class 1 words that are not themselves substitutes can be classified in one of three groups on the basis of their substitute forms (see table of correlation forms on pp. 120 and 121).

This grouping of Class 1 words in accord with the particular substitute forms with which they correlate [5] is important for the separation of the subject meaning "that which undergoes the action" from the subject meaning "that to or for which the action is performed." If the Class 1 word which is the subject is of the same substitute group as is the Class 1 word after the Class 2 word, then the subject meaning is ambiguous—it can be either "that which undergoes the action" or "that to or for which the action is performed."

Alice was given John as a partner.

Since both *Alice* and *John* belong to the same *he/she* group of substitutes it is impossible to determine from this sentence alone

---

[5] This grouping of the Class 1 words in accord with these substitute forms constitutes practically all there is of gender in present-day English. Such contrasts as *lion—lioness, actor—actress,* apply to very few words in English.

whether the subject meaning is "*to Alice* was given *John*" or "*Alice* was given *to John*." In sentences in which a Class 1 word which is subject comes from a different substitute group from the Class 1 word following, there is no ambiguity.

The *ladies* were given the *orchids*
   (he/she)   (it)

The *orchids* were given the *ladies*
    (it)   (he/she)

The *family* were (was) given the *money*
   (they-it)   (it)

The *money* was given the *family*
   (it)   (they-it)

The *boy* was given the *dog*
   (he/she)   (he/she-it)

The *dog* was given the *boy*
   (he/she-it)   (he/she)

In contrasts between a Class 1 word of the *he/she* groups and one of the *it* group, the Class 1 word of the *he/she* group is the one with the meaning, "that to or for which the action is performed," and the Class 1 word of the *it* group is the one with the meaning, "that which undergoes the action." In similar contrasts between a Class 1 word of the *he/she-it* or *they-it* group and one of the *it* group it is the Class 1 word of the *he/she-it* or *they-it* group that carries the meaning, "that to or for which the action is performed."

The *dog* was given the *food* [to the dog]

In a contrast between a Class 1 word of the *he/she* group and one of the *he/she-it* group, it is the Class 1 word of the *he/she* group that carries the meaning, "that to or for which the action is performed.'

The boy *was* given the *dog*   [to the boy]

Although it is true that an ambiguity results whenever the Class 1 words in this structure belong to the same substitute group, this ambiguity arises only when both Class 1 words have the same specific type of determiners, as in the examples above. All the Class 1 words there appear with the determiner *the*. If, however, one of the Class 1 words occurs with a specific determiner such as *the* and the other with a general determiner such as *a* there is no ambiguity even if both Class 1 words come from the same substitute group.

The *mother* was given *a son*
(he/she)   (he/she)

A mother was given *the son*
The child was given *a mother*
A child was given *the mother*

In a contrast between a Class 1 word with a specific type of determiner such as *the, this*, etc., and one with a general type of determiner such as *a, two*, etc., it is the Class 1 word with the specific type of determiner that carries the meaning, "that to or for which the action is performed."

These five different meanings for the subject—"performer," "that which is identified," "that which is described," "that which undergoes the action," and "that to or for which the action is performed"—are not just vague matters of the "context," but are definitely signalled by the contrasting selection and arrangement of (1) the Class 2 word with which the subject is bound, of (2) the substitute group to which the Class 1 words belongs, and of (3) the type of determiner with the Class 1 word.

The subject itself is simply that Class 1 word that is bound to a Class 2 word to form the basic arrangement of the sentence, and is identified and distinguished from other Class 1 words not by meaning but by certain contrastive arrangements, which will be outlined after we describe the other structures for Class 1 words.

II. "OBJECT"

One of the earliest structural meanings to which children learning English as their native language respond is the distinguishing between "performer" and "undergoer." By the time stories are read or told to them they have learned to react without the slightest hesitation to the signals that separate "undergoer" from "performer" in such statements as *Jack killed the giant, the kind lady fed the children, the hunters killed the wolf.* Later, in the schools, they learn to give a technical name, "object," to some of the words that represent the "receivers of the action"—as in the sentences above, *the giant, the children, the wolf.* The grammar they study, however, seldom describes the formal contrastive arrangements within the sentence that they have had to learn to respond to in order to grasp this meaning. They are usually taught not only that the technical name "object" has the meaning of "receiver of action" but that whatever has the meaning of "receiver of action" is an "object." The meaning is offered as the means of identifying the word to which the name is to be applied. Such a procedure not only gives us no insight into the mechanisms of the language, it leads to confusion, because we don't actually apply the name "object" to all "receivers of the action" in our utterances. As we have seen above, "that which undergoes the action" is one of the meanings of the "subject" of the sentence. Like the "subject," the "object" is a technical name for a structure in which a Class 1 word enters, and this structure signals a variety of meanings. Some of the diversity of meaning appears in the conventional names, "direct object," "indirect object," "object complement," "adverbial object," and, less frequently, "cognate object."

(a) "Direct object"

"Direct object" is the special term usually applied to the meaning, "that which undergoes the action," but, as with the linguistic use of the word "performer," "undergoer" is used very broadly. The meaning of "undergoes the action" in this kind of object includes *everything that is linguistically grasped in the pattern of "undergoer."* From a practical point of view there may be no actual "receiving" or "undergoing" of any action. The following examples show something of the range of meaning of "undergoer":

The students of the Institute *have* their *meals* in East Quad (401)

The car *turned* the *corner* on two wheels (921)

You'll have to *dig* the *holes* for the posts tonight (87)

Come over and we'll *light* a *fire* in the fireplace (392)

We'd have to *quit everything* else (250)

I only *saw him* from a distance (1095)

You really *swam* a swell *race* [6] in that two hundred (480)

P—— *swam* a good *hundred* this afternoon (467)

B—— *fears* that *examination* most of all (646)

---

[6] The category of "cognate object" in expressions like *run a race* seems to be mostly a lexical distinction not formally different from the other "direct objects."

(b) "Indirect object"

"Indirect object" is the special term usually applied to the meaning, "that to or for which an action is performed." Again this is the broad meaning of a linguistic structure and covers a variety of practical situations. The meaning, however, cannot be the means by which to identify "indirect object," for here too the meaning may be expressed by other means.[7]

I can furnish your *man* all the necessary tools (83)

Will you bring my *husband* the papers as soon as possible (527)

We could serve the *children* their dessert first (533)

I wonder if you would do *me* a favor (535)

She wants to sell *us* their own house (247)

We'd like you to give our *group* about a fifteen-minute talk (104)

Do you think there's any chance of getting this *boy* a job for his board (500)

(c) "Object complement"

"Object complement" is the special term usually applied to the meaning, "that which results from the action upon an undergoer." Here too the meaning cannot be the basis upon which to identify the Class 1 word in this structure. Very few examples occurred in the materials recorded.

[7] To call such expressions as *to the boy* an "indirect object" in the sentence *the man gave the money to the boy*, leads to confusion. The expression *to the boy* does express the same meaning as that of the indirect object, but this meaning is signalled by the function word *to*, not by the formal arrangement which constitutes the structure, "indirect object." The "subject" in the sentence *the boy was given the money* also expresses the same meaning as that of the indirect object, but we rightly call it "subject," not "indirect object."

> We were especially pleased when they appointed K——
> *dean* (44)
> The first time they elected V—— *senator* was . . . (830)
> I then appointed P—— *secretary* pro tem for the committee
> (427)
> It takes eight years to make a man even an *interne* (680)
> It's much easier to make a boy a good *swimmer* than to
> make him a good *competitor* (781)
> We've made the basement room a *study* for me (26)

(d) "Adverbial object"

"Adverbial object" is the special term usually applied to those Class 1 words in the meanings, "time," "place," "manner." Examples with the meaning, "time," were abundant; those with the other meanings, "place" and "manner," occurred very rarely.

> The committee approved the request last *Wednesday* (946)
> The matter will probably come up this *week* (952)
> Vacation begins the *end* of next week (724)
> Easter comes in March this *year* (428)
> Next *year* Christmas comes on Monday (582)
> How are you feeling these *days* (621)
> She worked all those *years* for very little (393)
>
> Will you be able to come this *way* on your way out (387)
> He started that *way* I know (560)
> We just can't continue to work this *way* (585)
> No it can't be done that *way* (628)

Each of these four kinds of "objects"—"direct object," "indirect object," "object complement," and "adverbial object"—has its particular meanings. These meanings, however, are also expressed by other devices in English and, therefore, the meanings cannot be used as the criteria by which to identify the structures to which we give these four names. These structures, like the one called "subject," are all structures of Class 1 words and are identified and distinguished by contrasting formal arrangements.

The so-called "object of a preposition" has none of the meanings of "object" described above.[8] The name "object" applied to the "word used with a preposition" seems to have arisen from the fact that the Class 1 words so used had in most instances the same inflectional endings as the "objects" having the special meanings which have been described.

III. "PREDICATE NOMINATIVE," "APPOSITIVE," "NOUN ADJUNCT"[9]

Other structures into which Class 1 words enter, structures which must be identified and distinguished from "subjects" and "objects," are those that are frequently called "predicate nominative" and "appositive," [10] and others that are here called "noun adjunct." All three of these structures have the meaning of "characteristics of identification." The "predicate nominative" and an "appositive" have the same referents as the Class 1 words to which they are attached; the "noun adjunct" never has the

[8] Those function words (most of which are called prepositions) usually simply make the Class 1 word into one type of "modifier." Modifiers in general will be discussed in Chapter X.

[9] The term "noun adjunct" rarely occurs in the conventional grammars. The words in this structure are most frequently just classed as adjectives. Sometimes grammars do speak of "the adjective use of the noun."

[10] The conventional definitions of "predicate nominative" and "appositive" are of little help even in stating the meanings of these structures, e.g.:

(Predicate nominative) "A noun that completes the predicate and explains the subject."

(Appositive) "A noun that is added to another noun to explain its meaning and denoting the same person, place, or thing."

same referent. An "appositive" and a "noun adjunct" may serve in the meaning of "identification" for a Class 1 word in any structure; the "predicate nominative" serves in the meaning of "identification" only for those Class 1 words used with a narrow list of Class 2 words of which the forms of *be* are the most frequent. "Predicate nominatives" and "noun adjuncts" occurred very frequently in the materials of this study. "Appositives" appeared very seldom.

> The only obstacle is the *attitude* of several of the ——— (468)
> Is Miss H—— the best *candidate* you have (435)
> That kind of a change in plan doesn't seem the right *thing* (89)

> . . . talking about their *childhood* days (86)
> Will you be able to take my *Friday* class (340)
> Then there'll be a *neighborhood* *pot-luck* supper over at the M——'s (126)

> J—— L—— my *assistant* will come for them about ten forty five (728)
> We want you to come for the banquet the farewell *dinner* (642)

All through the discussion of this chapter we have insisted that the terms we have centered attention upon are names for structures that must be identified and distinguished by formal contrasts. As structures, "subject," "direct object," "indirect object," "object complement," "adverbial object," "predicate nominative," "appositive," "noun adjunct," each signal a special meaning, and we have tried to indicate the chief features of each of these meanings and to illustrate them by the examples quoted. In all cases these

same meanings are expressed by other devices; we cannot, therefore, use the meanings as the criteria by which to identify and
distinguish the structures.

Apart from the concordance of form which at times distinctly
identifies a particular Class 1 word as bound to a particular Class 2
word as "subject," the formal contrasts that identify these structures are matters primarily of word-order patterns. The significant
units of these word-order patterns are a Class 2 word and the
Class 1 words whose structural relations are not shown by some
other device. Here I shall try to express these patterns of word
order by formulas and explain the significant contrasts in the
formulas by statements. In the formulas the necessary information
concerning the linguistic forms involved will be given by the
following symbols.

SYMBOL	MEANING OF SYMBOL
2	Any Class 2 word except those of the special list headed by the forms of *be*
2b	Any Class 2 word of the special list headed by the forms of *be*
1	Any Class 1 word except those substitutes compounded with *–self*
1-sf	Any Class 1 word substitute compounded with *–self*
3	Any Class 3 word
4	Any Class 4 word
1ᵃ, 1ᵇ, 1ᶜ . . .	The letter exponents put on each Class 1 word indi-cate whether the "referents" of two Class 1 words are "the same" or "different." Words with the same ex-ponent (1ᵃ, 1ᵃ) have the same "referent"; those for which the "referents" are different have different ex-ponents (1ᵃ, 1ᵇ). The order of the letter exponents has no significance.

1ª, 1ᵇ,   1ᶜ
he he/it it   The words under the number symbol for a Class 1
word indicate the "substitute group" to which it belongs (see Chapter VII, pp. 119–22, and this chapter,
pp. 180–82). Class 1 words for which in the particular
utterance no one of these substitutes is possible are

marked with *th*, as $\frac{1^a}{th}$, to represent such a substitute

1ª
th   as *then, thus, there.*

2=, 2-d, 2-ng   The symbols following the number representing a
Class 2 word indicate the form of that word: **2 =** is
the simple unchanged form (the "infinitive"); **2-d**
is the preterit as well as the so-called past participle;
2-ng is the form ending in *–ing*. Without these added
symbols a **2** represents the "present" form of a Class 2
word.

D, D, D
**   g s**   The symbol **D** represents any "determiner." The distinction between a determiner that is general or of a
class, like *a*, and one that is specific, like *the, this*, is
indicated by **g** or **s** under the **D**.

1, 2, 1, 2
– – + ±   The symbols **–, +, ±** under the figures for Class 1
or Class 2 words represent "number" forms: **–** for
singular, **+** for plural, **±** for a form that could be
either singular or plural.

f, f, f
** E F**   The symbol **f** represents any function word. The capital letter under the **f** indicates the function-word group
(here Group E and Group F) to which this particular
function word belongs (see Chapter VI).

The following ten formulas represent the formal contrasts in
patterns of arrangement of present-day English by which the
structures "subject," "direct object," "indirect object," "object
complement," "adverbial object," "predicate nominative," "appositive," "noun adjunct" are identified and distinguished.

Formula 1

$$D \quad 1 \quad 2\text{-d} \quad 4$$
$$+ \quad \pm$$

The single Class 1 word "tied" to the Class 2 word by the correspondence of number forms must be in the structure as "subject," and the subject meaning is "performer."

> The *pupils* ran out
> The *ships* sailed away

Formula 2

$$D \quad 1^a \quad 2b \quad D \quad 1^a$$
$$- \quad - \quad -$$

The single Class 1 word preceding the Class 2 word must be the subject. Both Class 1 words have the singular forms that correspond with the number form of the Class 2 word. The distinguishing feature here is the order. Here the arrangement of the Class 2 word of the special 2b list and the Class 1 word with the "same" referent following indicate that the subject meaning is "that which is identified." Examples of formula (2) are:

> One *difficulty* is the size
> My *husband* is the director
> This *girl* is my teacher

Formula 3

$$D \quad 1^a \quad 2\text{-d} \quad D \quad 1^b$$
$$- \quad \pm \quad +$$

Here again the order is the distinguishing feature. The Class 1 word that precedes the Class 2 word is the subject. Here the Class 2 word is not of the 2b list as in formula (2) and therefore the subject meaning is "performer."

Another significant difference between formula (3) and formula (2) is the fact that the referent of the Class 1 word following the Class 2 word in formula (3) is not the "same" as the referent of the Class 1 word preceding. In formula (3), therefore, the second Class 1 word is in the structure of "object." Examples of formula (3) are:

> The *dean* approved the *recommendations*
> The *boy* lighted the *lamps*
> The *guide* dug the *holes*

In formula (2), as shown by the letter exponents, the referent of the second Class 1 word is the "same" as that of the first. In this formula (2), therefore, the second Class 1 word is in the structure of "predicate nominative." Examples of the "predicate nominative" in formula (2) are:

> One difficulty is the *size*
> This girl is my *teacher*

Formula 4

$$D \quad 1^a \quad 2 \quad D \quad 1^b \quad D \quad 1^c$$
$$- \quad - \quad \quad - \quad \quad -$$

Formula 5

$$D \quad 1^a \quad 2 \quad D \quad 1^b \quad f \quad D \quad 1^c$$
$$- \quad - \quad \quad - \quad E \quad \quad -$$

Formula 6

$$D \quad 1^a \quad 2 \quad D \quad 1^b \quad D \quad 1^b$$
$$- \quad - \quad \quad - \quad \quad -$$

Formulas (4), (5), and (6) are alike except for the last item. The significant differences here are that in formulas (4) and (5) the referents of the Class 1 words following the Class 2 words are "different"; but in formula (6) they are "the same."

In addition, in formula (5) the Class 1 words following the Class 2 word have a function word of Group E between them.

In all three formulas the first Class 1 word is in the structure of "subject" (with the meaning of "performer") and the Class 1 words following the Class 2 word are in the structure of "object" —but of differing types. In formula (4), D $\underline{1^a}$ $\underline{2}$ D $\underline{1^b}$ D $\underline{1^c}$,

the 1^b is "indirect object" and the 1^c is "direct object."

> The school furnishes the *student* the *microscope*
> The foreman gives the *workman* his *machine*
> The committee gets the *boy* his *job*

In statement sentences, whenever two Class 1 words follow a Class 2 word, and the referents of the Class 1 words are different (and also not the same as that of the Class 1 word preceding the Class 2 word), and there is no function word of Group E between the last two Class 1 words, then the first of these Class 1 words is "indirect object" and the second, "direct object."

In formula (5), D $\underset{-}{1^a}$ $\underset{-}{2}$ D $\underset{-}{1^b}$ $\underset{E}{f}$ D $\underset{-}{1^c}$, there is a function word of Group E between the last two Class 1 words; therefore, the 1^b and the 1^c are both "direct objects." Examples of formula (5) are:

> The school furnishes the *microscope* and the *lamp*
> This fund provides the *teacher* not the *assistant*

In formula (6), D $\underline{1^a}$ $\underline{2}$ D $\underline{1^b}$ D $\underline{1^b}$, the two Class 1 words following the Class 2 word have the same referent. In this arrangement the first of the two Class 1 words is "direct object" and the second is "object complement." [11] Examples of formula (6) are:

> The board appoints a *teacher* the *secretary*
> This practice makes the *boy* a *swimmer*

Formula 7

$$D \quad 1^a \quad \text{2-d} \quad D \quad 1^b \quad D \quad 1^c$$
$$\underline{he/it} \qquad\qquad \underline{it} \qquad \underline{th}$$

This formula adds the symbols for the substitute groups to which the Class 1 words belong. They were omitted in the formulas above in order not to complicate the picture. The formulas there did not contain any contrasting arrangements in which the differences of substitute groups were significant. Among the symbols used, *he* stands for the *he/she* group as a whole and not simply for a word with the substitute *he* as distinct from *she* or *they*. The symbol *it* stands for the *it* group; the particular word may be a plural. The symbol *th* stands for a substitute not of any of the three groups *he*, *he/it*, *it*. It must not be mistaken for *they*. It represents a substitute such as *then* or *thus*. Examples of formula (7) are:

> The committee approved the request this *week*
> The publisher issued his bulletin last *Wednesday*
> This student began his vacation this *morning*
> My professor spent his holiday that *way*

---

[11] If one disregards a clear intonation difference, the formula (6) could also represent a "direct object" and an "appositive." With the "object complement" following the intonation curve on the "direct object" preceding is the ordinary one of continuation, 3–2–3; for the "appositive" following, it is usually a 3–2–4 with a pause. Compare the following utterances:

> The board appoints a ⌐tea⌐cher the⌐se⌐cretary

> The group attends the⌐ban⌐quet the⌐farewell din⌐ner

Formula 8

$$D \quad 1^a \quad D \quad 1^a \quad \text{2-d} \quad D \quad 1^b \quad \text{f} \quad D \quad 1^c$$
$$- \qquad - \qquad \pm \qquad + \qquad \text{E} \qquad +$$
$$\text{he} \qquad \text{he} \qquad \qquad \text{it} \qquad \qquad \text{it}$$

Formula 9

$$D \quad 1^a \quad D \quad 1^b \quad \text{2-d} \quad D \quad 1^c \quad \text{f} \quad D \quad 1^d$$
$$- \qquad - \qquad \pm \qquad + \qquad \text{E} \qquad +$$
$$\text{th} \qquad \text{he} \qquad \qquad \text{it} \qquad \qquad \text{it}$$

Formula 10

$$D \quad 1^a \quad 1^b \quad \text{2-d} \quad D \quad 1^c \quad \text{f} \quad D \quad 1^d$$
$$- \quad - \qquad \pm \qquad + \qquad \text{E} \qquad +$$
$$\text{it} \quad \text{he} \qquad \qquad \text{it} \qquad \qquad \text{it}$$

These three formulas differ only with respect to the first two Class 1 words. The Class 2 word in each is a preterit of one that is not on the special list; therefore, the meaning of subject will be "performer." Following the Class 2 word in each formula are two Class 1 words which do not have the same referent, and neither has the same referent as either of the Class 1 words before the Class 2 word. These two Class 1 words following the Class 2 words are "direct objects."

In formula (8) the two Class 1 words preceding the Class 2 word have the same referent, both have *he* group substitutes, and both have determiners; the first of these is therefore the "subject," the second, an "appositive." An example of formula (8) is:

This *student* my *assistant* brought the papers and the grades

In formula (9) the first two Class 1 words both have determiners, but they do not have the same referent, and the second Class 1 word has a substitute of one of the *he, he/it, it* groups. The first Class 1 word does not have in this particular sentence a substitute of one of the *he, he/it, it* groups. The second Class 1 word is there-fore the "subject" and the first Class 1 word is an "adverbial object." An example of formula (9) is:

> This *morning* my *assistant* brought the papers and the grades

In formula (10) the first two Class 1 words both belong to one of the *he, he/it, it* groups; their referents are not the same; but they have only one determiner, which is before the first Class 1 word. The second Class 1 word is therefore the "subject" and the first is a "noun adjunct." An example of formula (10) is:

> The *library assistant* brought the papers and the grades

The formulas given here have no use as matters to be learned. The purpose of presenting them in this way is simply to demon-strate that the actual signalling of the structures "subject," "direct object," "indirect object," "object complement," "adverbial object," "predicate nominative," "noun adjunct," is done in English by formal contrasts, primarily contrasts of arrangements of order. These structures have a range of meanings which are part of the total of the "structural meanings" signalled by our grammatical devices. One cannot use the English language with-out responding to and producing the signals of these essential meanings. In order to identify and to distinguish these particular structures one does not need to know the lexical meaning of the words, nor even what the sentence is about. He must be able to recognize the Class 1 and the Class 2 words and he must control enough of their meaning to know whether their referents are the "same" or "different," what "substitute group" they belong to, and whether a word of that substitute group is structurally substi-tutible in the utterance. The word-order patterns of these forms, the patterns that operate as the signals, are learned by the native speaker as a child; that is, he learns to respond to the meanings the patterns convey but is never conscious of the means by which the conveying is done. The formulas given here lay bare the structures themselves so that one can identify in the patterns the "subjects," "objects," etc., without knowing a single word of the sentence. In fact, many very different sentences can be made over the same patterns. The following formulas contain all these structures except "predicate nominative." Two formulas are given because "indirect objects" and "object complements" never, so far as I know, occur in the same sentence.[12]

$$D \quad 1^a \quad 1^b \quad D \quad 1^b \quad \text{2-d} \quad D \quad 1^c \quad D \quad 1^d \quad D \quad 1^e$$

```
D   1ᵃ   1ᵇ   D   1ᵇ   2-d   D   1ᶜ   D   1ᵈ   D   1ᵉ
    −    +        −     ±          −        −        −
    it   he       he               he       it       th
```

The caucus leaders the committee offered our candidate their support this Wednesday

```
D   1ᵃ   1ᵇ   D   1ᵇ   2-d   D   1ᶜ   D   1ᶜ   D   1ᵈ
    −    +        −     ±          −        −        −
    it   he       he               he       he       th
```

The caucus leaders the committee elected our candidate the chairman this Wednesday

---

[12] It is possible to make a sentence containing both "indirect object" and "object complement," but the ordinary speaker of English usually doesn't grasp the signal for "direct object" and becomes confused.

```
D   1ᵃ   1ᵇ   D   1ᵇ   2-d   1ᶜ   D   1ᵈ   D   1ᵈ   D   1ᵉ
    −    +        +     +     +         −        −        −
    it   he       it          he        he       he       th
```

The caucus leaders, the committee, elected us our candidate the chairman this Wednesday

Structural ambiguity of some sort will result whenever any of the essential signals indicated here do not appear in the utterance. Compare, for example, the following pairs of sentences:

1. The committee will accept the proposal *Wednesday*
2. The committee will accept *Wednesday*

3. The Romans constructed their arches this *way* later
4. The Romans constructed this *way* later

In (1) and (3) there is no structural ambiguity. The substitute *it* is not structurally substitutible in these utterances for *Wednesday* nor for *way*. These Class 1 words therefore cannot be in the structures of "direct object," "indirect object," or "object complement." They are "adverbial objects." In (2) and (4), however, *it* is structurally substitutible in that word order as well as *then* or *thus*, and in these sentences, as they appear in the word-order pattern in which they stand, *Wednesday* and *way* could be either "direct object" or "adverbial object."

The statements given above in the attempt to describe the significant contrasts that identify the structures of "subject," "object," "predicate nominative," etc., apply in all utterances except those in which the substitutes with *–self* are used—the so-called "intensive" and "reflexive pronouns," *myself, ourselves, yourself, yourselves, himself, herself, itself, themselves*. For these, some of the statements must be modified and several others must be added. The formulas must, therefore, have a symbol to mark the Class 1 words that are *–self* forms, 1-sf.

Formula 1

D	1ª	2-d	1ª-sf
	–	±	–
	he		he

Here the Class 1 word with the –*self* form, having as it must the same referent as the Class 1 word preceding it, may be either "predicate nominative" or "direct object." If the Class 2 word is one of the special 2b list, the Class 1 word with the –*self* form will be "predicate nominative"; if not, it will be "direct object."

> The man seemed *himself*
> The man hurt *himself*

Formula 2

D	1^a	2-d	1^a-sf	D	1^b
–		±	–		–
he			he		it

Formula 3

D	1^a	2-d	1^a-sf	D	1^a
–		±	–		–
he			he		he

In formulas (2) and (3) the significant contrasts in the –*self* form and the Class 1 word following are the same as those for words that are not –*self* forms. If the referents are different, the first is "indirect object" and the second, "direct object." If the referents are the same, the first is "direct object" and the second, the "object complement." The formulas differ from those without –*self* forms only in the fact that the referent of the –*self* form is necessarily the same as that of the Class 1 word preceding.

> (Formula 2)   The man made *himself* a *boat*
> (Formula 3)   The man made *himself* a *leader*

If, however, in formula (3) the Class 2 word is one of the special 2b list, then the last Class 1 word is "predicate nominative."

$$D \quad 1^a \quad 2\text{b-d} \quad 1^a\text{-sf} \quad D \quad 1^a$$

$-$	$\pm$	$-$		$-$
he		he		he

The man was himself a *leader*

Formula 4

$$D \quad 1^a \quad 2\text{-d} \quad D \quad 1^b \quad 1^a\text{-sf}$$

$-$	$\pm$		$-$	$-$
he			it	he

Formula 5

$$D \quad 1^a \quad 2\text{-d} \quad D \quad 1^b \quad 1^b\text{-sf}$$

$-$	$\pm$		$-$	$-$
he			it	it

These formulas (4) and (5) differ from those without –*self* forms in respect to the structure of the items that appear at the end. In formula (4) the –*self* form has the same referent as the "subject"; in formula (5) it has the same referent as the "object." Here the substitute group is significant.

> (Formula 4)   The man made the boat *himself*
> (Formula 5)   The man made the boat *itself*

Such a sentence as the following, however, is ambiguous, because there is no formal means of deciding whether the –*self* form has the same referent as the "subject" or the "object." Both belong to the same substitute group *it* and both have the same number form. A difference of substitute group or a difference of number form would resolve the ambiguity:

> (Ambiguous)   The wire made the contact *itself*
> (Unambiguous)   The wires made the contact *itself*
>   The wires made the contact *themselves*

Our conscious experience with language has served to overstress the part that words play in the conveying of meaning. We find it difficult to believe that one could understand the meanings of all the words in a language and yet not understand a single utterance in that language. Even when the meanings that are signalled by structures are pointed out, their importance for the whole process of communication usually escapes us. That these meanings really depend upon an intricate system of formal features apart from the words as vocabulary units is not grasped easily by those who seldom try to face the facts of language objectively. Part of the difficulty arises from the fact that the "grammar" we have experienced as pupils in the schools has led our thinking about language in an opposite direction. Nowhere is that more evident than in the usual treatment of "subjects" and "objects" in sentences. In this discussion, in contrast with the usual approach, we have insisted—

1. That the names "subject," "predicate nominative," "appositive," "direct object," "indirect object," "object complement," "adverbial object," "noun adjunct" are the names of structures in which Class 1 words appear;

2. That these structures are identified and distinguished by contrasting formal arrangements, not by the meaning;

3. That these structures are the signals by which we receive and convey such meanings as "performer," "identification," "that which undergoes the action," "that for which an action is performed," "that which results from the action."

X. Structural Meanings: "Modifiers"

Next to "subjects" and "objects," the common textbooks of grammar as well as the teaching in the schools have given most attention to "modifiers." The conventional definition of "modifier," however, provides very little understanding of what a "modifier" is and practically no help in distinguishing "modifiers" from a variety of other structures in present-day English.

> A modifier is a word or group of words that adds to the meaning of another word.[1]

But just how are we to decide whether a word "*adds to the meaning of another word*"? An examination of the instances usually given as examples of those words that "add to the meaning of another word" in contrast with those that are excluded from the definition leads to the conclusion that there must be some criteria of identification which are not stated in the definition.

1. They *should* put in a larger drainage field
2. They   put in a larger drainage field

To the ordinary student the word *should* certainly "adds to the meaning of" *put* and he sees no reason why, according to the definition, it should not be called a "modifier."

[1] Frank X. Braun, *English Grammar for Language Students, op. cit.*, p. 11.

1. Friction made the skin *red*
2. Friction   *reddened* the skin

Just why is *red* in (1) called a "modifier" and "reddened" in (2) excluded from that class? If the word *red* "adds to the meaning of" the word *skin* in the first sentence why does not *reddened* also add to the meaning of the word *skin* in the second sentence?

1. A fire *burns*   in the fireplace
2. A   *burning* fire is in the fireplace

In what way does *burning* in (2) "add to the meaning of" the word *fire* that *burns* in (1) does not?

The difficulty with this definition of "modifier" is precisely the same as that found in the other common definitions of our grammar. They all attempt to state the characteristics of a grammatical unit in terms of *meaning content* rather than in terms of *form*. The difference between *burns* and *burning* in relation to the word *fire* lies not in the meaning, but in the structural form. In the sentences preceding, *red* in relation to *skin* differs from *reddened* in relation to *skin* not in the meaning content but in the structural form.

For a grammar that will give an understanding of the working of a language we must turn aside from all definitions that strive to state the identifying characteristics of grammatical structures in terms of meaning content. Structures do signal meanings, it is true; and these meanings must be described. The meanings, however, cannot serve successfully to identify and distinguish the structures. Not only do structures usually signal several different meanings but, what is more important, there is probably in present-day English no structural meaning that is not signalled by a variety of structures. As we have seen above, the meaning of "performer of the action" is one of the meanings signalled by the structure we call "subject." We cannot, however, expect to define the structure "subject" as "performer of the action," for this meaning is signalled by a variety of other structures that are not "subjects." Compare, for example, the following sentences in each of which the word *committee* expresses the meaning "performer of the action" of "recommending." In only the first sentence is the word *committee* in the structure of "subject."

1. The *committee recommended* his promotion
2. His promotion was *recommended* by the *committee*
3. The *recommendation* of the *committee* was that he be promoted
4. The *committee's recommendation* was that he be promoted
5. The action of the *recommending committee* was that he be promoted

We cannot hope to define "modifiers" in terms of meaning content. We must begin with the understanding that "modification" is a structure, and that, like all structures, it must be described in terms of the formal units of which it is composed and the characteristic arrangements of these units.

The conventional discussions of grammatical matters call the modifying units "adjectives" and "adverbs."

> An adjective is a word used to modify (describe, limit, or qualify) the meaning of a noun or pronoun.

> An adverb is a word used to modify (i. e., describe, limit, or qualify) a verb, an adjective, or another adverb.[2]

According to the usual application of these definitions any word that modifies a "noun" or "pronoun" is an "adjective"; all other modifying words are "adverbs." The difficulty here lies in the fact that the units are defined in terms of the structure. We need

[2]Braun, *op. cit.*, p. 1.

rather to describe the structure in terms of the units. The definition of "adjective" says in effect that whenever we have a structure of "modification" with a "substantive" as one member, the other member of the structure is an "adjective" by definition. The definition of an "adverb" says in effect that whenever there is a structure of "modification" with a "verb," "adjective," or "adverb" as one member, the other member of the structure is by definition an "adverb." [3] Not only does it cause confusion to define the units of a structure in terms of the structure itself, but the confusion is increased because actual practice in the use of these names does not follow the implications of the definitions given.[4] In the following examples, although there is in each a structure of modification with a "substantive" as one member, the other members, the italicized words, are not in all grammars called "adjectives."

My *father's* house was a large stone building

The *appropriations* committee approved our department budget

The culture of the *plains* Indians differed from that of the East Coast Indians

Most of these students arrived only a few days *ago*

Some of the officers *there* are my friends

[3] Seldom do the ordinary grammar textbooks make any note of such modifiers as the following words attached to *like*, "preposition" and "conjunction."

In many ways Bob is *very much* like his brother
He even swims *just* like his brother does

[4] It is primarily because of this double confusion that I have found it impossible to use the ordinary names for the four parts of speech. "Substantive" and "verb" would not be too difficult to use practically, but the terms "adjective" and "adverb" at present are hopeless. The reader must not attempt to equate the names "adjective" and "adverb" as defined here with the parts of speech called above Class 3 and Class 4 words.

In the following example, although the structure of "modification" has a "verb" as one member, the other member is not in all grammars called an "adverb."

Most of those in this session will leave this *Friday*

Because of this double confusion in respect to the names "adjective" and "adverb" we shall avoid these words in describing the structures of "modification." Our task demands a description of the structure we call "modification" in terms of the functioning units which make up the structure and of the arrangements of these units by which the structure can be identified. We shall also need to indicate the meanings, as precisely as possible, which the structures signal.[5]

"Modification" is a structure in which each of the four parts of speech, and certain of the function words, described above in Chapters V and VI, can serve as the head or nucleus. Our discussion will therefore be clearer if we treat "modifiers" in relation to each of the kinds of structure head, in spite of the fact that this approach will necessitate some repetition.

I. "Modifiers" with a Class 1 word as head.
II. "Modifiers" with a Class 2 word as head.
III. "Modifiers" with a Class 3 word as head.
IV. "Modifiers" with a Class 4 word as head.
V. "Modifiers" with certain function words as heads.

[5] This procedure attempts to center attention primarily on the structures themselves, by pointing out the formal features by which they are identified and distinguished. One could, of course, take each part of speech and indicate all the structures in which it enters. Sometimes the description of the contrasting features which distinguish one structure from others in which the same form-classes enter leads to some overlapping of the two approaches and thus some repetition. See, for example, the description of the arrangement for "noun adjunct" in the treatment of "subjects" and "objects" and its treatment here.

"Modification" is a structure of connection, but it is a connection of a particular kind. Those forms that are connected *in this particular way* with a "head" are the "modifiers" of these head words. Just what are the characterizing features of the particular way of connection that we call by the technical name, "modification"? In each of the five types of head words we shall deal first with the structures of this modification, and, second, with the meanings of these structures.

I. MODIFIERS WITH A CLASS 1 WORD AS HEAD

(a) The structures of "modification" with Class 1 words as head

1. Class 1 words with Class 2 words as modifiers. We have seen above that a Class 1 word is "connected" with a Class 2 word by a concordance of form in a structure that we call "subject." The result of that kind of connection between a Class 1 and a Class 2 word is one of the basic patterns of a "sentence," which, by certain contrastive features of arrangement, signals the kind of utterance—whether the sentence is a question, request, or statement—and which can stand alone as a "situation stimulus" utterance unit at the beginning of a conversation.

A *fire* *burns* in the fireplace
The *friction* *reddened* the skin
The *committee* *recommended* his promotion

The particular kind of connection that is "modification" of a Class 1 word, however, differs sharply from this kind of connection of a Class 1 with a Class 2 word to form a sentence.

First, the forms of a Class 2 word connected with a Class 1 word by the structure of "modification" differ from those of a Class 2 word connected with a Class 1 word to make a sentence. In the structure of modification the Class 2 words are either of the *–ing* form or of the *–ed* form [6] and occupy "positions" other than that of the Class 2 word to make the structure of a sentence. Compare, for example, the following pairs of sentences. In each sentence there is a Class 2 word "connected" with a Class 1 word. In the first sentence of each pair, the Class 2 word is a "modifier" of the Class 1 word, but in the second sentence of each pair the Class 2 word is "tied" to the Class 1 word to form a basic pattern of a "sentence" with the Class 1 word as "subject."

(1) A *burning fire* is in the fireplace
     2-ng   1

(2) A *fire burns* in the fireplace
     1   2

(1) The *committee recommending* his promotion agreed
     1   2-ng

(2) The *committee is recommending* his promotion
     1   f   2-ng
       B

Second, the resulting structure of a Class 1 word with a Class 2 word connected as "modifier" stands alone as an utterance only as a "response" to a question, not as a "situation" utterance unit at the beginning of a conversation; and it does not by its arrangement signal question, request, or statement. The whole structure

---

[6] The term "*–ed* form" ("dental suffix") is used in this book as a convenient name for both what is conventionally called "past tense" form and the "past participle." The fact that for some Class 2 words the "past tense" form has a change of vowel rather than a "dental suffix" can be ignored for our purpose here, as well as the fact that a few "past participles" differ in form from the "past tense" form.

of a Class 1 word with a Class 2 word as "modifier" enters as a unit into any of the other structures of the sentence in which a Class 1 word alone is a constituent. It can be made a part of any of these other structures by simply placing the whole unit of the Class 1 word with its "modifiers" in the "position" in which the Class 1 word alone would appear.

The *recommending committee* (note structure: Class 1 word with Class 2 word as modifier)

1. The *recommending committee* approved his promotion
2. The dean approved the *recommending committee's* decision
3. The dean gave the *recommending committee* their instructions
4. Within the *recommending committee* there was no disagreement
5. The dean appointed those five men the *recommending committee*

The structure of "modification" with a Class 1 word as the head or nucleus includes not only Class 2 words as second members but also Class 3 words, other Class 1 words, and Class 4 words.

2. *Class 1 words with Class 3 words as "modifiers"*

an *excellent address*
   3   1

movable parts
3   1

a *longer vacation*
  3   1

the *coastal plain*
   3   1

all the *equipment necessary*
      1   3

his *messy room*
   3   1

at a *prohibitive cost*
   3   1

a more *rapid advance*
       3   1

3. *Class 1 words with other Class 1 words as "modifiers"*

	1	**1**		**1**	**1**
my	*fathers*	house	the	*health*	service
a	*ladys*	handkerchief		*Wednesday*	evening
my	*boys*	picture	a	*student*	advisor
the	*registrars*	letter		*automobile*	licenses
his	*mothers*	support	a	*boys*	school
the	*committees*	recommendation	a two	*weeks*	session
my	*home*	phone	the	*life*	guard
an	*eye*	shade	a	*paper*	knife

4. *Class 1 words with Class 4 words as "modifiers"*

	1	**4**	
For the	*work*	*thereafter*	he employed two assistants (888)
The	*conversation*	*meanwhile*	was practically zero (725)
The	*food*	*there*	was not what he needed (460)
The	*discussion*	*afterward*	proved the success of the talk (468)
His own	*study*	*abroad*	made him more understanding (976)
The constant	*racket*	*everywhere*	was annoying (382)
The	*walk*	*home*	was very tiring for her (381)

The "modification" structures with Class 1 words as heads may be formed of any of the four parts of speech or of all of them together.[7]

[7] See Aileen Traver, *The Modificational Patterns of the Substantive Head Construction in Present-Day American English* (unpublished dissertation, University of Michigan, 1944), for a summary of the range and frequency of the various modifiers of Class 1 words as they actually appear in a body of Standard English letters.

The *childrens constant deafening racket everywhere* kept the
   1   3   2-ng   1   4
younger ones from sleeping

This *candidates long concentrated manuscript study abroad* makes
   1   3   2-d   1   1   4
him ideal for that position

Not only do single words of each of the four parts of speech serve as "modifiers" of Class 1 words, but certain word-groups do also.

5. Class 1 words with "modifiers" consisting of a structure with one of the function words of Group F

The function words of Group F—*at, by, for, from, in, of, on, to, with,* etc.—each serve to make the Class 1 word following them into a "modification" structure. This word-group as a "modifier" may consist not only of the function word of Group F and a Class 1 word alone, but of any or all of the "modifiers" possible for the Class 1 word.

	1	(Mod.)
The	*carnival*	*over on the fair grounds* (239)
We'll have a	*crew*	*of fellows* come over (249)
There was a	*period*	*of being away* (237)
Is there	*anything*	*of importance* (225)
The	*examination*	*in the morning* will take until twelve (890)
A	*luncheon*	*at twelve-thirty* will open the series (890)
He had	*something*	*from his late trip to the Coast* to talk about (896)

I can furnish him some *tools*   *for that kind of a job* (833)

O.K. it's largely the   *report*   *of our conference with the dean* (226)

6. *Class 1 words with "modifiers" consisting of an included sentence, usually with one of the function words of Group J* (who, which, that, etc.)

	1	(Mod.)
They are the very	*ones*	*that should be invited* (875)
This is the first	*time*	*that the grounds been at all usable* (82)
The	*men*	*who came early* had to wait until the truck brought their tools (410)
The	*day*	*after you left* he came in (480)
The	*time*	*when you can do it best* is just before two (501)
The north	*end*	*which is our end* has plenty of light (861)

The "modifiers" of Class 1 words therefore consist not only of any of the four parts of speech or of all of them together but also of certain word-groups. Very seldom, comparatively, do Class 1 words occur with more than two "modifiers" in addition to a "determiner." (See Group A of the function words.) In the materials of this study examined here, 57 per cent of the Class 1 words occurred with no "modifiers" other than a determiner; 34 per cent with only one "modifier," and that in the position between the determiner and the Class 1 word; 7 per cent with word-group "modifiers"; [8] and only 2 per cent with two or more "modifiers."

---

[8] See Aileen Traver, *op. cit.*, p. 110 ff. for somewhat comparable figures. The chief differences seem to be in the relative number of Class 1 words with two or more "modifiers." It is to be expected, probably, that materials of informal oral conversations should show a very small number of instances with multiple "modifiers," in contrast with even informal written materials.

Never, in practice, does a Class 1 word occur with all the kinds of "modifiers" that are theoretically possible.

> Almost all/the/twenty-five/very famous/Army/*officers*/of the United States/listed in the catalog/who are still in active service/ . . .

Theoretically, a structure such as this of a Class 1 word together with its great range of modifiers can be substituted in any "position" in which a Class 1 word alone can appear.

The "modification" structures with Class 1 words as heads are identified and distinguished from other structures like "subject" and "object" in which a Class 1 word is a member, not only by the variety of the form-classes and word-groups that can serve as "modifiers" (i.e., as constituents of the "modification" structure with a Class 1 word as head), but also by the arrangements and forms of these constituents.

a. Most significant of all the features of arrangement to identify the structure of "modification" with a Class 1 word as head is the "position" between the determiner and the Class 1 word. Any word placed in this position, unless it is one of the degree "modifiers" of a "modifier" (see Group D of the function words and the discussion below), by its position, becomes one of the "modifiers" of the Class 1 word head.[9] Almost all single-word "modifiers" of Class 1 words occur in this position. In this position also occur more than 80 per cent of the total number of all kinds of "modifiers" of Class 1 words in the recorded materials.

b. The second significant feature of arrangement to identify the structure of "modification" with a Class 1 word as head is the "position" immediately following the Class 1 word.

[9] See Chapter XII for a discussion of problems of the immediate constituents of the structures.

(1). All word-groups as modifiers of Class 1 words (e.g., function words of Group F with Class 1 words, and function words of Group J with included sentences) always occur in this position; and all word-groups, with these constituents, that occur in this "position" become by that fact a constituent of the "modification" structure in which the Class 1 word is head.[10]

If both types of word-group occur in the same "modification" structure, then the one with the function word of Group F (so-called "prepositions") is always the first in order, and immediately after it is the one with the function word of Group J (sometimes called "relative pronouns" or "relative adjectives") and an included sentence.

If both types of word-group occur in the same "modification" structure, then, unless one of a narrow range of concordance "ties" is present, structural ambiguity will result with respect to the "modification" connection of the second word-group.

An	*examination*	of the	*students*	*who*	*are*	deficient
1			**1**	**1**	**2**	
–			+	±	+	
it			he	he		
(which)			(who)			

The word-group *who are deficient,* by both the form *who* and the form *are,* is made a "modifier" of the Class 1 word *students* rather than of the Class 1 word *examination.*

An	*examination*	of the	*students*	*which*	*is*	thorough
1			**1**	**1**	**2**	
–			+	+	–	
it			he	it/he-it		
(which)			(who)			

---

[10] Certain details necessary to make this statement complete will be given below in the discussion of the "modifiers" with Class 2 words as heads.

The word-group *which is thorough,* by both the form *which* and the form *is,* is made a "modifier" of the Class 1 word *examination* rather than of the Class 1 word *students.*

In the following sentence it is only the form *who* which definitely ties the group *who are here* to the Class 1 word *students.*

The examinations/ of the students/ *who* are here.

In the following sentences it is only the form of the word *are* which definitely ties the group *who are here* to the Class 1 word *students* in the first sentence and the form of the word *is* that attaches the same word-group to the word *teacher* in the second.

The *students* of the teacher who *are* here
The students of the *teacher* who *is* here

In the following sentences the concordance forms are not distinctive and therefore the "modification" connection of the last word-groups of each is ambiguous.

The students/ of the men/ who are members
The equipment/ of the group/ which is there
It is the beginning/ of a speech/ which is important
The requirements/ of the courses/ which are listed
A house/ of six rooms and a bath/ which they own

(2). Class 2 words as "modifiers" of Class 1 words frequently occur in the "position" immediately following the Class 1 word. This is also a significant position for a Class 2 word joined with a Class 1 word as "subject" to form the basic pattern of a statement sentence (the so-called "predicate verb"). In this position, the "modification" structure is identified and distinguished by formal contrasts other than position alone. Compare, for example, the following pairs of sentences.

("Modifier")   The men *listed* in the order sheet were all they needed
("Predicate")   The men *listed* in the order sheet   all they needed

("Modifier")   The students *nominated* for the committee were all their friends
("Predicate")   The students *nominated* for the committee   all their friends

("Modifier")   The students   *participating* in the parade were having fun
("Predicate")   The students were *participating* in the parade for fun

("Modifier")   The officers   *appointing* the committee were to do the work
("Predicate")   The officers were *appointing* the committee to do the work there

("Modifier")   A student *compiled*   report on betting was then presented
("Predicate")   A student *compiled* a report on betting which was then presented

(3). Class 4 words as "modifiers" of Class 1 words practically always occur in the "position" immediately following the Class 1 word.[11] Since this "position" also is a possible one for certain Class 4 words as "modifiers" of Class 2 words following, structural ambiguity concerning the connection of the Class 4 word "modifier" sometimes results. The distinguishing feature of the direction of the "modification" is here a contrast in the intonation pattern. For the Class 4 words that are "modifiers" of a Class 1 word preceding there is no pause or drop between the Class 1 word and the Class 4 word.

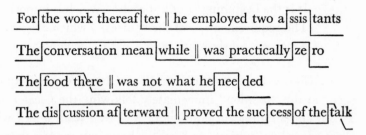

---

[11] There were in our materials no examples of another position for Class 4 words as "modifiers" of Class 1 words, but such expressions as *the above discussion* do occur fairly frequently in written material. The following example, however, should perhaps be noted here.

They worked only for the *inside* people (911)

His | own study abroad ‖ made him more under | stan | ding

The | constant racket ev | rywhere ‖ was a | nnoy | ing

The | walk home ‖ was very | ti | ring for her

(b) The meanings of "modification" with Class 1 words as head

To be of the greatest service the grammarian should not stop with a description of the functioning units of a "modification" structure and the significant arrangements of these units which distinguish this structure from others. The modification structure with a Class 1 word as head signals a variety of meanings, and it is desirable not only to indicate what these meanings are, but, as far as possible, to connect each meaning with the distinctive formal features which operate to distinguish it.[12] The following examples all consist of Class 1 words with "modifiers." The great diversity of the meanings in the relationship between the "modifier" and the Class 1 word to which it is attached will become consciously apparent to the native speaker of English upon even a very superficial examination.

a *black hat*   a *sofa cushion*
a *soft cushion*   a *sold hat*
a *hat sale*   an *embroidered cushion*
a *dancing girl*   a *sprained wrist*
a *working hypothesis*   a *hardened criminal*
the *opening day* of the sale   a *criminal action*
the *store clerks*   a *criminal lawyer*

---

[12] In this respect, as in many other matters, this study has not by any means solved all the problems. The reader will find it easy to raise questions for which no answers appear here. I am trying to present a broad outline with enough detail to illustrate the method of approach and the results that seem acceptable.

the *Christmas holidays*   a *corporation lawyer*

the *struck plants* (will not open until the men receive a new
    contract)

a *rug beater*   a *medical officer*

a *moving van*   a *perfect stranger*

the *up stroke*   *liquid measure*

utter darkness   the *telephone pole*

an *upstairs place*   the *water department*

a *hard worker*   the *hospital bill*

a *mathematics student*   the *New England atlas*

his *men friends*   a *speech map*

two *years service*   a *state university*

a *painless dentist*   *income tax*

an *inner spring mattress*   the *mountain areas*

heart disease   a *brain tumor*

his *study abroad*   a *package delivery*

the *talk thereafter*   *class admittance*

a *flat denial*

the precise *situation there* (cannot be explained easily)

student failures   *class absences*

atomic survival   a *body deformity*

an *unjust dismissal*   *student advice*

an *unfair foreman*   a *wireless operator*

the *mathematical processes* of *long division* and *short division*

his *rapid addition*   *committee authorization*

a *large addition*   an *algebra lesson*

an *easy addition*   a *complete anesthetic*

the *south addition*   a *partial anesthetic*

his *table companions*   this *Corona typewriter*

An attempt to list all of the various meanings in the "modifier"
structure, as shown in a body of examples such as these, is often
necessary to make a native speaker of English realize their great

diversity. In his usual elementary study of grammar, the narrow range of examples furnished often builds up the feeling that whenever a Class 1 word is "modified" the relation of the "modifier" to the modified head is always that of character or quality to a substance. A *black hat*, is, of course, a *hat* with this quality, *black*. A *black hat* is a *hat* that is *black*. A *soft cushion* is a *cushion* that is *soft*. Most of the examples given above, however, do not have this relation of character or quality to a substance. A *criminal lawyer* need not be "criminal"; a *perfect stranger* need not be "perfect"; a *liquid measure* need not be "liquid"; and a *hard worker* is not necessarily "hard." Our question here is whether the various meanings in the relationship of a "modifier" to a Class 1 word are tied to formal differences. We have insisted that the structure of "modification" itself is identified and distinguished from other structures such as "subject" by means of formal contrasts of arrangement. We have seen that within the structure of "subject" the various meanings of "subject" are also distinguished by formal contrasts of arrangement. To what extent are the various meanings of "modifier" of a Class 1 word also distinguished by formal contrasts?

The following formal characteristics within the "modification" structure provide significant contrasts to distinguish certain of the meanings that attach to the "modifier" relation.

1. Class 1 words with Class 2 words as modifiers: Meanings

a. When the "modifier" of the Class 1 word is a Class 2 word with the *–ng* form, the meaning in the "modification" structure is that the Class 1 word represents the "performer of the action" indicated in the "modifier." [13]

[13] This meaning of "performer of the action" indicated in the "modifier" has nothing to do with the meaning of "performer of action" or undergoer of action as shown in the "subject" or "object" structure. In such a sentence as *their barking dog prevented the burglary*, the Class 1 word *dog* has the *–ing* form "modifier" *barking*. It, therefore, has

	(Performer)
the *recommending*	*committee*
a *tiring*	*walk*
the *barking*	*dog*
a *raging*	*fire*
his *slowly reddening*	*face*

b. When the "modifier" of the Class 1 words is a Class 2 word with the *–ed* form (the so-called past participle) the meaning in the "modification" structure is that the Class 1 word represents the "undergoer of the action" indicated in the "modifier."

	(Undergoer)
the *recommended*	*procedure*
a *sprained*	*wrist*
the *dismissed*	*employee*
a *sealed*	*envelope*
the *broken*	*windowpane*

The difference between the structural meaning of the "modifiers" of Group (*a*) and those of Group (*b*) appears more clearly when the contrasting forms can be placed side by side as in the following groups.

CLASS 3	CLASS 2-D	CLASS 2-NG
MODIFYING CLASS I	MODIFYING CLASS I	MODIFYING CLASS I
(*character—substance*)	(*Class 1 is undergoer*)	(*Class 1 is performer*)
D **3** **1**	*D* **2-d** **1**	*D* **2-ng** **1**
The pure water	The purified water	The purifying water
An open book	An opened book	An opening book

---

the meaning of "performer of action" in relation to *barking*. But the whole structure *their barking dog* is in "subject" structure with relation to *prevented the burglary* and in this structure the word *prevented* has the formal characteristics that signal the meaning that *the barking dog* is the "performer of this action." In the sentence *they chained their barking dog*, although *dog* is still "performer of the action" of *barking*, the structure *their barking dog* is "undergoer of the action" *chained*. (See also note 14.)

The *water softened solution* was too weak to be effective
The *water softening solution* was too weak to be effective

In both the sentences of this pair the modifying structures each have the meanings of "performer" and "undergoer" of the same action. It is the contrast of the forms *softened* and *softening* that alone signals the differences between them. In the first, *solution* is the "undergoer" of the action of which *water* is performer; in the second, *solution* is the "performer" of the action of which *water* is the "undergoer." [14]

2. Class 1 words with Class 3 words as modifiers: Meanings

When the modifier of a Class 1 word is a Class 3 word the meaning in the modification structure is that of "quality" (represented by the Class 3 word) to substance (represented by the Class 1 word). This meaning is signalled in all these structures with Class 3 words—except in those structures that have certain special characteristics.

---

[14] Within this pattern an intonation contrast signals a significant difference in meaning.

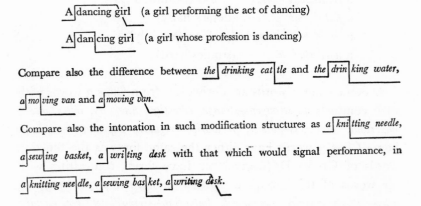

	(Quality)	(Substance)
	3	**1**
Those	*unsightly*	*wires*
His	*messy*	*room*
	Pure	*water*
The	*crooked*	*streets*

There are, however, three situations in which special characteristics signal meanings other than that of "quality of a substance."

a. Some of the Class 1 words (as shown in Chapter VII) are derivatives from Class 2 words, with such contrastive forms as *student—study, denial—deny, performance—perform, worker—work.* Some Class 3 words have the same shape as Class 4 words, as does *hard;* some others have a contrasting Class 4 form, as *continuous—continuously, rapid—rapidly, flat—flatly.* When such Class 3 words appear as "modifiers" of Class 1 words that are derivatives of Class 2 words, the meaning in the modification is not that of "quality of substance" but rather "manner of action," as in the following.

a *continuous worker*	(works continuously)
a *flat denial*	(denies flatly)
a *rapid performance*	(performs rapidly)
a *hard student*	(studies hard)

b. Some Class 1 words are derivatives from Class 3 words with such contrasts as *stranger—strange, necessity—necessary, importance—important, blackness—black, regularity—regular, supremacy—supreme.* Some Class 3 words have either the same form as the function words of Group D (degree), or have forms contrasting with *-ly* words of this group, as *absolute—absolutely, perfect—perfectly, utter—utterly, complete—completely, immediate—immediately, real—really.*

When Class 3 words of this type appear as modifiers of Class 1 words that are derivative of Class 3 words, the meaning in the modification is not that of "quality of a substance" but rather "degree of the quality."

a *perfect stranger*	(perfectly strange)
an *absolute necessity*	(absolutely necessary)
utter blackness	(utterly black)
complete supremacy	(completely supreme)
immediate importance	(immediately important)
perfect regularity	(perfectly regular)

c. Some Class 3 words appear fairly frequently with the markers of Class 1 words as Class 1 functioning units, as:

criminal in *a criminal*, in contrast with *criminal action*
liquid in *a liquid*, in contrast with *liquid food*
insane in *the insane*, in contrast with *insane man*
Spanish in *Spanish* (the language), in contrast with *Spanish architecture*

When Class 3 words like *criminal, liquid,* etc., appear as modifiers of Class 1 words for which lexical compatibility permits both uses, then the meaning in the modification structure is ambiguous. Ambiguity results whenever it is impossible to determine whether the "modifier" is a Class 3 word "modifier" or a Class 1 word "modifier."

these *Spanish students* (those who are studying the language, Spanish, *or* students from Spain)
a *deaf* and *dumb teacher* (one who teaches those who are deaf and dumb *or* one who is himself deaf and dumb)
a *criminal lawyer* (one who handles cases of crime *or* one who has committed crimes)

The following are not ambiguous, because lexical incompatibility excludes the meaning of the modifier as character to substance. From a formal point of view, in such examples the special characteristic of Class 3 words, "comparison," is impossible.

>an *insane asylum*
>*liquid measure*

3. *Class 1 words with other Class 1 words as modifiers: Meanings*

When the modifier of a Class 1 word is a Class 1 word, the meaning in the modification structure is usually "identification." [15] Certain special formal features in these structures signal several other meanings. The following examples show some of the diversity included in the meaning, "identification."

>the *budget committee*   a *pillow slip*
>a *state university*   my *insurance policies*
>an *army captain*   a *store clerk*
>his *bath robe*   the *license bureau*

In all of these as they occurred in the recorded materials the intonation pattern was similar.

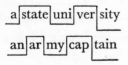

In two situations in which the modifier of a Class 1 word is another Class 1 word special formal features signal meanings other than "identification."

---

[15] The label "identification" is not a very satisfactory term for the somewhat diverse meanings generally signalled by this structure. I have not been able to find formal features that differentiate the more precise meanings included here.

a. Some of the Class 1 word heads are derivatives from Class 2 words with formal features contrasting with the Class 2 base, as, for example, *driver—drive, sweeper—sweep, sale—sell, delivery—deliver, enclosure—enclose, remembrance—remember, nourishment—nourish.* When Class 1 word modifiers occur with this type of Class 1 word head the meaning signalled by the modification structure is modifier as "undergoer of action."

a *truck driver*	the *milk delivery*
a *carpet sweeper*	the *garden enclosure*
a *rug sale*	a *birthday remembrance*
a *package delivery*	*body nourishment*

The intonation pattern here was similar to that of the preceding set of examples.

b. Some of these structures with a Class 1 word as head and another Class 1 word as "modifier" have a meaning in which the Class 1 word modifier indicates the "material" of which the head is composed. These seem to be differentiated by an intonation pattern, as in the following examples: [16]

a│stone wall

that│mud road

a│chocolate cake

The contrast of meaning as tied to a particular intonation pattern can be seen in the following example:

a│dust│mop (a mop used for dusting)

[16] In this chapter I have tried to note certain intonation contrasts that appeared. To generalize these contrasts requires a much more thorough study of intonation as a whole. The statements here can be only tentative.

The intonation a dust mop would signal the meaning, "a mop composed of dust."

4. Class 1 words with Class 4 words as modifiers: Meanings

When the modifier of a Class 1 word is a Class 4 word the meaning in the modification structure is "identification." Here too the modifier is tied to the head by an intonation pattern:

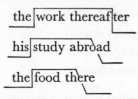

5. Class 1 words with a word-group as modifier having a function word of Group F (so-called "preposition"): Meanings

When the modifier of a Class 1 word is a word-group with one of the function words of the group containing *at, by, for, from,* etc., the meaning in the modification structure is usually "identification."

> the *money for the milkman*
> a *dog in the next apartment*
> *receptions for the new members*
> a *man from the FBI*

6. Class 1 words with a word-group as modifier which consists of an included sentence: Meanings

When the modifier of a Class 1 word is a word-group consisting of an included sentence, the meaning in the modification structure is either "identification" or "description," [17] depending upon the intonation pattern.

With no pause, and with no significant change of pitch level

[17] This label "description" is not a satisfactory term for the distinction here, but I cannot provide a better one.

after the Class 1 word, the meaning is "identification." With a pause and with a change of pitch level it is "description."

> Those| three men who are always grum|bling ("identification")

> Those|three men || who are always|grum|bling ("description")

Altogether the meanings in the structure of modification with a Class 1 word as head cover a considerable range. Here there have been some examples in which the Class 1 word head has the meaning of "performer," in others, of "undergoer." In some, the relation of the "modifier" to the Class 1 word head is that of "quality to substance"; in some it is "material of which the head is composed"; in some it is "identification." But all these meanings, diverse as they are, are tied to and thus signalled by certain formal arrangements of the Class 1 word and its "modifier."

II. "MODIFIERS" WITH CLASS 2 WORDS AS HEAD

A "modification" structure differs from other structures, as we have seen, in the fact that the whole structure enters into other structures as a complete unit and functions in these structures just as the single head word alone would function. A Class 2 word often serves as the head of a structure of modification. Class 1, 2, and 3, as well as 4,[18] words appear as "modifiers" of Class 2 words.

[18] In the structural analysis of Class 4 words a great deal of investigation remains undone. The very fact that it was necessary to resort to lists (short ones, it is true) of words that pattern like *often* or like *far*, with no other formal characteristics to distinguish them from other groups, seems to me evidence of unsolved structural problems. Harlan M. Hungerford attempted to deal with one of the many detailed problems that need study and reported his results in his dissertation *The Verb Head Construction . . . with Special Reference to the Marked Infinitive and Single-Word Adverbs* (Ann Arbor: University of Michigan, 1949).

1. Class 2 words with Class 4 words as "modifiers"

They should be asked to *support* their charges *formally* (174)
           2   **4**

It *usually runs* from sixty to eighty (190)
   4   **2**

I don't *particularly care* to go (875)
      4   **2**

The whole business *went along nicely* (89)
              2   **4**   **4**

I would have *gone* right *over* to see him except for my hay
fever (8912)   **2**   **4**

He didn't *say definitely* (89)
That *always happens* when we *plan ahead* (188)
He couldn't *absolutely assert* that they didn't (174)
We carry it *along religiously usually* (175)
    L—— talked with him and then *immediately reported* to
me (8910)

2. Class 2 words with Class 1 words as "modifiers" [19]

I've *thought* of you a thousand *times today* (84)
   2   **1**   **1**

[19] Here we are including only those Class 1 words for which, in the utterance as
it stands, the substitutes *he, she, it* are not possible. The so-called "objects" could be
included as "modifiers" inasmuch as the resulting construction functions as the head
alone could function, but it is not necessary to include them here. From a practical
point of view their contrastive arrangements appear more satisfactorily in the preceding chapter.

It *worked* a little *while* (82)
  2   **1**

Then this *morning* I *got up* early (85)
        1   **2**

I've *been* away all *afternoon* and *evening* (87)
   2   **1**   **1**

Maybe he'll *come*   some other *time* (90)
        2   **1**

The abstract *came*   *Wednesday* (240)
        2   **1**

And now, the very next *time* it doesn't *work* (83)
               1   **2**

We *had* a perfectly wild time last *night* (84)
  2   **1**

He *told* me this *noon* (89)
  2   **1**

I *took* him down a little *while* ago (89)
2   **1**

This structure of a Class 2 word with a Class 1 word as "modifier" occurs very frequently in the materials.

3. Class 2 words with Class 2 words as "modifiers"

Both the boys *came running* when C—— yelled (838)
        2   **2**

4. Class 2 words with Class 3 words as "modifiers"

(1292)   We make a long incision and *lay open* the whole muscle
                                      2   **3**

Most of the group will *remain loyal* (430)
                        2   **3**

*5. Class 2 words with a so-called "phrase" modifier—a function word
of Group F* (at, by, for, from, *etc.*) *and a Class 1 word*

The luncheon *will begin*   *at twelve-thirty* (89)
             2   **mod.**

They *worked* only *for the inside people* (911)
     2   **mod.**

We'll *have* our banquet *on Thursday night* (9114)
      2   **mod.**

Miss T—— *is coming*   *from Battle Creek* (9012)
               2   **mod.**

*6. Class 2 words with a word-group as "modifier" which consists of an
included sentence* [20]

Can you *come*   *after your meeting is over* (840)
        2   **mod.**

He *worked* here *until he was sent to Brazil* (862)
   2   **mod.**

Just *get* there *as soon as you can* (1006)
     2   **mod.**

[20] See, however, the discussion of "Sequence Sentences and Included Sentences"
in Chapter XI, and of "Immediate Constituents" in Chapter XII.

The arrangements of the various modifiers of Class 2 word heads are distinctive but more complex than those of modifiers of Class 1 words.

1. In general, the modifier of a Class 2 word appears in a position following the Class 2 word. All types of modifiers of Class 2 words can occur in the positions following the Class 2 word.

2. In general, the modifiers of Class 2 words appear in positions not only following the Class 2 word but also following any Class 1 words in the structures of the various types of "object." [21]

A typical example of this basic arrangement is the following.

We   carry   it   along   religiously   usually (175)
2   1   4   4   4
       (object)

We must not assume, however, that the various "modifiers" are all on the same level or that "objects" and "modifiers" belong to the same layer of structure.[22]

3. The various types of the Class 4 words as modifiers of Class 2 words can be classified in accord with the other positions in which they can appear. This means that although all Class 4 words, as modifiers of Class 2 words, very frequently follow the Class 2 word, some pattern like *along;* others like *religiously;* and still others like *usually.* Each of the three groups can occur in positions in which the others do not, as illustrated in the following sentences:

[21] Except, of course, the so-called "adverbial object" which is here included among the "modifiers."

[22] The statements in this chapter concerning the characteristic arrangements of modifiers must not be interpreted in any way that will deny the principle of levels or layers of structure. The purpose of this chapter is to describe simply the units that enter into these various structures and their features of arrangement, leaving to Chapter XII the significance of "immediate constituents."

Usually we carry it *along religiously*
We *usually* carry it *along religiously*

But we do not find the order of the following:

Along we carry it *religiously usually*
We *along* carry it *religiously usually*

Each of the three groups of Class 4 words as modifiers occurs in positions in which the others do not appear. By far the largest group of Class 4 words are those that pattern like *religiously* and have a similar formal contrast with Class 3 words, *religiously* (Class 4)—*religious* (Class 3). Those that pattern like *along* are of four groups:

1. Those with the same shape as the words of Group F of the function words: *in, out, down, above, below, over, under,* etc.

2. Those having the distinct contrastive form with the prefix *a, along—long,* such as *away, ahead, across, around, abroad.*

3. Those having the distinct contrastive form with the suffix *-ward,* as *homeward, seaward, forward, backward, outward, upward,* etc.

4. Those compounds ending with *-where,* such as *everywhere, somewhere, nowhere,* etc.

Those that pattern like *usually* seem to have no common distinguishing features except the fact that they occur in the same positions. The members of this group, however, are not many, and can be listed with some completeness. Some examples of this group as they appeared in our materials are *often, again, hourly, annually, twice, already, seldom.*

The fact that, in general, the word *there* can operate as a substitute for practically all of the Class 4 words in the group that patterns like *along,* that *thus* can operate as a substitute for practically all of the Class 4 words that pattern like *rapidly,* and that *then* can operate as a substitute for all words that pattern like *already*, leads to the conclusion that the meanings in most of the modification structures with Class 2 words as heads are those of "place," "manner," and "time." The separation of these meanings seems to be a matter of the lexicon, not of the structure, except perhaps for broad distinctions of position.

III. "MODIFIERS" WITH CLASS 3 WORDS AS HEAD

In the materials examined many Class 3 words appeared with modifiers. All these modifiers except the word *enough* occurred in the position immediately before the Class 3 word. It is the words that have frequently been used in this "position" before the Class 3 word and that have lost their lexical meanings which have become the function words listed in Group D of Chapter VI. They have a variety of shapes and must be learned as particular words belonging to this list. No matter what the lexical meanings of these words were earlier the meaning of this structure as "modifier" of a Class 3 word is that of some "degree" of a quality expressed in the Class 3 word.

1. Class 3 words with function words of Group D as "modifiers"

The tank is in *real good* shape (163)
    D 3

I'm *awfully glad* you have a place for me (232)
    D   3

We're *awfully short* of help right now (249)
    D   3

It isn't *very good* but it's over three hundred a month (246)
    D 3

The other house is *pretty good* but we're not enthusiastic
            D   **3**

(726)

It's *too big* for the three of them (730)
    D   **3**

They haven't *quite enough* money to handle the one on
         D   **3**

W—— (728)

He's a *rather serious* student (173)
       D   **3**

2. Class 3 words with Class 1 words as "modifiers"

It was only *house high* as it crossed the road (780)
      1   **3**

The hole must be a *foot larger* each way (164)
       1   **3**

They have a one *year old* boy in addition (410)
        1   **3**

A *paper thin* sheet of copper separates the two layers (480)
   1   **3**

It really can't be *that small* (731)
       1   **3**

When we got back all the stuff was *stone cold* (506)
           1   **3**

3. Class 3 words with Class 4 words as "modifiers"

> They're *entirely wrong* about the basis of the agreement
>   **4**   **3**
> (240)

> C—— was *decidedly worse* this afternoon (816)
>   **4**   **3**

> We want the top *nearly white* but the bottom a bronze (908)
>   **4**   **3**

> You've really done an *exceedingly good* job (917)
>   **4**   **3**

> Was it *sufficiently hot* for you (928)
>   **4**   **3**

> They guarantee them to be *strictly fresh* (139)
>   **4**   **3**

4. Class 3 words with other Class 3 words as "modifiers"

> All the windows had been *tight shut* all night (460)
>   **3**   **3**

> They're going to make the walls a *soft blue* color (480)
>   **3**   **3**

> A—— had been out in that *icy cold* shanty all after-
>   **3**   **3**
> noon (603)

In all of these instances of the structure of modification with a Class 3 word as head, the intonation pattern tied the two units together. No pause is possible between them.

pretty good

house high

strictly fresh

soft blue

icy cold shanty

5. Class 3 words with Class 2 words as "modifiers"

In the morning . . . the cottage was *freezing cold*
$\quad\quad\quad\quad\quad\quad\quad\quad\quad\quad\quad\quad$ **2** $\quad$ **3**

6. Class 3 words with word-groups as "modifiers"

There is one small patch *ready   for planting* (1026)
$\quad\quad\quad\quad\quad\quad\quad\quad\quad\quad$ **3** $\quad\quad$ **mod.**
All the other boats are *bigger   than he can manage* (96)
$\quad\quad\quad\quad\quad\quad\quad\quad\quad\quad$ **3** $\quad\quad$ **mod.**

The meaning of the modification structure with a Class 3 word as head is consistently that of "degree" despite the great diversity of the lexical meanings of the "modifiers."

IV. "MODIFIERS" WITH CLASS 4 WORDS AS HEAD

The "modifiers" with Class 4 words as head present a picture very similar to that of the "modifiers" with Class 3 words as head. The same function words that operate as modifiers of Class 3 words, those of Group D—*very, quite, pretty, rather, awfully, too,* etc.

—operate also as modifiers of Class 4 words. The meaning, in the modification structure with Class 4 words as heads is also that of some "degree." And the distinct intonation pattern duplicates that of the structures with Class 3 words as heads.

1. Class 4 words with function words of Group D as "modifiers"

We're awfully short of help *right now* (249)
                                 D   4

I know he'll be in *pretty soon* (189)
                    D   4

Go *right ahead* with the mimeographing (191)
   D   4

And it has *pretty well* saturated the soil (944)
            D   4

She would do *very well* if she just had more shorthand (190)
              D   4

I would have gone *right over* to see him (8912)
                   D   4

2. Class 4 words with Class 1 words as "modifiers"

We really shouldn't go *that far* yet (193)
                        1   4

He got to the office *somewhat late* that morning (828)
                      1   4

Three of them came in at least a *day early* (912)
                                  1   4

3. Class 4 words with other Class 4 words as "modifiers"

They had to go *away out* to the lake to get it (981)
4   4

We should have moved the other desk *farther over* toward
4   4

the window (732)

4. Class 4 words with word-groups as "modifiers"

P—— swam *faster* in his last hundred *than he did in the first*
(1328)

V. "MODIFIERS" WITH CERTAIN FUNCTION WORDS AS HEAD

The "modifiers" with function words of Group F and Group I as heads are also similar to the "modifiers" with Class 3 words as heads—and like the "modifiers" with Class 4 words as heads. The same words operate here as "modifiers" and the meaning in the modification structure is that of some "degree." The intonation pattern also duplicates that of these preceding modification structures.

1. In many ways Bob is very *much like* his brother (623)
The materials will be ready *along about* February (194)
The path was planned to go *right between* the posts (296)
Our paper had fallen *just over* the wall (1296)
That vine has grown rapidly *right up* the side of the house (314)
We used to plow it *almost to* the fence (698)

His footprints were very clear *directly beneath* the window (8119)

Mr. F—— built not *far up* the road from us (9013)

2. He even swims *just like* his brother does (623)

And then *immediately after* the play was over we went to the League (8911)

A—— came in *right when* I was in the midst of everything (682)

The point of view maintained here differs sharply from that of the conventional grammars in the matter of "modifiers." We have insisted that *a "modifier" as a "modifier" is not a part of speech. Modification is a structure* in which there are always at least two units—a "head" and a "modifier." In present-day English the "head" can be any of the four parts of speech or of the function words of Group F or Group I. *The "modifier" can also be any of the four parts of speech or of the function words of Group D.* The meanings in the structure of modification—the meaning relationships between the "modifier" and the "head"—vary widely, but the specific differences of meaning in this variety are on the whole tied to the formal make-up of the modification structure.

Most of the modification structures examined in this chapter consisted of a head and only one "modifier." The modifiers of a single head consist at times of several units, and then there arises the problem of the signals of the various layers of modification. This problem involves the principle of "immediate constituents," the topic of the discussion in Chapter XII.

XI. "Sequence" Sentences and "Included" Sentences

The definition that provided the working start for this investigation, the statement accepted as the basic description of the language unit we sought to isolate and examine, came from Bloomfield.

> It is evident that the sentences in any utterance are marked off by the mere fact that each sentence is an independent linguistic form, not included by virtue of any grammatical construction in any larger linguistic form.[1]

This statement, however, although it offered a satisfactory brief indication of the chief characteristic of the unit we wanted to examine, did not furnish the criteria necessary to determine whether any particular amount of talk was an "independent" linguistic form or whether it was included in any larger structure. As a practical procedure we used the mark of a change of speaker to isolate "utterance units." We assumed that these "utterance units" (unless they were interruptions) were "free" or "independent" linguistic units, but we did not assume that they were necessarily "single" free units or sentences. The "utterance units" marked by a change of speaker consisted of one of the following:

[1] Leonard Bloomfield, *Language, op. cit.,* p. 170.

1. A single minimum free utterance.
2. A single free utterance, expanded, not minimum.
3. A sequence of two or more free utterances.

Single free utterances are the "sentences" we have isolated and examined in the preceding chapters. The chapter on "modifiers" dealt especially with various expansions of the units that constitute a minimum free sentence. Here we are concerned especially with the sequences of two or more free utterances that make up some of the "utterance units," and the particular "utterance units" for our immediate consideration are those that begin conversations. Some of these utterance units represented a rather considerable stretch of continuous discourse on the part of one speaker. In these, all the single free utterances or sentences, after the one at the beginning, constitute our "sequence" sentences. In general, the forms of these "sequence" sentences differed from those that stood first in a "situation" utterance unit only in the fact that the "sequence" sentences contained certain signals that tied them to preceding utterances. The forms that thus tie following sentences in the same utterance unit to the sentences that precede them I have called "sequence" signals. These sequence signals consist of a variety of linguistic forms. Some are the substitutes for Class 1 words; some are from the function words called "determiners"; others are forms that have conventionally been classed among the "adverbs." The substitutes for Class 1 words will provide the illustrations for a statement of some of the general features of the situation.

I. SUBSTITUTES FOR CLASS 1 WORDS AS "SEQUENCE SIGNALS"

To be unambiguous as a "sequence" signal the form of a substitute must tie it specifically to a particular Class 1 word in the preceding sentence. It is not enough that a so-called "antecedent" be present in the sentence that precedes; the precise form of the substitute must be that which correlates with only one unit of the preceding.

(Situation sentence)	(Sequence sentence)
The *boy* has just brought the evening *paper*	*It* is at the door

The connection of the "sequence" sentence to the second part of the "situation" sentence rather than to the first is made through *it* as the form correlating with *paper*. In the following the form *he* connects the "sequence" sentence to the first part of the preceding.

(Situation sentence)	(Sequence sentence)
The *boy* has just brought the evening *paper*	*He* is at the door

In the following the form *they* connects the "sequence" sentence to both parts of the preceding. The plural form *they* correlates with *boy* and *paper* together.

(Situation sentence)	(Sequence sentence)
The *boy* has just brought the evening *paper*	*They* are at the door

In the following, however, the form *they* is the correlating form for *papers* alone and also for *boy* and *papers* together. The connection of the "sequence" sentence is, therefore, ambiguous.

(Situation sentence)	(Sequence sentence)
The *boy* has just brought the *papers*	*They* are at the door

In similar fashion, inasmuch as *they* is the correlating form for both *boys* alone and for *boys* and *paper* together, the same "sequence" sentence would also be ambiguous in the following:

(Situation sentence)   (Sequence sentence)

The *boys* have just brought the *paper*   *They* are at the door

The following examples display in simple form something of the variety of the clear as well as the ambiguous connections established between separate sentences through the use of these Class I substitutes as "sequence" signals.

(Situation sentence)	(Sequence sentence)
The *boy* has called his *mother*	*She* is waiting now
	He is waiting now
	They are waiting now
The *boys* have called their *mother*	*She* is waiting now
	They are waiting now [2] (ambiguous)
The *boys* have called their *mothers*	*They* are waiting now (ambiguous)
The *police* have just brought in a *man*, and his *wife*, and three *children*	*He* is in bad condition
	She is in bad condition
	They are in bad condition (ambiguous)
	They had no trouble with *them* (ambiguous)
	It is a disgrace [3] (ambiguous)

[2] Throughout the rest of this discussion only those instances in which the "sequence" signal makes an ambiguous connection are labeled. In all the other instances the "sequence" signal establishes a clear connection.

[3] The ambiguity here arises from the fact that the form *it* is a form that can serve as a substitute for several parts of the sentence—that they have brought in the whole family, or that the police have done it, or that they have just now done it and not earlier.

The *boy* threw a *stick* over the *fence*	*That* accounts for the barking of the dog (ambiguous) *It* made the dog bark (ambiguous) *He* made the dog bark
The *boy* threw several *sticks* over the fence	*These* made the dog bark *This* made the dog bark
The *boy* brought his *friends* inside	*He* expected some refreshments *They* expected some refreshments (ambiguous) *That* excited the dog *They* excited the dog (ambiguous) *They* played with the dog (ambiguous)

A—— M—— has introduced an ordinance which would limit fraternities or sororities to income zones
Now *that* would mean that *they* would be limited in *their* purchases to the very close in-campus region
I called Mr. S—— the ——— man today and asked him what he knew about *this*
He didn't even know *it* was happening (264)

In the three "sequence" sentences above, *that*, *this*, and *it* are ambiguous as signals; *they*, *their* and *he* make unmistakably clear connections.

The *houses* we saw this afternoon didn't impress us particularly
Each had some advantages
Both had disadvantages (266)

I talked with Mrs. —— this afternoon about putting
   in a large new seepage bed
That wouldn't be a guaranteed permanent solution but
   it's probably the best you can do (946) (*That* and *it* are
   ambiguous)

I wonder whether your wife knows anybody that knows
   anything about *houses*
They're really very difficult to find you know (255)

My *son* will be a senior medic this coming year
He's gone out to the hospital at Y—— for the summer
They thought it would be good experience for him (251)
   (*They* is ambiguous)

D—— and B—— landed in here for lunch
Well I started getting *it* for *them* right away
Before I finished *that they* called me from the bus station
   (85) (*That* and *they* are ambiguous)

I'd like to talk to you about teaching this summer
I prefer to do *it* with you personally in the office if I could
   (259) (*It* is ambiguous)

The real-estate people don't seem to be much help these
   days
There's one *man* though that has done a lot for our
   foreigners
You might call *him* and say I told you to call (254)
The pine trees are getting so big they're interfering with
   the wires
I want to raise with Mr. —— the question of putting
   them underground and how much *it* would cost (214)
   (*Them* and *it* are ambiguous)

II. THE SO–CALLED "DEFINITE ARTICLE" AND THE "DEMONSTRATIVES" AS "SEQUENCE SIGNALS"

(Situation sentence)

(Sequence sentence)

A *policeman* has just brought in a *man* a *woman* and three *children*

The policeman is making his report now

The man is over by the window

The woman is being sent to the hospital

The children are being cared for by the matron

Sunday we're going out in our boat for a picnic and we'd like to have you go with us

That is *the* boat that is over near M—— C—— (9108)

I heard that you stopped over one day last week to see me

That day I was in Detroit to see the Immigration people (882)

An IBM machine like the one we saw yesterday has a standard keyboard and can be operated by any experienced typist

This machine would make it possible to prepare copy in our office (1046)

The quoted price of the books we need is sixty-five dollars

That amount is just about what we figured (898)

Our moving took all afternoon and most of the night

The next day we slept till noon (450)

They stayed inside all day Sunday and didn't even go swimming

The day before they got badly sunburned

III. FREE COMBINATIONS WITH *ELSE* AND *OTHER* AS "SEQUENCE SIGNALS"

The free combinations with *else* and those with *other* serve primarily as "sequence signals"—as connectives between sentences. The common free combinations with *else* are *anyone else, someone else, everyone else, anybody else, somebody else, anything else, something else, everything else, nothing else, no one else, nobody else, everybody else, anywhere else, somewhere else, everywhere else, any place else, some place else, every place else*. The common free combinations with *other* are *any other* (one) (person) (place) (time), *some other* (one) (person) (place) (time), *every other* (one) (person) (place) (time).

(Situation sentence)	(Sequence sentence)
I am trying to find out about the possibility of sending some funeral flowers today	*Any other time* I would know who to call (1026)
R—— says the committee is going to consider only budget matters today	*Everything else* must wait (1480)
Mr. K—— wants to know whether Dr. —— can come to a meeting of the L—— committee on Wednesday	*Everybody else* can come at that time (1086)
There are several difficulties with having the farewell dinner in E—— Q——	*Somewhere else* might be better all around (840)
Mr. W—— asked us to meet in his office tomorrow at nine	I think *some other place* would be better especially at *that* hour (733)
After this summer I'm going to cut down on the number of things I try to do	*Someone else* will have to take over the running of the L—— I—— (1401)

IV. SOME SO–CALLED "ADVERBS" AS "SEQUENCE SIGNALS"

There are a number of words, which usually appear in lists of "adverbs," that operate primarily as "sequence signals." Their structural use as "sequence signals" is not that of the usual modifier with a Class 2 word as head. The difference appears in the following sentence:

Later the men went away *early*

Here *early* operates as a regular modifier. The word *later*, however, serves as a connective to an utterance that must have preceded the one given. The contrast in the form *later* can have meaning only with reference to a practice of these men at some former period—the content of a preceding sentence. This form *later* does not appear at the beginning of a sentence that begins a conversation. It appears only in a "sequence" sentence. The same shape, *later*, could of course appear both as a modifier and as a sequence signal.

Later the men went away *later*

It is the sequence signal that stands at the beginning of such a sentence, not the modifier. If only one *later* occurs, and that at the beginning, it is a sequence signal.

Later the men went away

If only one *later* occurs, and that at the end of the sentence, it can be either a modifier or a sequence signal. The intonation pattern can be used to distinguish the one from the other.

The men went away la|ter   (modifier)

The men went a|way la|ter   (sequence signal)

The modifier and the sequence signal can both appear at the end of the sentence. Then the first *later* is a modifier and the second the sequence signal.

The men went away *later later*

In similar fashion the sequence signals can be distinguished from the modifiers in the following sentences:

The men went away earlier *later*
The men went away later *earlier*
Earlier the men went away later
Afterwards the men went away early
Heretofore the men had gone away late

The contrastive position is a marker of these sequence signals, but only a limited list of forms operate in these positions, and, so far as I see now, they must be learned as distinct items of a list just as all the function words are learned. They are distinguished from one another lexically, but structurally in these distinct positions they are the "same"—they serve as sequence signals connecting a following sentence to one that precedes.

The items from our materials that operate in this way as sequence signals are the following: *then, afterwards, hereafter, thereafter, henceforth, hitherto, heretofore, meantime, meanwhile, later, earlier.* The words *before* and *since* serve as sequence signals primarily when they appear at the end of a sentence. At the beginning of sentences these words *before* and *since* as sequence signals do sometimes occur, but then they have special stress, with a 3–2–3 intonation, and are followed by a pause.

I'm afraid you don't remember me I've been in the ———
office for six months *Before* ‖ I was with the Red
Cross (61)

Up to 1945 L—— was with the ———
Since ‖ he has worked with us (1030)

I think I talked to you yesterday about an IBM machine
Afterwards ‖ I looked up a catalog (879)

The checks will be delayed again this month
Hereafter ‖ you should try to get the letter in by the
twentieth (874)

Two other words usually called "adverbs" operate primarily as
sequence signals. They are *there* and *elsewhere*.

In the time schedule my class in ——— is listed as two
hours
Elsewhere it has three hours (1030)

V. SOME SO–CALLED "CONJUNC-
TIONS" AS "SEQUENCE SIGNALS"

There are a number of words that often appear in lists of "conjunctions" and called "co-ordinating" conjunctions; they operate
chiefly as "sequence signals." These words include *however, yet,
nevertheless*,[4] *also, moreover, besides, likewise, otherwise, therefore, thus,
consequently, accordingly, furthermore, similarly*.

[4] There seems to be considerable confusion in the labels attached to the words of
this list. In the *American College Dictionary*, for example, *yet* in the sense of "nevertheless"
is labelled "conjunction," but the word *nevertheless* in the sense of "however" is called
"*adv.*" On the other hand, *however* in the sense of "nevertheless" and "yet" is labelled
"*conj.*" *And* in the sense of "moreover, also, besides," is labelled "*conj.*"; but *besides* and
also and *moreover* are all called "*adv.*" *Therefore, thus, consequently, accordingly, also, moreover, besides, likewise, otherwise, furthermore* are all labelled "*adv.*"

Our rented typewriters are in pretty bad shape
Besides we need at least one with a longer carriage (1085)

They'll bring the abstract in tomorrow
The deed *however* won't be ready until Thursday (240)

With this big group we should have a piano in the dining
room
Therefore I'd like you to look into what's available both
from the ——— and for rent downtown (73)

An objection may be raised that these formal devices that have
here been called "sequence signals" connecting separate sentences
are really the marks of a "compound sentence"—part of the structural devices by which units having the formal characteristics of
a sentence are included in larger sentence units. Although the
illustrations given above consist only of a single following sentence
containing a sequence signal to connect it with the one preceding,
such signals are not confined to pairs of sentence units. All sentence
units that follow the one that begins a conversation practically always contain some type of sequence signal. Not only do all the
"sequence sentences" within the continuous speech of one person
contain these sequence signals, but the "response utterances" of a
second speaker continuing the conversation also have them.

X———: This is ——— ———
Do you have a return on *my* request for a reserva-
tion to New York and back
That was for the twenty-seventh leaving the
twenty-seventh and returning the first

Y———: Let's see, *that* was for the Wolverine wasn't it

X——: No *something else* going down

It was the Wolverine coming back

Besides I think you said there was no chance on the Wolverine for that day

Y——: *That*'s right *it* was number seventeen at three forty-two

It's here all right roomette E

Let's see *though* there's a note attached here

Oh *it*'s just the request for the one coming back

That hasn't come in yet

You might call again *later* (260, 261)

"Sequence" sentences in general have the same formal characteristics as those that begin conversations except for the items that have here been called "sequence signals." These items are formal structural matters—correlating substitutes, certain determiners like *the*, *this*, *that*, free combinations with *else* and *other*, and "function words" of a special group. Structurally these items signal the fact that the sentence unit in which they appear is a "sequence" sentence, connected with a sentence unit that precedes.[5] These sequence signals all look back to a preceding sentence; they are retrospective. The various practical connections between sequence sentences and those that precede them are matters of the lexical content of the items that serve as sequence signals; the structural meaning is the particular direction of the connection.

In addition to these devices that signal a connection between free sentence units there are in English the function words (Group J) and formal word-order arrangements by which word-groups having the formal characteristics of free sentence units are

---

[5] The so-called "compound" sentence seems to be primarily a matter of the punctuation of written materials. In the mechanically recorded materials of speech examined here only a very few instances occurred with a clear 3–2–3 intonation before one of these sequence signals. These were only with the words *and* and *but*.

included in larger sentence units. These are the signals of "included" sentences. In other words, in some sentences there are devices that signal the inclusion of two or more separate sentences within the structural pattern of a single free sentence unit. These signals of inclusion consist primarily of the following function words, standing before the included sentence unit: *after, although, as, because, before, in order that, if, since, when, where, while, that, what, who, how, why, which, whenever, wherever, whatever, whoever, whichever, whether.*

Perhaps the most significant difference between these function words as signals of "inclusion" and the forms given above as signals of sequence lies in the fact that these function words of inclusion at the beginning of a sentence look forward to a coming sentence unit, while the signals of sequence look backward to the preceding sentence unit.

> *While* I was over at the Administration Building I checked the payroll with Mrs. —— (8910)
> *If* it would be of any use we'll arrange to have your Dr. —— talk to you by telephone (8913)
> *When* K—— was at the dinner last week we talked a good deal about the house business (9015)
> *Before* the regular students arrived the L—— cafeteria was a very comfortable place to lunch (9015)
> *Since* they came it is horribly crowded and not at all relaxing (9015)

Whenever words of this group appear at the beginning of an utterance with the form-classes and arrangement of a statement, these words, acting as function words, signal the structural fact that the unit they introduce is to be included, with the one immediately following, in a larger single sentence unit. Inasmuch as they are prospective when they thus stand at the beginning of an utterance, they frequently occur in "situation" sentences—the sentence units that begin conversations.

These same function words also signal the inclusion of the structure following them, together with the unit preceding, in a larger unit. In these situations the intonation pattern at the end of the preceding unit is the 3–2–3 curve that signals continuation.

> I understand you were out here yesterday afternoon *after* you cleared up the luncheon (941)
>
> Mr. P—— advised us to change the whole layout *whenever* we could afford it (942)
>
> The boys we've had out there couldn't do anything satisfactory with the lines *because* they're all clogged with roots (1002)

When sentence units are included in larger units they can fulfill a variety of structural functions. In the structure of the larger sentence unit in which they are included, they often operate as a single unit substitutible for one of the single parts of speech. For example, in the preceding chapter we have already seen word-groups of this kind as one of the units in some of the structures of modification.

1. An included sentence can thus be a modifier with a Class 1 word as head.

> The boys have been working on the *tile that was plugged* (942)
>
> Some of the *guests who are coming to the picnic* are . . . (113)
>
> The *place where he lived* was near a swamp (819)

2. An included sentence can be a modifier of a Class 2 word.

> The desire of the committee for the appointment of R—— *was expressed as vigorously as we could* (224)
>
> We *worked until the watchman came in at midnight* (1210)

3. An included sentence can be a modifier of a Class 3 word or of a Class 4 word.

> All the other boats are *bigger than he can manage* (96)
> P—— swam *faster* in his *last hundred than he did in the first* (1328)

4. Included sentences can also appear in the structure of "subject" or in that of "object."

> *Whatever you decide to do about the place of the dinner* will be all right with us (190)
> In the layout of the bed I think *that you should stay away from the willow tree* (942)
> The best suggestion so far was *that we should get a quonset hut* (1190)
> *How J—— got elected to that job* none of us ever found out (908)
> I wanted to know *whether there would be an assistant in my —— this semester* (541)

Determining the precise layer of structure of which an included sentence is a unit is part of a large problem. Here we have simply indicated that such an inclusion can serve as a modifier of a Class 1 word, without touching the question of the structural relation of this kind of modifier to the other modifiers of this part of speech. We have simply said that an included sentence could serve as a modifier of a Class 2 word, without questioning the structural effect of the position of such a modifier. These matters, as well as the structural bearing of certain included sentences at the beginnings of utterances, constitute part of the problems of "Immediate Constituents."

XII. Immediate Constituents: "Layers" of Structure

Speech acts that are language always consist of lexical items in some kind of structure. The view that children begin to "talk" with words only, not in structure (the so-called "naming" things stage), and that they later put these words into structures, rests upon an inadequate understanding of the features of structure. For the baby, the process that results in "talking" begins just as soon as he learns (not consciously of course) *that vocal noises make things happen.* "Talking," as distinct from babbling, and as distinct from the mere imitative production of such sound sequences as *da-da, ma-ma, ba-by,* aims to produce results—to elicit the co-operative responses of others. *The predictable responses to language that constitute social co-operation come not from lexical items alone, words as words, but from structural frames with words as content.* It is not the lexical item *come*—the word alone—that will elicit from your friend the response of a motion of approach. It is the form *come* as contrasted with the forms *came* and *comes;* it is this form, *come,* with a 2–4 intonation as contrasted with a 3–2 intonation; it is this form *come* as belonging to a distinct functioning class, and as fitting the pattern of one type of English utterance—it is these structural features in which the lexical item *come* is placed that elicit the action response. Any other lexical item of the same class given these same structural features would also elicit an action response.

Throughout this book we have been concerned with the structural features of English—those formal features that operate as the signals of structural meanings. We have found that these formal matters are significant only as they are contrastive items in a structural pattern. We have been concerned, then, with describing the structural patterns of English in terms of the units of which they are composed and of the contrastive features, of the form and the arrangement of these units, which constitute the pattern itself. The units which make up the structural patterns, the constituents of these patterns, have not been words as lexical items, words as meaning units, but words as parts of speech. The basic units of each structure have been either parts of speech (form-classes) alone, or parts of speech and function words. The significant contrastive features of the structural patterns have been matters of (1) the selection of the part of speech units, (2) the forms of these items, (3) the arrangements of position, and (4) the intonation or sequences of pitch.

We come now to the task of seeing these various structural patterns not simply as separate parts within the practical utterances of conversation but rather as operating together to form the complete utterances. It is not enough to list all the units of all the structural patterns that occur in an utterance and to describe their contrastive features. If one is to arrive at the complete structural meaning of any utterance he must in some way determine how the separate constituents are to be grouped.

In many other matters a similar problem confronts us. In simple mathematics the grouping of the items makes considerable difference. What, for example, is the answer to the following mathematical problem given orally?

"Five plus four times six minus three." Here there are four numbers as constituents—5, 4, 6, and 3—and three operations—addition, multiplication, subtraction. The answer will vary with each different grouping of the constituent items; that is, there will be a different answer whenever the "immediate constituents" of each operation differ. To this particular mathematical problem there may be four different answers:

$$(5 + 4)(6 - 3) = 27$$
$$5 + 4(6 - 3) = 17$$
$$5 + (4 \times 6) - 3 = 26$$
$$[(5 + 4) \times 6] - 3 = 51$$

Even in a simple mathematical problem with only four constituents there must be a clear understanding of the structural grouping of the items—an agreement as to the *immediate constituents of each operation*—before there can be agreement concerning the correct answer. In the written statements of such problems the structural groupings are usually indicated by parentheses. In oral statements of these problems the structural groupings are usually shown by intonation and pause.

It is not only in the statement of mathematical problems that a grasp of the structural grouping of the items is necessary to a clear understanding. Descriptions of processes—the recipe for a cake, for example—must indicate not simply the constituents, the ingredients, and the operations, but also the "layers" of the operations, the "immediate" constituents of each operation.

Many books explaining games like football or baseball are of no use to those who do not already know how to play the game, because the authors have ignored the principle of "immediate" constituents. The following portion of a description of the game of baseball, a description designed for those who know nothing about the game, will serve as an illustration.

Baseball is played with a bat and a ball on a level field at one end of which is a square, or "diamond," 90 feet on a side. One point of this square is home plate and the sides of the playing field extend at least 250 feet from the point of the square which is "home plate." The other three points of the 90-foot square are the three bases — first, second, and third in counterclockwise order. There are nine players on each team. One team is in the "field" while the other team is "at bat."

The bat is made of wood not more than 42 inches long (usually not more than 36 inches) and not over $2\frac{3}{4}$ inches in diameter at the thickest part. The "home plate" is five-sided, 17 inches wide across the front, and $6\frac{1}{2}$ inches long on each of the two sides adjacent to the 17-inch front edge. From these two $6\frac{1}{2}$-inch sides two twelve inch sides meet in a point at the back of the center of the plate. Each of the three bases is 15 inches square.

The "catcher" stands behind "home plate." The "pitcher" stands at a spot on a direct line from home plate to second base. In addition to these two players there are a "first baseman," a "second baseman," and a "third baseman," who stand near their respective "bases." A "shortstop" covers the area between second and third base. The "right fielder" covers the area beyond first base, the "center fielder" the area beyond second base, the "left fielder" the area beyond third base. The nine members of the opposing team are the "batters" who take regular turns in batting. Each batter when he is "at bat" stands in a marked space on either side of the home plate.

The game begins when the pitcher throws the ball toward the home plate. The batter may or may not attempt to hit the ball with his bat. If he does not attempt to hit it and it passes over the plate at a height between his knees and his shoulders it is a "strike." If it passes outside the boundaries of the plate or below the knees or above the shoulders of the batter it is a "ball." If the batter attempts to hit the ball with his bat and misses it completely it is also a "strike." If the batter hits the ball and it drops to the ground outside the right or left boundaries of the playing field it is a "foul" but counts as a "strike" if the batter has not already had two "strikes" against him. If the batter has three strikes against him he is "out" and another batter takes his place "at bat." If the batter has four "balls" he proceeds to first base.

If the batter hits the ball and it is caught by a player of the opposing team before it touches the ground the batter is "out." If, however, the ball falls to the ground inside the playing field, then the batter must run to first base. If he reaches first base before the ball is thrown to the first baseman and before the first baseman having the ball in his possession touches the base with his foot, the "runner" is "safe." If the first baseman, having the ball in his possession, touches the base before the "runner" does, the "runner" is "out." If the "runner" over-runs first base after touching it with his foot he may return "safely" to the base if he turns to the right at the end of his running. If, however, he turns to the left and the first baseman tags him with the ball before he returns to the base he is "out." If he reaches first base "safely" and no "error" has been committed by the members of the opposing team he is credited with a "hit," a "single."

This description then goes on, giving the details of a "two-base hit," a "three-base hit," a "home run," a "sacrifice hit," an "infield fly," a "bunt," and a "stolen base." The author ends with a detailed statement of scoring and the number of "innings" that constitute a "game."

Readers to whom we have submitted this description, readers who had never played baseball and who did not understand the game, have never been able to proceed beyond the fourth or fifth paragraph of this material without being completely confused. The difficulty with this description is not that it has too much detail, as one might suspect at first, nor that it does not proceed in an orderly fashion. The author of this description has tried to pursue a time sequence in the playing of the game, with explanations of each of the details as they are met in that sequence. The details are all constituents of the various patterns that make the game of baseball, but *there is no effort to grasp the structural relationship of these patterns in the whole system.* The author has not sought, he certainly has not displayed, the immediate constituents for each level of structure. An understanding of the game depends upon, consists of, really, *a grasp of the immediate constituents of each layer of structure.*

The beginning of a description which is based upon a clear grasp of such immediate constituents is the following:

> Baseball is a contest between two teams of nine players each, the winning of which is decided by the number of "runs" each team has made by the end of a legal game. A legal game of baseball usually consists of nine co-ordinate "innings" or nine turns "at bat" of each team. The team that is having one of its turns at bat is on the offensive; it is seeking to make "runs." Runs are made as follows . . .
>
> The team that is not "at bat" is "in the field." When it is in the field it is on the defensive; it is seeking to prevent the other team from making runs. Runs are prevented by making "outs" because when the defensive team in the field makes three outs the turn at bat of the other team ends. Outs are made as follows . . .

This description attempts to keep the matters of each structural area of baseball together and distinctly separate from those of another structural area. "Runs," for example, belong to the "offensive" structures of the game, "outs" belong to the "defensive" structures. To attempt to describe "runs" and "outs" together so mixes the layers of structure that a reader, new to the game of baseball, never grasps this fundamental division and relation, throughout the various activities of the contest.

The significance of the principle of immediate constituents for understanding and for all levels of language use cannot be over-emphasized. Most of the failures of communication seem to be tied up, in one way or another, with the problems of immediate constituents. In the matter of grasping the whole arrangement of the structural patterns in each of our sentences as complete units, it is essential that we keep each layer of structure separate and that we grasp the immediate constituents of each layer. Just as the naïve native speakers of a language are practically always entirely unconscious of using any special devices to signal structural meanings in general, so more sophisticated speakers often refuse to believe that formal devices signal structural groupings. In accord with the principles we have adopted for this study, we must assume that in each language some formal features attach to the various groupings of structural constituents, features that the speakers of the language learn to respond to and to produce.[1] We must assume, however, that each language will have its own system of structural grouping, just as it has its own set of signals for structural meanings generally. If the history of English is typical, then we must assume also that the signals of structural grouping for any particular language may change over a period of years.

The task then of discovering the means used by any language to signal its structural groupings will differ with each language. Resources available in the study of one language will be lacking in others. The investigator will use all the resources in order to arrive at and test his conclusions concerning the descriptive facts. In English, the historical records of the language at earlier periods

---

[1] The problems of "immediate constituents" have justly received increasing attention in recent years. Leonard Bloomfield touches the matter in several parts of his book *Language*. See pp. 158–69, 184–97, 227–46. See also Kenneth L. Pike, "Taxemes and Immediate Constituents," *Language*, 19 (1943), 65–82; Roulon S. Wells, "Immediate Constituents," *Language*, 23 (1947), 81–117; and Eugene A. Nida, "The Analysis of Immediate Constituents," *Language*, 24 (1948), 168–77. In this connection see also Zellig S. Harris, "From Morpheme to Utterance," *Language*, 22 (1946), 161–83.

permit a comparison and contrast that will often point to significant structural features of the living language of today.[2]

For example, the Modern English rendering of the Old English *an lytel sæs earm* must be rearranged to signal the structural grouping indicated in the Old English sentence. It cannot remain in the order *a little sea's arm* but must be changed to *a little arm of the sea*. The Old English *ealle þara nytena frumcennedan* must be rendered in the rearranged form *all first born [offspring] of the animals*.

See also the examples given earlier, pages 58, 59.

Even such a brief comparison of Old English structures of modification with their Modern English equivalents suggests tentative conclusions concerning the use of word order as a signal of the direction of modification and the differing positions of single words and of word groups like *of the monastery, of the sea,* and *of the animals*.

In general, the basic procedure of arriving at and testing significant features of structural grouping has been that of systematic substitution with enough control of meaning to decide whether any two arrangements were the "same" or "different"—i.e., whether the "response" of the native speaker was the "same" or "different."

Over and over again in the discussions of this book we have pointed out that, in present-day English, the word-order arrangements of the various form-classes furnished many of the significant contrasts which constitute our structural signals. It is the contrastive arrangement of Class 1 and Class 2 words for example that form the basic signals of the kind of utterance—a question, a request, or a report. These word-order contrasts are not matters of an absolute order of words as words, but an order of selected form-classes or parts of speech. In order then to grasp a word-

[2] This use of historical material is not a mixing of the synchronic and diachronic points of view. The picture of the present-day language is not distorted by any historical considerations. It is simply using the tool of contrast with earlier forms to bring to one's attention differences that must then be tested by substitution techniques to determine their significance.

order arrangement, we have found that it is first necessary to recognize the various form-classes.[3] The first step then must be the identification of these form-classes.

Some words—a few—must be learned as separate items that in themselves signal certain structural meanings. These "function words" must be recognized and identified with their particular structural signal. We must know that in English such a function word as *at* or *in* with a Class 1 word following will constitute a word group, and that on one layer the group as a whole forms a single constituent.

In English a layer of structure has usually only two members. Each of these members may of course be composed of several units, but on any single layer the immediate constituents of the structure of that layer are usually only two. On the level of a whole utterance such as the following the immediate constituents are those indicated by the lines.

The recommending committee | approved his promotion

On the level of the following structures the immediate constituents are again those indicated by the lines.

the other things | of the monastery

a little arm | of the sea

approved | his promotion

In some structures the precise division to separate the two immediate constitutents may seem doubtful. For many such instances the intonation furnishes the necessary marks.

the king of England's empire

[3] It is, perhaps, unnecessary to insist again that this "recognition" of the form-classes does not mean a conscious identification, nor does it imply any naming of them. "Recognition" here means simply that one has learned to respond in the same way to all the items of a single form-class in the structural patterns.

The intonation pattern, in such an expression, would determine whether the two constituents are those marked in (1) or those in (2).

1. the king| |of England's empire
   ‾‾‾‾‾‾‾‾‾

2. the king of England's| |empire
   ‾‾‾‾‾‾‾‾‾‾‾‾‾‾‾‾‾‾‾‾

The precise division in the following structures is shown not by word order but by the correlation of certain word forms.

an examination of the students| |which is thorough
‾‾‾‾‾‾‾‾‾‾‾‾‾‾‾‾‾‾‾‾‾‾‾‾‾

an examination| |of the students who are here now
‾‾‾‾‾‾‾‾‾‾‾‾

the uniforms of the regiment| |which are there
‾‾‾‾‾‾‾‾‾‾‾‾‾‾‾‾‾‾‾‾‾

the uniforms| |of the regiment which is there
‾‾‾‾‾‾‾‾‾

In the following examples, however, the forms of the words in the last group could correlate with either of the Class 1 words preceding, and therefore the structural grouping is ambiguous. With no other clues we cannot decide just what the immediate constituents of the structures are.

the requirements of the courses which are listed
the dependents of the men who are members
the equipment of the class which is there

In English the arrangement of the modifiers of Class 1 words makes possible a mechanical marking of the various layers of structural grouping once the details of the function words, of the correlations of forms, and of the special intonation sequences have been noted. The direction of the modification is forward toward the Class 1 word for those units that precede, and backward toward the Class 1 word for those units that follow. In each case, the modification is cumulative, with the outer layer being the last of the modifiers following the Class 1 word.

an | oral | examination | of the students | which is thorough

The shifting of the position of modifiers thus produces a different alignment of the immediate constituents and thus a different structural grouping with a different structural meaning.

a good book | to read

a book | good to read

a heavy box | to lift

a box | too heavy | to lift

In English the arrangement of the modifiers of Class 2 words also makes possible a mechanical arrangement of the various layers of structural grouping, after the details of the function words, of the correlation of forms, and of the special intonation sequences have been noted. Again the modification is directional and cumulative. The outside layer here is the first of those that precede the Class 2 word.

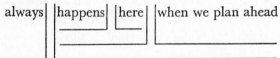
always | happens | here | when we plan ahead

The result of this approach has been a series of steps for the analysis of present-day English sentences that seem to reveal the immediate constituents of each structure in its proper structural layer and thus the relation of structure to structure. These procedural steps use formal contrasts for all matters except those particular items in which, in the structural descriptions above, we have had to resort to lists—function words, for example. It is assumed that the utterances to be examined are those that have occurred in actual conversation.

1. The first step is an identification of the parts of speech and the function words.[4] This operation includes the noting of the inflectional forms and other similar formal features of the form-classes.

2. The second step is the marking of the special ties that are signalled by a concordance of forms or by particular intonation contrasts.[5]

3. The third step is the identifying of the particular arrangement of the Class 1 and Class 2 words that signal the kind of sentence.

4. The fourth step is the identifying of the particular arrangement of the Class 1 words (not in word-groups with function words) before and after the Class 2 word.

5. The fifth step is the cutting off of any "sequence" signals that stand either at the beginning or at the end of the sentence. The relation of these sequence signals is to the sentence as a whole, not to any particular part.

6. The sixth step is the cutting off of an included sentence that stands at the beginning of the utterance in which it is included. An included sentence in this position is related to the whole of the unit that follows.

7. The seventh step is the cutting between the Class 1 word and the Class 2 word that form the basic arrangement of the sentence.

8. The eighth step is the cuttings separating the various modifiers of the Class 1 word that is "subject." These cuttings can proceed mechanically in accord with the use of word order in

[4] As indicated in the Introduction, this study attempts to center attention upon the structural features of English sentences other than intonation. Intonation is not ignored. All utterances must occur with some intonation. Here we have explored the contrasting patterns of structure that occur with similar intonation features. Only those contrasting intonation patterns have been noted that differentiate the structural meanings of similar arrangements of forms.

[5] These are the particular intonation contrasts that have been indicated in the descriptions of the various structures above.

present-day English. With multiple modifiers the modification is cumulative and directional. Postmodifiers are cut off first, beginning with the last one. Word groups as modifiers are treated on this level as whole units in relation to the head to which they are attached. The analysis of the arrangement within the group is of a different structural layer.

9. The ninth step is the cuttings separating the various modifiers of the Class 2 word. These cuttings can also proceed mechanically in accord with the use of word order in present-day English. With multiple modifiers the modification here too is cumulative and directional. Premodifiers are cut off first. Postmodifiers are cut off next, beginning with the last. On this level, word-group modifiers are treated as whole units.

10. The tenth step is the cuttings, following a similar procedure, within the word groups that have been treated as whole units on the level above.

For this type of analysis it is not necessary to know the lexical meanings of the words nor to know what the sentence is about. One must, however, in determining the structure of Class 1 words, either know whether the referent is the "same" or "different," or have another special list of Class 2 words. The following sentences will serve to illustrate the procedure here outlined:

1. The identification of the parts of speech and function words and marking of any special intonation patterns

D	3	3	1ᵃ	f	D	1ᵇ	4	2	D	3	1ᶜ	f	D	1ᵈ	f	2	f	1ᵉ
				−	F		−		−			−	F	+	J	+	F	−
			it			it					it		he	he				it

In these symbols the numbers **1, 2, 3, 4** represent the four parts of speech; **D** is any "determiner"; **f** represents a function word, and the capital letter under the **f,** the particular group to which the function word belongs (see Chapter VI). The letter exponents are the same as those used in Chapter IX, as are the other symbols under the Class 1 words. The type of function word in each case here indicates the items that belong to the group it introduces.

2. The marking of the special ties that are signalled by a concordance of forms and the groups that are tied by special function words

$$D\ \ 3\ \ 3\ \ \frac{1^a}{\text{it}}\ \left(\frac{f}{F}\ \ D\ \ \frac{1^b}{\text{it}}\right)\ 4\ \ \frac{2}{}\ \ D\ \ 3\ \ \frac{1^c}{\text{it}}\ \left(\frac{f}{F}\ \ D\ \ \frac{1^d}{+\,\text{he}}\right)\left(\frac{f}{\text{he}}\ \ \frac{2}{J}\ +\ \left(\frac{f}{F}\ \ \frac{1^e}{\text{it}}\right)\right)$$

The Class 4 word is not tied to **1ᵇ** as a modifier by means of the special intonation that would be necessary. If such a special intonation feature were present it would have to be marked in the preceding step.

3. The identifying of the particular arrangement of the Class 1 and the Class 2 words that signal the kind of sentence

$$D\ \ 3\ \ 3\ \ \frac{1^a}{\text{it}}\ \left(\frac{f}{F}\ \ D\ \ \frac{1^b}{\text{it}}\right)\ 4\ \ 2\ \ D\ \ 3\ \ \frac{1^c}{\text{it}}\ \left(\frac{f}{F}\ \ D\ \ \frac{1^d}{+\,\text{he}}\right)\left(\frac{f}{\text{he}}\ \ \frac{2}{J}\ +\ \left(\frac{f}{F}\ \ \frac{1^e}{\text{it}}\right)\right)$$

Here the arrangement is 1 ⟷ 2 tied—a statement sentence.

4. The identifying of the particular arrangement of the Class 1 words not in word-groups with function words, before and after the Class 2 word

Here **1ᵃ** is "subject"; **1ᶜ** is "direct object."

5 and 6. Cutting off of "sequence" signals and included sentences

In this sentence there are no "sequence" signals at the beginning and end to be cut off, nor is there an included sentence at the beginning to be cut off.

7. The cut between the Class 1 word, with its premodifiers and its postmodifiers as one unit, and the Class 2 word, with its modifiers as the second of the units

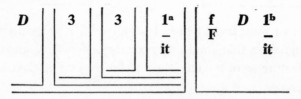

8. The cuttings separating the various modifiers of the "subject" Class 1 word

$$
\mathbf{D} \quad \mathbf{3} \quad \mathbf{3} \quad \begin{matrix}\mathbf{1^a}\\-\\\text{it}\end{matrix} \qquad \begin{matrix}\mathbf{f}\\\mathbf{F}\end{matrix} \quad \mathbf{D} \quad \begin{matrix}\mathbf{1^b}\\-\\\text{it}\end{matrix}
$$

9. The cuttings separating the various modifiers of the Class 2 word

$$
\mathbf{4} \quad \begin{matrix}\mathbf{2}\\-\end{matrix} \quad \mathbf{D}\ \mathbf{3}\ \begin{matrix}\mathbf{1^c}\\-\\\text{it}\end{matrix} \left(\begin{matrix}\mathbf{f}\\\mathbf{F}\end{matrix}\ \mathbf{D}\ \begin{matrix}\mathbf{1^d}\\+\\\text{he}\end{matrix}\right) \left(\begin{matrix}\mathbf{f}\\\mathbf{J}\\\text{he}\end{matrix} + \left(\begin{matrix}\mathbf{f}\\\mathbf{F.}\end{matrix}\ \begin{matrix}\mathbf{1^e}\\-\\\text{it}\end{matrix}\right)\right)
$$

10. The cuttings within the word-groups that have been treated as whole units

$$
\begin{matrix}\mathbf{f}\\\mathbf{F}\end{matrix} \qquad \mathbf{D}\ \begin{matrix}\mathbf{1^b}\\-\\\text{it}\end{matrix}
$$

$$
\mathbf{D} \qquad \mathbf{3} \qquad \begin{matrix}\mathbf{1^c}\\-\\\text{it}\end{matrix} \qquad \left(\begin{matrix}\mathbf{f}\\\mathbf{F}\end{matrix}\ \mathbf{D}\ \begin{matrix}\mathbf{1^d}\\+\\\text{he}\end{matrix}\right)\ \left(\begin{matrix}\mathbf{f}\\\mathbf{J}\\\text{he}\end{matrix} + \left(\begin{matrix}\mathbf{f}\\\mathbf{F}\end{matrix}\ \begin{matrix}\mathbf{1^e}\\-\\\text{it}\end{matrix}\right)\right)
$$

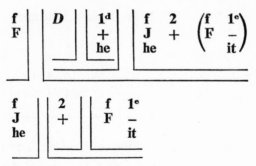

The particular sentence that was here analyzed in accord with the procedure of these ten steps was the following. Many words could have appeared in each of the "positions" of this sentence, and the structural meanings would have been the same.

>This particular social event of the season usually claims
>the full attention of the students who stay in town

The steps in the procedure are valid in so far as they represent the actual layers in the structural grouping within our utterances. The main features of that structural grouping show themselves as follows:

1. On the top layer the immediate constituents consist of (a) the modifiers of the sentence as a whole and (b) the body of the sentence.

| When K—— was at the dinner last night | we talked a good deal about the house business (9015) |

| Before the regular students arrived | the L—— cafeteria was a very comfortable place to lunch (9015) |

2. On the next layer the immediate constituents consist of (a) the Class 1 word with its modifiers and (b) the Class 2 word with

its modifiers, the units that form the basic arrangement of the sentence.

The salary checks for the staff of the Institute	came from the payroll office this morning

3. On the next layer are the modifiers of the Class 1 word and the modifiers of the Class 2 word. But these modifiers do not operate in a direct word by word relation to the head. In general the immediate constituents of a structure are only two in number. Sometimes there are several co-ordinate members of one of the constituents, but this situation is always specially signalled.

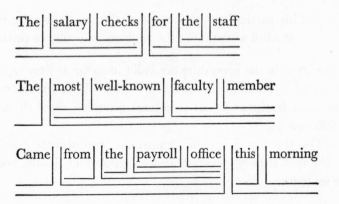

In all of these various layers of structure the determination of the direction of the modification, the grasp of the precise units that form the immediate constituents of each structure, come as an automatic response to those who know the language. These groupings are not vague, but precise and sharp. The seeming vagueness arises when we try to describe them and indicate the features that as native speakers we use to mark them. When the necessary distinguishing marks are absent ambiguity results.

Sometimes the force of the formal arrangement produces groupings that are lexically incompatible or logically humorous:

The house consists of six rooms and a bath which they own

The signals of these groupings are therefore not the meanings themselves. On the contrary it is the features of correlation of forms and of order that convey the meanings.

XIII. Practical Applications

In its method, this introduction to the structure of English utterances turns away from the usual procedures of analysis that the schools have taught for more than a hundred and fifty years, and to which they still devote a tremendous amount of time.[1] It very definitely attempts to challenge the validity of those procedures. And this challenge applies not only to matters of detail in the conventional approach, but to the very basis upon which the whole structure of the conventional approach depends. A vigorous discussion of the use and value of "grammar" has extended over the last half century. In the schools, ever since the end of the eighteenth century when "English" first became a subject of study, "grammar" has consisted of two different sets of activities. Both, however, have had the same general aim, the ancient one expressed by Julius Caesar Scaliger and quoted from him in many of the older textbooks: *"Grammatici unus finis est recte loqui."* [2]

[1] After visiting, in the capacity of special investigator for the United States Bureau of Education, a great many classrooms from Virginia to the State of Washington, and from Los Angeles to Rhode Island, and later, for the Regents of the State of New York, some fifty representative towns in that state, Dr. Dora S. Smith reached the conclusion that "more time is being spent in high school English classes of America today upon grammar and usage than upon any other single phase of instruction." See "English Grammar Again," *English Journal*, 27 (1938), 647.

[2] "The one end of grammar is to speak correctly."

See also the "definitions" of grammar collected by Rollo La Verne Lyman, in *English Grammar in American Schools before 1850* (Department of the Interior, Bureau of Education, Bulletin No. 12 [1922], p. 105).

One set of activities attempted to develop "correct speaking and writing" by the direct approach of rules to be memorized, and examples to be corrected in accord with the rules. This set of activities, although often still called "grammar," has acquired a separate name, "usage," which occurs frequently in the phrase, "grammar and usage." [3] The other set of activities attempted the more indirect approach of developing a correct use of language by the method of sentence analysis, often using "diagramming" and "parsing." This other set of activities has acquired the special name, "formal grammar."

The traditional grammar in the sense of "rules for correct usage" has been challenged frequently during the last fifty years. It was inevitable that the greater understanding of the nature of language change through the historical approach of modern linguistic science should gradually be brought to bear upon the problems arising from differences of language usage.[4] This challenge of the grammar of "usage" consisted not only of the controlled experiments which demonstrated that "knowledge of rules" had very little relation to "habits of language practice," but also of the historical evidence that most of the rules themselves were unsound linguistically.[5] Basically, as far as the leadership of English teaching in the schools is concerned—the leadership represented in the National Council of Teachers of English—this challenge of the traditional grammar of "usage" has been successful. Much certainly remains to be done. The general public still furnishes a

---

[3] See for example, the quotation in footnote 1 of this chapter.

[4] See, for example, Thomas R. Lounsbury, *The Standard of Usage in English* (1908), and Brander Matthews, *Parts of Speech* (1901).

[5] See, for example, C. C. Fries, "The Periphrastic Future with *Shall* and *Will* in Modern English," *Publications of the Modern Language Association*, 40 (1925), 960–1040; C. C. Fries, "The Rules of the Common School Grammars," *PMLA*, 42 (1927), 221–37; S. A. Leonard, *The Doctrine of Correctness in English Usage* (Madison: University of Wisconsin Press, 1929); C. C. Fries, *The Teaching of the English Language* (New York: Thomas Nelson & Sons, 1927).

lucrative market for unscrupulous publishers of cheap dictionaries based on materials that are old enough to be no longer protected by copyright. There is still a financially profitable field for rapid courses in the traditional rules for "correctness," and for even those handbooks whose makers ignore all the descriptive studies of the actual practice of the language, including the great *Oxford English Dictionary*. But among the leaders of our English teachers there has been a constantly increasing effort to grasp the significance of the descriptive studies of usage in terms of practical classroom practice.[6] In the grammar of "usage" the last twenty-five years have thus seen a tremendous change in attitude.

In the set of activities called "formal grammar" no such progress has been made. The usefulness of the materials and of the study of "formal grammar" has been challenged and many have insisted that school programs should "eliminate as much as possible" of this type of grammar. But the defenders of "formal grammar" seem to be just as numerous and as articulate as those who would cast it out. The most often expressed compromise position seems to be that which agrees in retaining in the schools a certain minimum of "formal grammar." Specifically, those who hold this position maintain that certain "grammatical concepts" are essential; [7] that to deal with these essential grammatical "concepts" a minimum number of the usual grammar terms are necessary; and that these "concepts" and these terms can best be mastered through a study of "formal grammar." Those who hold this compromise position usually agree that the study of "formal grammar" is so "difficult" that we should attempt to teach it only to students with a special aptitude for language and then only in their later school years. Some would limit its study to prospective

---

[6] See, for example, Robert C. Pooley, *Teaching English Usage* (National Council of Teachers of English, 1946).

[7] See C. D. Thorpe, *Preparation for College English* (1945); Thorpe, "How much grammatical terminology?" *Modern Language Journal*, May, 1948.

teachers of English or of foreign language and place it in the college or in the graduate school.

Throughout all the discussions of the value or usefulness of the study of "formal grammar" there appears no challenge of the validity of the material itself. Those who have concerned themselves with the scientific study of language, especially those who have engaged in the descriptive analysis of American Indian languages, have sometimes condemned the procedures of the traditional "formal grammar." This condemnation of the procedures of "formal grammar" by these linguists, however, has had no effect upon the treatment of "formal grammar" in the schools. In fact, very few of those concerned with the practical teaching of English or other languages even know that anyone has ever insisted that the materials and procedures of "formal grammar" are basically false.

The challenge of "formal grammar" which this book on English structure offers makes no compromise. From the point of view underlying this study, the principles, the procedures, the definitions, of "formal grammar" are unsound. This does not mean, of course, that every statement of a detail in the traditional "formal grammar" is false; it means that the conventional "formal grammar" is, like the Ptolemaic astronomy, falsely oriented. The study of the usual "formal grammar," then, has much the same sort of value and usefulness as the study of the astronomy of Ptolemy, or of the medical beliefs and practices of Galen, the great Greek physician. Being falsely oriented, "formal grammar," as it is studied in relation to English, cannot be expected to provide any satisfactory insight into the mechanisms of our language or any grasp of the processes by which language functions.

Only those who have not grasped the thoroughly different basic orientation of the modern scientific approach to language could suggest that pupils begin the study of grammar with the materials of the traditional "formal grammar" and then later (in some proposals, much later) pass to a "scientific analysis." One might just as well insist that an introductory course in chemistry begin with alchemy, or that astrology provide the introduction to astronomy. It is true that the mechanisms of English structure are intricate, and that the statement of their operation cannot be both accurate and simple. The descriptions of the forms of life in terms of the various phyla as the science of biology presents them are also intricate and complicated, but thirteen year old boys often find their introduction to a scientific biology, as adjusted to their experience, highly fascinating. Electricity is a complicated and intricate matter, but an introduction to an understanding of its operation through simple but perfectly sound steps has often been achieved in the junior high school. A sound descriptive approach to one's native language—with a laboratory full of living specimens on every hand—by means of a step by step procedure adapted to the linguistic experience of pupils of similar age is certainly equally possible of achievement.

The special question for our consideration concerns the value or usefulness of this "new" grammar—this descriptive analysis of the formal contrastive features of English that comprise its system of devices to signal structural meanings. There is no question concerning the necessity of "knowing" this grammar in the sense of automatically responding to these patterns of form and arrangement in the practical use of the language. Developing the unconscious habits of these responses must constitute some of the earliest steps in learning to talk English. The question for us is not one of "knowing" the grammar of English in this sense of ability to respond automatically to our system of signals; our question concerns the value and usefulness of "knowing" in the sense of a *conscious grasp and understanding* of the precise patterns that operate as our structural signals.[8] In its usual meaning our question would

---

[8] It is probably not necessary to point out that the studies that have been made concerning the value or lack of value of "formal grammar" have no significance whatever for our question of the value or usefulness of this grammar of an entirely different kind.

turn attention to possible immediate, measurable results of such a conscious grasp and understanding in terms of special language skills. In that connection it seems worth while to discuss briefly five separate matters: (1) language learning, (2) structural ambiguity, (3) punctuation, (4) structural resources, (5) total meaning.

I. LANGUAGE LEARNING

In two areas, descriptive material such as that offered here has already proved indispensable. If adults of foreign speech are to learn English they must, among other things, learn to respond to and to give the signals by which our language conveys its structural meanings. The most efficient materials for such learning are those that are based upon an accurate descriptive analysis of the structural patterns. Such an analysis need not constitute in itself any part of the material to be learned, although many adults find help in such descriptive statements.[9] But an analysis of this kind must precede and furnish the groundwork for the building of the specific exercises to be practiced and the ordering of them in a proper sequence.

In addition, in this country, whatever foreign language is taught is practically all directed to those who speak English as their native language. Many of the problems of this foreign language teaching arise out of the special features of the English language. It is not enough to have teaching materials based upon a descriptive analysis of the language to be learned. Such a descriptive analysis must be carefully and systematically compared with a similar description of English structure—the native language of the learner. Only in this way will one arrive at the kinds of new habits

---

[9] As I have insisted elsewhere, however, "A study of the statements of the patterns, making them matters of conscious knowledge, must never be allowed to become a substitute for practice of the sentences themselves." C. C. Fries, *Teaching and Learning English as a Foreign Language* (Ann Arbor: University of Michigan Press, 1945), p. 34.

to be formed, and, perhaps more important still, at the kinds of things the student must learn to ignore in dealing with the foreign language. It is not enough, also, for the teachers of foreign language to be able to speak English; to be efficient, they should "know" the structural system of English from the point of view of a sound descriptive analysis. In teaching, in learning, and in testing achievement and progress,[10] in the mastery of English by foreigners as well as in the mastery of a foreign language by native speakers of English, a sound description of English structure is indispensable.

II. STRUCTURAL AMBIGUITIES

Time after time, in the descriptive statements of the forms and arrangements that constitute the various sets of structural signals, particular situations were pointed out in which structural ambiguities commonly occur. In these instances, it was always possible to state specifically the precise features of the signals that were not present or which overlapped. There were, for example, such expressions as the following:

the requirements of the courses which are listed
the dependents of the men who are members
the equipment of the class which is there

The structural ambiguity of each of these expressions is not just a vague matter of "failure to place the modifiers as near as possible to the words they modify." The following expressions made in the same pattern have no such ambiguity:

[10] See the basic principles for the building of sound measures of progress and achievement in the mastery of a foreign language as developed by Robert Lado, *Measurement in English as a Foreign Language* (University of Michigan, 1950. Doctoral dissertation).

the uniforms of the regiment which is there
the uniforms of the regiment which are there
an examination of the students which is thorough
an examination of the students who are here now

In English the pattern of a Class 1 word with a so-called "phrase" modifier followed by a word-group such as that at the end of each of these expressions is very frequent. Often such expressions are ambiguous, sometimes humorously so. The structural signal of grouping (the direction of the modification) is not simply a matter of position. Wherever this pattern occurs, unless the last word-group contains one of a narrow range of distinctive correlating forms, tying the word-group to only one of the Class 1 words preceding, structural ambiguity is inevitable.

A sound descriptive statement of the structural signals of English makes clear the places where such ambiguities are likely to occur and the precise nature of the distinctive features involved. The descriptive analysis can thus become the means through which a user of the language becomes aware of the common sources of structural ambiguity, as well as the precise formal devices for resolving them.

III. PUNCTUATION

1. Throughout the discussion of the question, "What is a sentence?" and at times elsewhere in the materials, it seemed necessary to remind the reader that we were discussing the structures of the sentences of living speech, not those of writing. The punctuation of written material had no part in our treatment of the sentence. The schools, however, have on the whole been primarily concerned with the *writing* of sentences—especially with the graphic signals of the beginnings and the ends of "sentences." Teachers often insist that to cast out the teaching of "formal grammar" would rob them of their chief tool for teaching punctuation.

As a matter of fact the rules for the use of the various marks of punctuation are practically always stated in terms of "grammar." Sometimes there appears a recognition of the fact that punctuation is in some respects related to the "tones of the voice" —that "in reading aloud what has been written" the voice should "fall" at the places marked by a period or a semicolon, that it should rise at an interrogation point, and that it should "remain suspended" at a comma. Such statements as these, however, have been offered as guides for reading what has been written, not as rules for placing the marks in the written material. From the very beginning of the use of modern punctuation in English writing and printing, the definitions of the various marks—period, comma, semicolon, colon—as well as the statements of their use, have been based on grammatical structure.[11]

Basically, then, the marks of punctuation are graphic devices which can operate in a limited way as structural signals in written materials which lack such features as intonation, pause, and stress. This does not mean that punctuation does or can represent the sound features of intonation or stress; it means simply that punctuation can provide a device to supplement the features of form and arrangement in some of those situations for which, in speech, intonation provides the distinguishing features. For the use of punctuation in this way we need first a descriptive analysis of the signals of structural meaning as they operate in the language itself, in speech. Given that description as a base, we can then use certain of the marks of punctuation [12] as substitutes for some of those

[11] See the quotations from the early textbooks, especially those of the sixteenth century, in C. C. Fries, "Shaksperian Punctuation," in *Studies in Shakspere, Milton and Donne* (Ann Arbor: University of Michigan Language and Literature Series, 1924), I, 76-79. See also discussion of the so-called "rhythmical" use of punctuation in the 1623 folio of Shakspere's plays.

[12] We are not concerned here with such marks of punctuation as those for which our use can be stated in a purely arbitrary rule, as, for example, quotation marks and the mark of the genitive.

features not present in writing and also for some purposes beyond those of the signals of speech.

Three uses of punctuation need comment.

1. The descriptions above have pointed out that the distinctive signal to separate certain structures consisted of an intonation contrast. In most of these instances, graphic marks of punctuation provide a substitute for the intonation signal.

Those three men *who are always grumbling* . . .

There is no question about the fact that the italicized word group is a unit of a structure of modification, and that *those three men* constitute the other unit, the head. In this type of modification the structural meaning is that of "identification" only if there is no change of pitch level between the Class 1 word *men* and the function word *who*. The meaning is that of "description" if there is at this spot a change of pitch level with a possible pause. In this expression the use of commas provides a substitute for the change of pitch level.

The three men, who are always grumbling, . . .

The commas in this written expression serve to mark this as a "descriptive" modification structure as contrasted with one of "identification" in the same expression with no commas.[13]

The discussion *afterward* proved the success of the talk

In this sentence as it occurred the connection of *afterward* with the word *discussion* as a postpositive modifier was clearly marked by the intonation.

The dis|cussion af|terward ‖ proved the success of the talk

[13] The use or non-use of commas here in these expressions with so-called "restrictive" and "non-restrictive" clauses is solely a matter of providing a graphic signal as a substitute for a significant intonation contrast. It should not be treated as on a level with the strictly arbitrary uses of the comma in the writing of dates and numbers, etc.

Here the substitute for the intonation signal can be the graphic sign of the comma:

The discussion afterward, proved the success of the talk

The contrasting structure would appear as follows:

The discussion, afterward, proved the success of the talk

As indicated above also, the modifiers of Class 3 and Class 4 words, and of certain function words in which the meaning of the modification structure is degree, are all "tied" to their heads by a distinctive intonation pattern. Again the comma can provide the graphic signal for such a contrast. Compare the following pairs of sentences as written with the commas inserted at different places:

1. They are to come to the office, directly after the play
2. They are to come to the office directly, after the play

3. They'll be ready to move it, along about February
4. They'll be ready to move it along, about February

In each of these pairs of sentences the comma as placed in (1) and (3) *does not indicate the intonation*, but serves as a graphic signal which operates as a substitute for the feature of pitch sequence.

In similar fashion the comma serves as a graphic signal that can substitute for a distinctive intonation contrast in separating an "object complement" from an "appositive" of the "direct object."

The board selected our teacher their secretary
The board selected our teacher, their secretary

In discussing the structural patterns of sentences it was pointed out also that in a few situations an intonation sequence superceded the arrangement of form-classes in signalling the kind of sentence. This was true in the examples following:

R—— usually wrote his own speeches

[Response] He wrote his own speeches

Here the graphic signal of a "question mark" at the end of the response sentence is essential to overcome the statement signal in the arrangement *he wrote*. . . .[14]

Of a slightly different type of contrast are the following:

Will he be surprised   Will he be sur prised

Is that ever good   Is that e ver good

Here the order arrangement of the sentences in both columns is that of a question, but the intonation pattern of the sentences in the first column supercedes the signal of arrangement, and the sentences are not questions.

Here too the graphic marks of punctuation offer a substitute for the distinguishing intonation pattern:

Will he be surprised!   Will he be surprised?
Is that ever good!   Is that ever good?

In all of these instances we must stress the fact that the signals of the various structural meanings are formal features in the living

[14] As shown in Chapter VIII, the signals of the kind of sentence are features of form and arrangement other than intonation. Only in a very few instances is a contrast in intonation a distinguishing feature. The so-called "question mark" at the ends of sentences is an essential graphic signal only in those few situations in which intonation is the distinctive signal. The use of a "question mark" for all questions is a good demonstration of the fact that the graphic signs of punctuation are not tied to intonation sequences as such, for more questions occur with falling intonation than with rising intonation.

language of speech. Their description in speech must come first. Afterward we can find and describe the uses of certain marks of punctuation to substitute for those features of speech which are necessarily absent in written materials.

2. The preceding chapter attempted to stress the importance of the signals of structural grouping within the sentence. Most of these signals are matters of arrangement, supplemented in certain structures by concordance of form. Not often does intonation furnish the deciding signal of structural grouping. Sometimes it does, however, as in the following expressions.

The | president of the univer | sity's com | mit | tee on educational policies . . .

The | pre | sident of the uni | ver | sity's com | mit | tee on educational policies . . .

Here the use of the graphic sign can serve to signal the contrast in structural grouping.

> The president, of the university's committee on educational policies, . . .

In most situations, stress and intonation serve primarily to emphasize other means of structural grouping and thus provide against a false preliminary grouping before all the signals have been given. This is especially true in the use of certain of the sequence signals which have the same shape in two structural uses. In these instances the punctuation mark provides an unmistakable sign in writing.

> I'm afraid you don't remember me I've been in the ———
> office for the last six months
> Before, I was with the Red Cross

Up to 1945 L—— was with the ————
Since, he has worked with us

Our materials are not ready
Besides, the time is too short

The structural grouping in the following written sentences would be ambiguous without commas as special grouping signals.

We request that we be advised as to whether or not you desire separation at least eight weeks preceding the date on which you are eligible for separation.

We request that we be advised, as to whether or not you desire separation, at least eight weeks preceding the date on which you are eligible for separation.

Within the sentences of written materials, the punctuation marks comma and semicolon can supplement effectively the other signals of structural grouping.

3. In the textbooks of English composition much is made of the writing of good sentences and the writing of good paragraphs. In line with the traditional approach to language the writers of these texts attempt to define not only the sentence,[15] but also the paragraph, in terms of meaning content. Just as the sentence is defined as "the statement of a complete thought" so the paragraph is defined as "the smallest unit of developed thought." It is important to recognize that neither the sentence, *as set off by punctuation in written materials*, nor the paragraph are units of the living language of speech.

One cannot find in speech the signals that will mark unmis-

[15] See Chapter II.

takably the divisions of sentences as they might appear in the marks of written representation. Groups of teachers, asked simply to record the number of sentence units as the paragraph quoted in Chapter II (p. 11) was read to them, differed greatly in their conclusions as to the number. Every number from three to nine was indicated. The marking of written materials into separate sentences by the marks of "end" punctuation does not find its inevitable and complete guide in the "grammar" of English—in the formal signals of structural meanings.

A comparison of the sentence divisions as marked in the two paragraphs following [16] will provide an illustration of the point to be stressed here.

The Need of a New Physics Laboratory at Our High School

It is a clearly shown fact that a new physics laboratory is greatly needed at our High School. At present both the chemistry and the physics laboratories are in the basement of East Wing. This arrangement is very inconvenient in many ways. First, the rooms are small, so the stations are close together. With the increased number of students in these courses the rooms are often crowded. This makes it very inconvenient to perform experiments. At times it causes errors in the work. The rooms are not very well lighted, because they are partly beneath the ground. This makes it difficult to obtain correct results in some experiments, especially when using the telescope. If there were a new physics laboratory better work would be done.

The sentences, as marked by the punctuation in this paragraph, each have the formal characteristics of single free utterance units in English. There is no question of grammatical incompleteness.

---

[16] These paragraphs were both written by a freshman student just after his entrance to college.

They are short, it is true. Their average length is 12.5 words. Some teachers to whom this paragraph was submitted have insisted that the sentences were "too short," were "insignificant," but they could offer no communicable criteria for "insignificance" and nothing except an arithmetical average of the number of words as a measure of "shortness."

One begins to touch the heart of the problem if one asks, after a rapid reading of the paragraph, just how many inconveniences are mentioned and precisely what they are. The expression in this paragraph fails to communicate easily the answers to these questions, not because it does not present all the constituents of each of the inconveniences which constitute the need of a new laboratory, but because it has not grasped these constituents in their structural layers. The principle of immediate constituents can be applied on the level of the marking of sentence divisions in the written material of a paragraph. Small rooms, for example, are not necessarily an inconvenience in themselves, although, joined with other conditions, they may be one of the constituents of an inconvenience. But small rooms, with stations close together, crowded with students, joined with the fact that these students are trying to perform experiments, together do obviously constitute an inconvenience.

The following is the paragraph in which the student tried to apply the principle of immediate constituents to the punctuation of the sentence divisions. He sought such a grouping of the constituents that each sentence would represent the same structural layer of the material.

The Need of a New Physics Laboratory at Our High School

The inconveniences of the present arrangement of having both the chemistry and the physics laboratories in the basement of East Wing show clearly that our High School needs a new physics laboratory. In the present small rooms with their stations close together, and the consequent crowding due to the increasing number of students in these courses, the performing of accurate experiments becomes nearly impossible, and the performing of any experiments very inconvenient. The lack of light, due to the fact that the present rooms are partly beneath the ground, also increases the difficulty of accurate work, especially with such instruments as the telescope. A new physics laboratory, therefore, will produce better work.

Paragraph divisions are solely matters of the punctuation of written materials. The formal graphic mark is an indentation on a written or printed page. The paragraph itself is simply the amount of written or printed material that stands between two indentations. The grouping of material into paragraphs can also apply the principle of immediate constituents. Failure to do so results in the kind of writing illustrated by the explanation of baseball quoted early in Chapter XII (pp. 258–60). The paragraph divisions would signal a different structural layer from that of the sentence divisions. But each paragraph would represent the comparable structural levels.

Applied to written materials, in the marking of sentence divisions and paragraph units, the principle of immediate constituents has been considerably extended. It has been used here to illustrate the possibility of employing some of the principles of our approach to structural signals, in our efforts to deal with the larger problems of written composition.

IV. STRUCTURAL RESOURCES

The language of those that are not educated differs from that of those who have a formal education, not primarily in the matter of so-called errors or wrong forms, but in the fullness of the use that is made of the resources of our language.[17] A comparison of the sentences of these two social groups in the matter of mere length seems to show some significance.[18]

Altogether the Standard English materials included 1,153 sentences and the Vulgar English materials 914. The raw arithmetical average seemed to indicate that there was very little difference in length of sentence between these two groups. For the Standard English sentences the average number of words was 23.46; for the Vulgar English sentences, 23.16. This surprising similarity does not, however, represent the significant facts. The following chart gives the distribution of the frequency of the sentences of various lengths.

Length by words	1–9	10–19	20–29	30–39	40–49	50–59	60–69	70–79	80–89	90–100	100+
Standard English	84	369	373	165	105	29	19	5	0	2	2
Vulgar English	205	338	156	84	42	27	20	17	8	3	14

In the Standard English sentences the most frequent length was 21 words (50 instances); in those of Vulgar English it was 11 words (51 instances). Second in frequency for Standard English were sentences of 23 words (47 instances); for Vulgar English, 8 words and 16 words (with 41 instances for each number). In the group of sentences with one to nine words each, Vulgar English has two and a half times as many as Standard English (Standard English

---

[17] See C. C. Fries, *American English Grammar* (New York: Appleton-Century Co., 1940), Chapter XI.

[18] The materials for this comparison are not the recorded conversations used for the study of structure described in this book, but the letters used for my *American English Grammar*. See Chapter III of that book. The recorded conversations contained only the speech of those who could be classed as speakers of Standard English and thus furnished no basis for such a comparison. The problems involved in the mere counting of the sentences were many. In the Standard English materials, punctuation could be used as a check. In the Vulgar English materials the punctuation was often absent. The basic criterion of the unit to be counted was "a structure not included by any formal device in any larger structure."

84, Vulgar English 205). On the whole, the sentences of the Vulgar English materials were shorter than those of the Standard English letters. Vulgar English, however, had more very long sentences than did Standard English. The frequency of those sentences with 50 to 70 words was about the same, with 48 for Standard English and 47 for Vulgar English. But for sentences of more than 70 words the Vulgar English materials had nearly five times as many (Standard English 9, Vulgar English 42).

Part of the difference shown in these figures arises from the fact that many of the Vulgar English sentences are either the very brief statements of "constituents" without any representation of the different layers in which these "constituents" belong,[19] or the very long sentences in which these "constituents" are added in loose succession, without any grasp of the layers of structure in which the "constituents" function. This conclusion seems to be supported also by the much greater frequency in the Vulgar English sentences of the connectives *and* and *so*.

	Standard English	Vulgar English
and	474	707
so	17	105

On the other hand, it is in the sentences of the Standard English materials that one finds the frequent illustrations of the kinds of structural grouping that have used fully the resources of our structural signals. Simply to have a description of what these resources are and how the structural signals operate is of course not sufficient. It is one thing to discover and describe what the structural signals of English are; it is quite another to start from such a descriptive display of the resources of the language and provide the exercises, the actual activities, by which a native speaker of English can develop a greater and greater control and use of these

---

[19] See above, the illustration of "insignificant" sentencing in writing (p. 288).

resources to the full. We are assuming here that the discovery and description of the resources themselves must precede and furnish the basis for an effective approach to the problems of such a practical mastery as characterizes those who have the greatest competence in communication.

V. TOTAL MEANING

The vigorous condemnation of the use of meaning as employed in the linguistic studies of an earlier generation has tended to make the very mention of the word *meaning* anathema among some present-day linguists. To assert that any present linguistic study is "based on meaning" is tantamount to impeaching the scientific integrity of the author of that study. The wholesale and uncritical repudiation of all bearing of "meaning" upon the work of linguists seems to have become a conventional attitude of some who are counted among linguistic scholars.[20] On the other hand, those who oppose the recent developments in the methods of linguistic study nearly all assume, as a matter of course, that *all use of every type of meaning* has been rigidly excluded from linguistic studies made in accord with these methods, and often make that assumed fact the basis of their opposition and criticism.

In this book, I have challenged the traditional uses of meaning as the tool of analysis in dealing with sentence structure. I have insisted over and over again that we cannot use definitions that are based on meaning content rather than on form, that we gain no insight into the way our language works if our analysis of sentence structure consists solely of giving technical names to portions

[20] See the impression gained by Dr. John B. Carroll in his interviews with linguists throughout this country, and stated in *A Survey of Linguistics and Related Disciplines, A Report Prepared at the Request of the Carnegie Corporation of New York* (Cambridge, Massachusetts, 1950), p. 15: "A general characteristic of the methodology of descriptive linguistics, as practiced by American linguists today, is the effort to analyze linguistic structure without reference to meaning."

of a total meaning of an utterance which we must know in detail before we can begin. I have not, however, repudiated "all uses of meaning" in linguistic analysis, and I have deliberately insisted that all substitution procedures demand for their use the control of certain aspects of meaning. One cannot determine whether one item is substitutible for another in any frame without in some way knowing whether the result is "same" or "different." That the precise lexical meanings of the "words" are unnecessary is proved from my use of formulas with symbols to represent whole form-classes.

Throughout this book we have been concerned with the signalling of one type of meaning and we have tried to show as precisely as possible what meanings, what "structural meanings," were signalled by the various patterns of formal contrasts. The signals of structural meanings, however, do not account for all the meanings in our utterances. In Chapter IV we especially pointed out the obvious difference between structural meaning and lexical meaning. These two types of meaning constitute what I have called "linguistic meaning." Linguistic meaning is important, vitally important, for every use of language; but it does not constitute *the total meaning* of our utterances.

You will remember that Rip Van Winkle, after his twenty years sleep, returned to his village in the midst of an election. With his rusty gun and his ragged clothes he made his way to the inn at which the voting was taking place. There one of his utterances almost caused a riot:

> "Alas! gentlemen," said Rip, "I am a poor quiet man, a native of the place, and a loyal subject of the King, God bless him!"
>
> Here was a general burst from the bystanders — "A tory! a tory! a spy! a refugee! hustle him! Away with him!" It was with great difficulty that the self-important man in the cocked hat restored order. . . .

It was not the linguistic meaning of the utterance that produced the vigorous response. Twenty years before, when Rip started out on his tramp in the mountains, such a statement would have elicited no such reaction. It would have meant simply that he was a "good" citizen. But there had been twenty years of history, including the Revolutionary War. The linguistic meaning of the utterance was the same as it would have been twenty years earlier, but its "social" or "cultural" meaning had changed. Rip's statement now meant (in its social meaning) that he was an "enemy" of the newly established government. The reader of the story of Rip Van Winkle has missed its "meaning" unless he grasps at once the significance of the reaction of the group to Rip's words. The total meaning of our utterances consists not only of the linguistic meaning—the lexical meaning and the structural meaning—but also of the "social" meaning.[21] To grasp only the linguistic meaning is "mere verbalism."

If I say to you, "John Smith can swim a hundred yards in forty-five seconds," the linguistic meaning will probably be perfectly clear. You will know the type of motion designated by the word *swim*, the distance represented by a hundred yards, and the span of time covered by forty-five seconds. But is this fast or slow swimming? Is there any significance in this statement? You miss the "social" meaning of this utterance unless you can fit the linguistic meaning of this sentence into a social frame of organized information—unless you know, for example, that this time is four seconds better than the world record for this distance.

The problems of getting and conveying meaning through the medium of language are various and complex. When we insist that our students cannot understand what they read, or that they cannot comprehend what they hear in lectures, the difficulty may

---

[21] "Social" meaning is not a completely satisfactory term. It is the best word I have found to cover all the varieties of meaning other than the linguistic meanings signalled by structural arrangements and by the "words" as lexical items.

be a matter of the lexical meaning, the experience which the vocabulary units represent. It may be a matter of the structural meanings, the signals that we have been describing in this book. It may more often be a matter not of linguistic meaning at all, but of the "social" meaning, of the social-cultural significance of the utterances. One of the practical values of the materials that form the body of this book lies in the fact that these materials present the formal arrangements, the signals, upon which one of the important types of meaning depends. They serve thus to aid in the diagnosis of difficulties in the struggle with meaning, and in providing the special means of dealing with meanings of this special kind. The problems of other types of meaning will be more clearly grasped if we can remove from consideration the complex set of matters that constitute structural meanings and their signals.

The chief use and value of a descriptive analysis of the structure of English, however, does not seem to me to lie in any of the five matters just discussed, or in all of them together. I believe fundamentally in *education* as distinct from *training*. Training seems to measure usefulness or value in terms of output or product, with the individual person as the means. His skills are developed so that he can do things. Education, in contrast with training, seems to stress the individual himself as the end, and measures usefulness and value in terms of contribution to the freedom and development of individual personality. From this point of view, I should insist that the chief value of a systematic analysis and description of the signals of structural meaning in English is the insight it can give concerning the way our language works, and, through English, into the nature and functioning of human languages.

Index

All references are to pages. Subject entries are in roman type; words and groups of words are in italics; proper names are in small capitals.

adjective, 67, 87, 204, 206
adverbial object. *See* structures
adverbs, 87, 204, 205, 206, 248
after, 99
afterwards, 249, 250
AIKIN, JANET RANKIN, 13, 31
along, 232
ambiguity. *See* structural ambiguity
American English Grammar, vii, 162
analysis by meaning, 7, 8, 15, 18, 183, 186
and, 94
answers, 158, 165, 172
appositive. *See* structures
assumptions, 24, 37, 39, 51, 58, 59, 74, 110, 262
at, 95

BAIN, ALEXANDER, 13
baseball
    patterns, 60, 72, 140
    structural layers, 258
BARKER, RUSSELL H., 12, 15
be (and reversal), 148
besides, 249, 251

BLOCH, BERNARD, 22
BLOOMFIELD, LEONARD, ix, 8, 20, 21, 22, 33, 35, 240, 262
-body, 116
both, 244
BRAUN, FRANK X., 55, 173, 202
BROWN, GOOLD, 66
BRYANT, MARGARET, 32

calls, 44, 51, 53
CARROLL, JOHN B., 293
Class 1, 76–79, 89, 111–22, 173–201, 201–38, 263–69
Class 2, 80–82, 90–92, 96, 123, 124, 135–37, 201–38, 254, 263–69
Class 3, 82–83, 201–38, 255
Class 4, 83–86, 132–39, 210–38, 255
clauses, restrictive, non-restrictive, 283
comma, 283, 284
complete thought, 9, 10, 13, 15
compounds of *-one, -body, -thing, -self*, 116
compounds with *-where, -time, -way, -while*, 134

concordance ties, 144–48, 176, 214

conjunctions, 250

conservative, 6

correctness, 6, 275, 276

cultural lag, 1

CURME, GEORGE O., 30, 32

CURTIS, ROY G., 22

cuttings, for immediate constituents, 267–70

definitions, 68, 173, 174, 187, 203, 204

DELBRUCK, B., 14

dental suffix, Class 2, [d], [t], or [ɪd], 124, 208, 220

determiners, 89, 118, 196, 213

dialect, 5

did, 96

direct object
  See structures
  conventional definition, 174

direction of modification, 265, 272

do, 96, 148, 149

does, 96, 148, 149, 151

DOUCE Ms., 66, 103

each, 244

echo, 157, 158

education, 296

–else, 247

–er, *–est*, 130, 138

exclamations, 53

form-classes. *See* parts of speech

formal clues, 72, 79, 104, 262

formal grammar, 275, 276

formulas
  for immediate constituents, 268–71
  for sentence patterns, 145–48
  for "subject," "object," etc., 189–201
  special, 91
  symbols of, 189, 190, 198

frames, 70, 75, 76

FRIES, C. C., 91, 275, 279, 282, 291

function words, 87–109, 172
  basis for name, 104–09
  Group A, *the, a,* etc., 88, 89
  Group B, *may, be, get,* etc., 90, 91
  Group C, *not,* 92
  Group D, *very, pretty,* etc., 92, 93, 94
  Group E, *and, or, but,* etc., 94, 95
  Group F, *at, by, for,* etc., 95, 96
  Group G, *do,* 96, 97
  Group H, *there,* 97, 98
  Group I, *why, when,* etc., 98, 99
  Group J, *after, because,* etc., 99–101
  Group K, *well, oh, now, why,* 101–02
  Group L, *yes, no,* 103
  Group M, *say, listen, look,* 103
  Group N, *please,* 103
  Group O, *lets,* 103, 104
  number of, 104
  percentage of, 105

some uses of, 118, 119, 125, 131, 148–57, 160–62, 190–200, 267–69

GALEN, I, 277
GARDINER, ALLEN H., 14, 17
grammar
  analysis, 2–3, 54–64, 279
  basic units of, 61–64
  conventional, 2, 54–57, 65–69, 87, 173–75, 202–06, 239, 274–77
  definition of, 56, 72
  "formal" grammar, 276, 277
  knowledge of, 57, 278–79
  "new," 2
  usage, 275–76
  value of, 274, 278–96
grammar and usage, 275
greetings, 42, 51

HARRIS, ZELLIG, 75, 262
HARVEY, WILLIAM, I
have, 91, 149, 150
he, 242, 243
hereafter, 249, 250
how, 154
how many, 153
HUNGERFORD, HARLAN M., 227

included sentences, 100–01, 240, 252–55
independent linguistic form, 21, 22
indirect object. *See* structures

informant, 4
interjections, 53
interruptions, 23
intonation, 26–28, 93, 143, 144, 152–58, 162–64, 194, 216, 217, 221, 225, 227, 236, 237, 248, 254, 258, 264, 267, 268, 283, 285
it, 242, 244

jabberwocky, 70
JESPERSEN, OTTO, 3, 7, 17, 20

LADO, ROBERT, ix, 280
language of the people, 4
later, 248
layers of structure, 256, 264, 271, 272
leave-taking, 42
length of sentences, 291
LEONARD, S. A., 275
let us, 103
lets, 103
lexical meanings, 55, 56, 75, 268
lexically compatible, 79, 224, 273
liberal, 7
linguist, 4–7
linguistic community, 35
linguistic meaning, 56, 294
list, 2b, 135–37
listen, 103
literature, 4, 5
look, 103
LOUNSBURY, THOMAS R., 275
LYMAN, ROLLO LA VERNE, 274

man/men, 117
markers (part of speech), 62, 65–69, 74, 78, 89, 118
MATTHEWS, BRANDER, 275
meaning
  analysis by, 7, 8, 15, 18, 183, 186
  as situation and response, 34
  control of, 8, 74, 79, 294
  definitions by, 18, 175, 189, 203, 293
  kinds of, 55, 294, 295
  lexical, 55, 56, 75, 268
  linguistic, 56, 294
  social, 295
  structural, 56, 57, 74, 106–09, 196, 252, 294
  substitution technique, 74
  total, 55, 293–96
  traditional use, 293
  See also meanings
meanings
  and form, 117, 239
  degree, 223, 236, 237
  description, 179, 226, 227
  identification, 179, 188, 191, 201, 224–27
  lexical, 233, 268
  manner, 222, 223
  number, 117, 118
  of function words, 105–09
  of words, 146, 201
  performer, 103, 177, 178, 191, 192, 201, 204, 219, 227
  place, 233

possession, 117, 118
  quality, 219, 221, 222, 223, 236, 238
  result, 185
  time, 233
  to or for which, 180
  undergoer, 180, 184, 218, 220, 225
  use of, 18, 54, 74, 203
  See also meaning
MEILLET, A., 20
MILL, JOHN STUART, 65
minimum free utterance. *See* utterances
modification, 202–39, 262–73
modifiers, 202–39, 262, 273
more, 131
most, 131

NATIONAL COUNCIL OF TEACHERS OF ENGLISH, 275
negative, 92, 97, 159, 167, 172
–ng form, 190, 219
NIDA, EUGENE A., 262
no, 102, 165
non-communicative utterances, 52
not, 92
noun, 66, 67, 87
noun adjunct. *See* structures
now, 102

object
  See structures
  conventional definition, 174

object complement. *See* structures

oh, 102

one, 116

oral responses, 42

oral signals of attention, 42

other, 247

Oxford English Dictionary, 36, 276

paragraph divisions, 290

paragraph units, 290

parts of speech, 61–64, 65–86, 110–41

    as functioning units, 61–64, 73, 74

    Class 1, 76–79, 89, 111–22, 173–201, 201–38, 263–69

    Class 2, 80–82, 90–92, 96, 123, 124, 135–37, 201–38, 254, 263–69

    Class 3, 82–83, 201–38, 255

    Class 4, 83–86, 132–39, 210–38, 255

    common definitions of, 67–69, 204–06

    markers, 62, 65–69, 74, 78, 87, 118, 131, 141

    names for, 75, 78, 80, 82, 83, 87, 205, 206

    number of, 65–66, 86, 104–09, 110

    words as, 64, 257

    See also function words

patterns, 60, 61, 72, 73, 74, 79, 111–13, 140, 145, 176, 183, 189, 196, 201, 228, 278

PENDLETON, C. S., 12

phonemic notation, 7

PIKE, KENNETH L., ix, 26, 143, 262

please, 103, 164

polite formulas, with request, 164

POOLEY, ROBERT C., 276

positions, 71, 72, 74–86, 88–105, 125, 126, 134, 139, 141, 208, 212–16, 231, 232, 271

predicate, 14

predicate nominative. *See* structures

PRIESTLEY, JOSEPH, 66

PRISCIAN, 9

procedures, viii, 26, 30, 32, 35, 36, 74–79, 88–105, 110, 111, 206, 263, 266

pronoun, 68

PTOLEMY, 277

punctuation, 9–12, 24, 144, 281–90

    substitute for intonation, 283–89

question, 31, 32, 45–47, 51, 53, 96–99, 142–72

    mark, 285

    negative in, 151, 172

radicals, 6, 7

recorded speech, 3, 4, 21

recurrent partials, 39, 40

referent, 189

reflexive pronouns, 198

request, 47, 51, 143, 145–48, 164

response utterance units, 37, 40,
41, 165
responses, 22, 32–53, 72, 142,
145, 154–58, 172, 272
See also answers
reversal, 148, 150, 158–62
ride/rode, 124
RIES, JOHN, 17

"s" ending, 77, 80, 117, 125
"same" or "different," 8, 74, 75,
79, 294
SAVAGE, SHIRLEY PAYNE, 10, 11,
14
say, 103
SCALIGER, JULIUS CAESAR, 274
SEIDEL, EUGEN, 14, 17
–self, 116, 198–200
sentence
analysis, 54, 57, 59, 266
fragments, 9, 10
included, 100–01, 240, 252–
55, 269
kinds of, 29, 53, 143–48, 172
length, 291
patterns of, 142–72
sequence, 101, 240–52
what is, 9–28, 64
See question, statement, request, call, answer, greeting
sequence sentences, 101, 164, 240–
52
sequence signals, 165, 241–53
shall, 150
she, 243

SHEFFIELD, ALFRED WHITE, 13
SHEN, YAO, ix
signals of structural meaning, 8,
58, 59, 61, 69–71, 74, 91,
106–09, 111, 144, 145, 153,
165, 169, 172, 206–07, 252–
53, 263, 267, 269, 286, 296
since, 250
situation and response as meaning, 34
situation utterance units, 37, 40,
41, 164, 165
social meaning, 295
speech community, 36
stand alone, 19, 20, 22, 23, 207
Standard English, 5, 210, 291
statement, 50, 51, 143, 145–48
structural ambiguity, 57, 61–63,
65, 138–39, 146, 169, 178,
180–82, 200, 214–17, 223,
241–45, 265, 272, 280–81,
286
structural grouping, 253–54, 256–
73, 286
structural meanings. *See* meanings
and signals
structural resources, 290
structural signals. *See* signals
structures
"appositive," 187, 194, 195,
201, 284
immediate constituents of, 256–
74
"modification," 202–39
"noun adjunct," 187, 196, 201

"object," 183–87, 196, 255
  "adverbial," 186, 194, 196, 198, 201
  "cognate," 184
  "complement," 184, 194, 201, 284
  "direct," 184, 192, 193, 194, 199, 201
  "indirect," 185, 193, 199, 201
  "of preposition," 187
  "predicate nominative," 187, 192, 201
  "subject," 173–83, 191, 195, 196, 201, 225
subject. *See* structures
substitutes, 118–20, 180–83, 194, 196, 200
substitution, 74, 80, 263, 294
SUNDÉN, KARL F., 17
symbols. *See* formulas
syntactic form-classes, 141

terminology, 2
test frames, 74–75
that, 245–46
the, 88
then, 249
there, 97, 160–62
there comes a time, 161
therefore, 251
they, 242, 243
thing, 116
this, 246
THORPE, C. D., 10, 11, 14, 55, 276

time, 134
total meaning, 55, 293–94
training, 296
TRAVER, AILEEN, 210, 212
two-word verbs, 96

usage, grammar of, 275
usually, 232
utterance units, 23–25, 36–41, 52, 164–65, 240–41
  response, 37, 40, 41, 99, 101, 102, 165
  situation, 37, 40, 41, 164, 165, 207, 241
utterances, 21–26, 36–53, 142–44
  expanded, 25, 37, 75, 78, 241
  free, 25, 29–31, 36, 39, 52
  minimum, 25, 29–30, 37, 74–78, 105, 241
  noncommunicative, 52–53
  of continued discourse, 42, 49–51, 52
  response, 105, 154–58
  sequence, 30, 39, 49, 164, 241
  situation, 105
  that start conversations, 164, 241
  with action responses, 41, 47–49, 53
  with oral responses, 41–47, 53
  See also sentence

VARRO, 66
verb, 87

very, 92
Vulgar English, 5, 291

WALCOTT, FRED G., 10, 11, 14
WARD, WILLIAM, 66
WATTS, BERTHA M., 30
well, 102
WELLS, ROULON S., 262
were, 154
were they, 162
what, 153, 154
when, 98, 153, 154
where, 134, 153

which, 121, 153, 154
while, 134
who, 107, 153
who, which, 121
why, 102, 134, 153, 154
will, 150
words
   as parts of speech, 64, 257
   words understood, 16, 17
written composition, 290

yes, 102, 165